MW01293504

A Momentum Publication

THE ART AND PRACTICE OF LIVING
WONDROUSLY

Edited by Dr. Ronit Ziv-Kreger
Momentum's Director of Education
With articles by thirty-seven incredible contributors

Hebrew calligraphy by Avshalom Eshel

MAGGID

A Momentum Publication

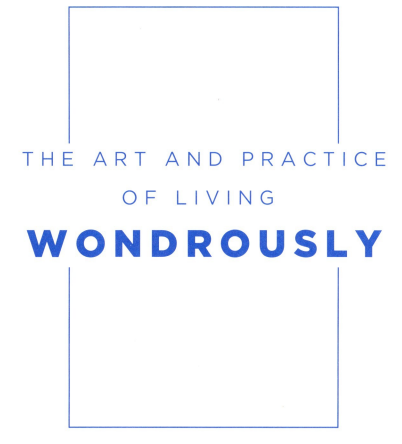

THE ART AND PRACTICE

OF LIVING

WONDROUSLY

Edited by Dr. Ronit Ziv-Kreger
Momentum's Director of Education
With articles by thirty-seven incredible contributors

Hebrew calligraphy by Avshalom Eshel

מגיד

MAGGID

The Art and Practice of Living Wondrously
First edition, 2025
Maggid Books
An imprint of Koren Publishers Jerusalem Ltd.

PO Box 8531, New Milford, CT 06776-8531, USA
& PO Box 4044, Jerusalem 9104001, Israel
www.korenpub.com

Copyright © 2025 Momentum Unlimited Inc.
Introduction to chapter on Taking Leadership, pages 198-200, copyright © Ronit Ziv-Kreger.
Other introductions (to book, sections, and chapters) copyright © 2025 Momentum
Unlimited Inc. and Ronit Ziv-Kreger.
All rights reserved.
Full copyright for each article remains with its writers, who have given permission for
their article to be included in this book.
Hebrew calligraphy by Avshalom Eshel, a *sofer stam*, calligrapher, and artist living in
Ein Karem, Jerusalem. Design of the art and the English writing in the book's section
openers by Ronit Ziv-Kreger; copyright © 2024 Ronit Ziv-Kreger.
All rights reserved.
Please note that this volume includes sacred texts and should be treated
accordingly.

Original book and cover design by Ira Ginzburg.

The creation of the book was made possible with the generous support
of The Zalik Foundation.

Considerable research and expense have gone into the creation of this
publication. No part of this publication (content or design) may be reproduced,
stored in a retrieval system, or transmitted in any form by any means, electronic,
mechanical, photocopying, or otherwise, without the prior written permission of
Momentum Unlimited, except in case of brief quotations embedded in critical
articles or reviews.
Hardcover ISBN: 978-1-59264-711-8
Printed in the USA

For our parents, who always reminded us
that "we are not Russian, we are Jewish."

Thank you for teaching us that
"we are a gift from God."

Love,
Helen and David Zalik

There's no single playbook for a world of increasing complexity, uncertainty, intensity, and ambiguity, but that doesn't mean we are without options or collective wisdom to guide us forward. *The Art and Practice of Living Wondrously* offers present-day reflections, questions, and practices from revered spiritual, organizational, and communal leaders to help us create more positive, productive, and hopeful futures.

— **Lisa Kay Solomon, Futurist in Residence at the Stanford d.school, best-selling author, and award-winning civic innovator**

This book is for anyone seeking to live Jewishly with joy and pride. Its articles, introductions, and practices are gems, offering accessible wisdom to elevate your daily life.

— **R. David Aaron, best-selling author of *Living a Joyous Life: The True Spirit of Jewish Practice* and *Endless Light: The Ancient Path of Kabbalah***

This transformative work illuminates a path toward rediscovering life's purpose, showing us how to move from disconnection to wonder, from fear to openness. For anyone seeking to live fully awake to life's possibilities, this book is an essential companion for the journey.

— **Sarah Waxman, CEO and Founder of At The Well Project**

This inspired collection by leading Jewish voices will guide you to realize that, rather than searching for miracles, you and your life are the greatest miracle of all.

— **Dr. Zohar Raviv, International Vice President of Education Strategy for Taglit-Birthright Israel**

Dr. Ronit Ziv-Kreger has put together the ultimate book to support your quest for a fulfilling life. This is a book that you will have occasion to turn to again and again.

— **R. Joseph Telushkin, author of *Jewish Literacy: The Most Important Things to Know About the Jewish Religion, Its People, and Its History; Rebbe: The Life and Teachings of Menachem M. Schneerson, the Most Influential Rabbi in Modern History;* and *Words That Hurt, Words That Heal: How the Words You Choose Shape Your Destiny***

In our business we are dedicated to promoting holistic well-being and empowering people to lead healthier, happier lives. *Living Wondrously* deepens our understanding of well-being and revives the art of finding wonder in our everyday lives.

— **Sammy Rubin, Founder and CEO of YuLife**

In an era of uncertainty and complexity, this book illuminates our path, inviting us on a journey of spiritual renewal and connection to eternal Jewish values, offering practical tools for a life of meaning.

— Dr. Aliza Lavie, former Member of Knesset, social entrepreneur, and best-selling author of the National Jewish Book Award winner *Iconic Jewish Women: A Jewish Women's Prayer Book*

You, me, and our entire generation of Jews need this book. We all know there is great wisdom in Judaism, but it takes vision and skill to bring it to bear on issues that are of real concern to people today. This book does just that, and you will find yourself tapping it time and again as a rich handbook for becoming a better parent, friend, student, and leader — Jewishly!!

— Alan Morinis, Founder of The Mussar Institute; author of *Everyday Holiness: The Jewish Spiritual Path of Mussar*

The Art and Practice of Living Wondrously is an extraordinary collection of life wisdom. This is a book to be read slowly, discussed with a partner, and shared with those you care about or would like to care about.

— R. Dr. Zvi Grumet, author of *Genesis: From Creation to Covenant* and co-author of the commentary in *The Koren Lev Ladaat Humash*

Through its masterful weaving of ancient Jewish wisdom and contemporary insights, this book provides a refreshing and profoundly practical road map for transforming everyday experiences into opportunities for meaning and connection.

— Joanna Landau, Founder and President of Vibe Israel and co-author of *Ethical Tribing: Connecting the Next Generation to Israel in the Digital Era*

This book is a feast of the best of Jewish and general wisdom about the most important issues in life. What a gift!

— R. David Jaffe, Founder and Director of Kirva and author of the National Jewish Book Award winner *Changing the World from the Inside Out: A Jewish Approach to Personal and Social Change*

It's not our struggles that give us wisdom — it is rather our tradition's wisdom that lifts us through the struggles to joy. Each time you struggle, this book will invigorate you with that wisdom, told through a tapestry of insights and stories, so you can rise through pain and confusion to find wonder.

— Deborah Gilboa, MD, author of *From Stressed to Resilient: The Guide to Handle More and Feel It Less*

The greatest asset we will ever have is ourselves. This fantastic book takes us on a journey through relationships, challenges, and hope — three of the most important areas of our lives. Embrace *The Art and Practice of Living Wondrously*, for through it you will embrace life, with all the incredible goodness it has to offer, and you will find life embracing you in return!

— **R. Dr. Benji Levy, CEO of Share**

Who knew that Judaism is bursting with wisdom for every aspect of our life? Every author in this book knew; what a joy that each shared a precious treasure with us all.

— **Lori Palatnik, author and Founding Director of Momentum**

For anyone seeking the chutzpah to live authentically and intentionally, this book is your road map. *The Art and Practice of Living Wondrously* fuses timeless Jewish teachings with practical guidance, transforming everyday challenges into moments of wonder and profound connection.

— **Julie Silverstein and Tami Schlossberg Pruwer, co-authors of the bestselling book** *Chutzpah Girls: 100 Tales of Daring Jewish Women*

Teaching our teens the "art and practice of living wondrously" is a legacy parents can bestow upon their children. It is a forever gift.

— **Dr. Bruce Powell, Head Emeritus of de Toledo High School and author of** *Raising A+ Human Beings: Creating a Jewish School Culture of Academic Excellence and AP Kindness*

These pages pulse with a vision of vibrant Jewish living that is truly transformative. The writings are deep and yet accessible. They are presented in an interactive framework that encourages the reader to personalize and integrate the wisdom directly into their daily lives. Read and be transformed!

— **Chaya Lester, psychotherapist, co-director of the Shalev Center for Jewish Personal Growth, and author of** *Ink from Ash: Healing & Empowerment from the Oct. 7th War,* *Lit: Poems to Ignite Your Jewish Holidays,* **and** *Babel's Daughters: From the Bible Belt to the Holy Land*

Table of Contents

195　Being an Agent of Hope

THE WONDERS OF YOUR TEACHINGS

OPEN MY EYES THAT I MAY PERCEIVE

— PSALMS 119:18

GOD OF ISRAEL, WHO ALONE

WORKS   WONDERS

— PSALMS 72:18

פלא

— LITURGY

FLESH WHO DOES WONDERS

BLESSED ARE YOU, GOD, HEALER of ALL

I WILL GIVE THANKS TO YOU, GOD WITH ALL MY

HEART; I WILL TELL OF ALL YOUR WONDERS

— PSALM 9:2

THE ART AND
PRACTICE OF LIVING
WONDROUSLY

Introduction

What Is Living Wondrously?

This book invites readers to open themselves up to a new way of living, one in which they greet the world and welcome the wonder they find in it. In living wondrously, we add an extra portion of vitality, connection, and purpose to our existence. It is a mindset that is about embracing life and uncovering pathways to wisdom and wholeness.

Abraham Joshua Heschel wrote poignantly about wonder and the Creator: "Who lit the wonder *before* our eyes and the wonder *of* our eyes?"[1] The magnificence in creation is not necessarily what we regularly see before us; in order to see it we must open our eyes and look. Our ability to do so is itself a magnificent gift.

Not all types of sight expose wonder. In looking at the world around us (or the news about it), people often see a dark and dim reality — and miss a deeper, concealed beauty. The Hebrew language seems to acknowledge this. The letters for the Hebrew word for dark or dim, *afel* (אפל), spell the word for wonder when put in a different order: *peleh* (פלא).

Further, the Hebrew word for world, *olam* (עולם), is related to the word hidden, *alum* (עלום). It hints to an essential fact of living: Precious gems are often concealed. We are sometimes oblivious to unseen wonder and beauty that lie below the surface.

The Hasidic master Rabbi Mordechai Yosef Leiner of Izhbits teaches that this is the message embedded in the biblical story of the twelve scouts[2] whom Moses sent to tour the Land of Israel.[3] The trouble didn't begin when ten of the twelve scouts returned with a scathing report. It began with their outlook. He asserts: "Moses instructed the scouts to gaze into the inward depths, telling them to 'tour [the land].' Had they done so, they would have seen that in the depth the land

---

1 Abraham Joshua Heschel, *Man Is Not Alone: A Philosophy of Religion,* New York: Farrar, Straus and Giroux, 1951, p. 75.

2 Also known as spies.

3 Numbers 13–14.

is filled with goodness, but they only looked at the externalities and saw it as a 'land that consumes its inhabitants.'"[4]

Rabbi Leiner is aware that perceiving wonder is not simple. He laments that the scouts didn't call for help as King David did: "Open my eyes, that I may perceive the wonders of Your teaching."[5]

Living wondrously begins with your outlook, with seeing yourself, the people in your life, and the world around you in a deeper manner. You can uncover wonder anywhere and everywhere. It is near you, even *in* you. There is wonder in how your body functions, in parts of you that you do not usually appreciate. You can find nobility beneath foibles and struggle when you offer a patient gaze of caring to yourself and the people around you. Wonder can be discovered by tuning in to the most minute aspects of your immediate environment, such as the intricacy of a leaf or an insect under a magnifying glass. But it can also be sensed when looking at the night sky, a majestic view, or towering architecture.

In everyday life, we find ourselves needing to attend to concrete and practical reality. Should we relegate searching for wonder to vacation or weekends? Recent research has shown that frequently encountering awe and wonder, even for brief moments, is beneficial for mind, body, and overall well-being.[6] The search for wonder should not be curbed to special occasions but intentionally incorporated into daily living.

In fact, research has shown that experiencing awe and wonder reduces stress and inflammation, bolstering long-term health.[7] Regularly experiencing awe in nature alleviates symptoms of post-traumatic stress disorder and aids healing.[8] Wonder helps people feel more connected to one another and promotes pro-

4   Mei HaShiloach, Torah portion Shelach..

5   Psalm 119:18.

6   Barbara L. Fredrickson, "The Role of Positive Emotions in Positive Psychology: The Broaden-and-Build Theory of Positive Emotions," American Psychologist, 2001, 56(3), p. 218–226.

7   Jennifer E. Stellar, Neha John-Henderson, Craig L. Anderson, Amie M. Gordon, Galen D. McNeil, Dachner Keltner, and David DeSteno, "Positive Affect and Markers of Inflammation: Discrete Positive Emotions Predict Lower Levels of Inflammatory Cytokines," Emotion, 2015, 15(2), p. 129–133.

8   Craig L. Anderson, Maria Monroy, and Dacher Keltner, "Awe in Nature Heals: Evidence from Military Veterans, at-Risk Youth, and College Students," Emotion, 2018, 18(8), p. 1195–1202.

social behavior.[9] Awe has been shown to foster curiosity, problem-solving, and creativity.[10] And, by shifting attention away from the self toward something greater, wonder encourages us to prioritize the well-being of others, leading to more ethical behavior.[11]

Acclaimed researcher Dr. Dacher Keltner explains, "How does awe transform us? By quieting the nagging, self-critical, overbearing, status-conscious voice of our self, or ego, and empowering us to collaborate, to open our minds to wonder, and to see the deep patterns of life."[12]

This book is designed to guide you as you bring wonder and awe into your life in ways that resonate with what is important to you. The book's first section is about fostering connection and belonging in relationships. Its second section relates to perceiving hidden nobility in the challenges we face. And its third and final section explains how we can become agents of hope, fortifying the world and the people who surround us.

How to Use This Book

Each chapter in this anthology explores an aspect of daily life as an invitation for inquiry into living wondrously. This book is meant to provide practical insights and offer guidance into practices for cultivating awe and well-being.

Each chapter has articles from three or four authors of different backgrounds who collectively bring personal stories, valuable insights from social science research and Jewish wisdom to provide different pathways into personal and spiritual growth.

To make the most of what this book can offer you, rather than read passively and intellectually, engage with the insights. Consider reading with a pencil and mark what strikes you, argue with the ideas, weigh them against other ideas and

---

9   Paul K. Piff, Pia Dietze, Matthew Feinberg, Daniel M. Stancato, and Dacher Keltner, "Awe, the Small Self, and Prosocial Behavior," Journal of Personality and Social Psychology, 2015, 108(6), p. 883–899.

10 Yang Bai, Laura A. Maruskin, Serena Chen, Amie M. Gordon, Jennifer E. Stellar, Galen D. McNeil, Kaiping Peng, and Dacher Keltner, "Awe, the Diminished Self, and Collective Engagement: Universals and Cultural Variations in the Small Self," Journal of Personality and Social Psychology, 2017, 113(2), p. 185–209.

11 Melanie Rudd, Kathleen D. Vohs, and Jennifer Aaker, "Awe Expands People's Perception of Time, Alters Decision Making, and Enhances Well-Being," Psychological Science, 2012, 23(10), p. 1130–1136.

12 Dacher Keltner, Awe: The New Science of Everyday Wonder and How It Can Transform Your Life, New York: Penguin Press, 2023, p. xix.

your own experience, discuss them with your friends. Let the process stir your emotions and challenge your current mindset and habits. Find something in every chapter to grab on to. Consider the practices I have added to each article. You can also craft your own practices to find steady steps toward bringing your chosen insights into your life.[13]

Give yourself time to integrate what is meaningful to you before moving on to the next article or chapter. The goal is not to rush through the book but to grow through engaging with the book; to allow for a richer and more meaningful process of discovery. The chapters and articles need not be read in order. Allow yourself the freedom to explore what captures your interest in areas of life where you seek to draw in more wonder.

Momentum and the Backstory of This Book

Momentum is committed to making Jewish living and learning accessible for parents around the world in ways that are most relevant to them. Past-president of the board Helen Zalik and her husband, David Zalik, envisioned an accessible and inspiring gateway to the treasure trove of Jewish wisdom — namely, a book not categorized by traditional themes such as holidays or Torah portions, but by what people care about most in their day-to-day lives. We surveyed thousands of past alumna of Momentum programs, asking what topics would be most helpful to them. The ten chapters of this book are the top ten topics they selected from three dozen options.

In the face of rising antisemitism, deepening our knowledge of beautiful and applicable Jewish teachings helps foster pride and identity. Rabbi Jonathan Sacks aptly said, "The best response to antisemitism is to strengthen Jewish identity, to live our values, to build communities strong enough to stay true to their faith while contributing to the common good."[14]

Wonder As a Lifeline

The work on this book has spanned two intense and painful experiences — the COVID pandemic and the horrific trauma of October 7, 2023, and its aftermath. Our world has changed. In the face of the devastation, we've witnessed

---

13   This paragraph is adapted from the introduction to *Everyday Holiness: The Jewish Spiritual Path of Mussar* by Alan Morinis.

14   Rabbi Jonathan Sacks, *Not in God's Name: Confronting Religious Violence*, New York: Schocken Books, 2015, p. 259.

heroes and heroines stepping forward in extraordinary ways, especially in Israel and also around the world. Momentum alumni not only took action but mobilized others for communal action in wonderous feats. Pausing to take notice of such heroism and moral beauty is especially important at these times. The sagacious, Holocaust survivor, psychologist, and author Dr. Edith Eger described it this way in an interview: "In the face of trauma and despair, wonder becomes a lifeline. It reminds us that beauty exists, even in the darkest of places. When we cultivate a sense of wonder, we shift our focus from what we have lost to what is still possible. Wonder invites us to look beyond our pain and opens our hearts to the beauty of connection and community. It teaches us that hope is not just a feeling but an active choice we can make each day."[15]

May this book offer you pathways to living wondrously or, as Rabbi Abraham Joshua Heschel famously suggested, "Our goal should be to live life in radical amazement."

Ronit Ziv-Kreger
Director of Education and Evaluation, Momentum

---

15   Dr. Edith Eger, interviewed by Dr. Ronit Ziv-Kreger, January 2021.

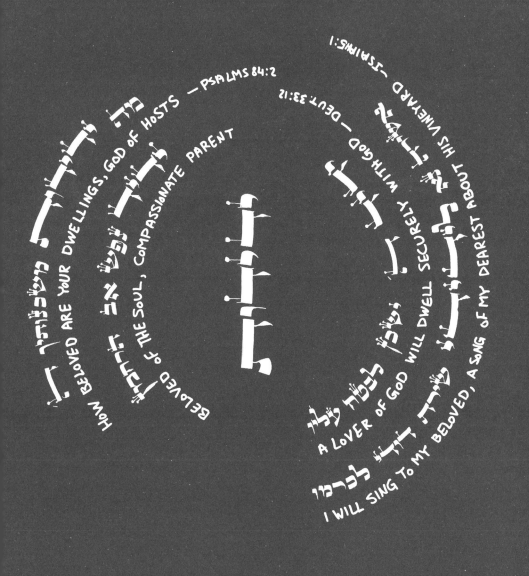

NURTURING
RELATIONSHIPS

It is no secret that the foundation of a fulfilling life — far more than wealth or accomplishments — are strong relationships.[16]

Nurturing relationships, however, isn't always easy. In fact, loneliness is so pervasive that the U.K. government went so far as to establish a Ministry of Loneliness.[17] No kidding.

Research has indicated that warm relationships keep bodies physically stronger and minds sharper as people age. Data shows that those with good friendships are less likely to be depressed or to develop diabetes or heart disease, that they regulate stress more effectively, and that they recover faster from illness.[18] The converse is also true. "Loneliness has a physical effect on the body. It can render people more sensitive to pain, suppress their immune system, diminish brain function, and disrupt sleep, which in turn can make an already lonely person even more tired and irritable."[19]

The challenge of nurturing relationships is an inherent part of the human experience. Drawing on centuries of insights, Jewish guidance for living[20] abounds with examples of what it means to nurture relationships.

The narratives about our matriarchs' and patriarchs' interpersonal relationships serve as both examples and as warnings. Through their interactions with God and with one another, we learn profound lessons about parenting, marriage, friendships, and our responsibilities vis-à-vis our own parents.

Nor are these marginal topics in Jewish teachings; relationships take center stage even in rabbinic literature. The great sage Rabbi Akiva, in fact, asserted that the guiding principle of the Torah is the

16 https://www.ted.com/talks/robert_waldinger_the_secret_to_a_happy_life_ lessons_from_8_decades_of_research.

17 https://www.bbc.co.uk/programmes/articles/2yzhfv4DvqVp5nZyxBD8G23/ who-feels-lonely-the-results-of-the-world-s-largest-loneliness-study.

18 https://www.ted.com/talks/robert_waldinger_the_secret_to_a_happy_life_ lessons_from_8_decades_of_research.

19 Robert Waldinger and Marc Schulz, "What the Longest Study on Human Happiness Found Is the Key to a Good Life," *The Atlantic*, January 19, 2023, https://www.theatlantic.com/ideas/archive/2023/01/harvard-happiness-study-relationships/672753/.

20 Written and Oral Torah.

Golden Rule — the reminder to "love your neighbor as yourself."[21]

The first chapter in this section focuses on fostering and maintaining our friendships, including with life partners and adult children. The next chapter addresses raising resilient and spiritual children — because our parenting has a significant influence on their ability to develop healthy relationships. The third chapter delves into caring for parents, a pivotal moment in our lives that may call on us to grow, serve as role models for our own children, and ease what can be the loneliest times for those we love.

As you dive into this section remember the words of Rabbi Nachman of Breslov, who taught us: "If you believe that you can destroy, believe that you can repair."[22] May these chapters help you live wondrously, inspiring you to nurture, and even repair, the relationships in your world.

---

21   Leviticus 19:18; Bereshit Rabbah 24:7.

22   Meshivat Nefesh #38.

FOSTERING AND MAINTAINING
FRIENDSHIPS

The story of Creation echoes with the refrain "it was good" — but the Torah also defines things as "not good." The first negative in the Torah is aloneness. "It is not good for a person to be alone,"[23] God says of Adam. The renowned psychoanalyst and social philosopher Erich Fromm expressed it this way: "The deepest need of man is the need to overcome his separateness, to leave the prison of his aloneness."[24]

Friendship and close relationships are where people feel seen, heard, known, and cared for in good times and bad. But these days people spend less time fostering relationships. Between 2010 and 2013 Americans spent an average of six and a half hours per week with friends. But by 2014 time spent with friends began to decline — and by 2022 it had dropped by more than fifty percent to less than three hours a week.[25]

The authors in this chapter offer skills that are helpful in deepening various relationships — connecting with a friend, a co-worker, or a family member. Adrienne Gold Davis, Momentum's director of experience and engagement, shares a powerful secret for maintaining respectful relationships and explores one of the most challenging friendships to navigate: the relationship between a parent and their adult child. The founder of Encounter-Centered Couples Therapy, Hedy Shleifer, describes how family relationships, especially an intimate partnership such as a marriage, offers a laboratory for experimentation as she teaches about three connectors that are necessary for a flourishing friendship. Dr. Orit Kent taps into wisdom from the age-old partnership learning mode of Jewish study to help build skills that are relevant to fostering friendships. And Dr. Alan Morinis introduces the art of self-knowledge and personal character development, which fosters traits such as patience, persistence, playfulness, curiosity, humility, and creativity as a path toward establishing and sustaining deeper friendships.

---

23   Genesis 2:19.

24   Erich Fromm, *The Art of Loving*, New York: Harper & Row, 1956.

25   https://www.washingtonpost.com/opinions/2022/11/23/americans-alone-thanksgiving-friends/.

Respect and Reciprocity

Adrienne Gold Davis

Adrienne Gold Davis is the director of experience and engagement for Momentum and an international Jewish educator. She was a Canadian TV personality specializing in fashion, style, and beauty before falling in love with all things Jewish and making a major career pivot. She spent 15 years as a senior lecturer and community liaison for the Jewish community before joining the Momentum team. Today she also hosts a top-rated podcast, Rise and Shine *with Adrienne Gold Davis, and leads Momentum trips to Israel.*

I want to share a most powerful secret for maintaining respectful relationships. It doesn't matter if they are romantic or platonic, with your parents or with your children. At work or at home. With friends or with colleagues. It's a simple two-word formula that ensures the dignity of your fellow and keeps your focus on your own issues. It is simply this: LOOK. AWAY.

Now, this seems to fly in the face of the model of analysis, magnification, and dissection that we currently indulge in. Perhaps we labor under the delusion that when we truly understand the MOTIVATION for someone else's untoward behavior, when we truly SHARE with them what they are doing that is annoying us, when we list and elucidate the *unpleasant* in our view, then we can somehow make it stop. Or make THEM stop. Or control the things that trigger us in any way. But that is all that it is. A delusion. Because fellowship and friendship, love and intimacy, are not based on staring at that which offends or annoys us in the other. Those emotions are best served by looking away.

There is a famous biblical story that became the very prayer we say when we walk into a synagogue. It is the story of a prophet for hire named Bilaam, who was engaged to curse the Jewish people as a nation. When he overlooked our encampment and tried to speak words of curses, what came out instead was this: *Mah tovu, ohalecha Ya'akov, mish'k'no'techa Yisrael.*

Or in English: How lovely are your tents, O Jacob, Your dwelling places, O Israel.

What exactly did Bilaam see that made words of praise fall from his lips unintentionally? One of the thoughts we learn is from the biblical commentator Rashi. He tells us that in the Israelite encampment none of the people's tent doors faced anyone else's, so no one could peer into their neighbors' tents. The Jewish mandate for privacy, for not looking where you are not invited, is a profoundly healing behavior. And it comes up time and again in our sources.

When I was first married, I thought that to truly know my husband meant that I should know his every thought. His every whereabouts. His every weakness. And I made a point of searching for them. I think I thought that love meant seeing everything and even letting the other know you could see. For their BEST INTEREST. Because YOU CARE. BECAUSE you love them! I have come to learn that the very opposite is true. And if we feel the inclination to do this with our spouses, how much more so do we believe we have the right — the obligation — to do this with our children. But something happened with one of my children that taught me about the value and dignity of looking away in order to spare someone the embarrassment of being seen while not at their best.

I was watching a soccer match when one of my boys was about five. He was very excited to be a legendary goalie in his own mind! He didn't make a move without looking to see if I was watching. He could tell from across the field if I averted my attention for even one moment. One evening during a game, I happened to have a seat right behind the goal and watched a player moving quickly on the net. I knew the kid was good and that he would likely score a goal. And that it would break my son's heart. And he would hate that I saw. So as if by impulse, as the ball went into the net, I swiveled around and pretended to be talking to the woman sitting behind me. I looked away so as not to witness what I knew he would not want me to see in his five-year-old machismo. On the way home that night we went for ice cream after his team's crushing defeat. It was a double scoop on a school night just before bed kind of defeat. As we groaned and waddled back to the car, my little one took my hand and, in a moment of unfettered honesty, said, "Mom, thanks for not seeing me lose the game." I stayed silent. I did not know if even he understood what he was saying but, in that moment, I understood it was an act of love for him that made me turn around. And that it was something I had never done for my husband! It was a revelation. I looked away. I chose to see him only at his best.

Consider a behavior from someone in your close environment for which you would like to experiment with looking away.

The years pass quickly, as they do, and the stakes grow higher than missing a save in goal. It becomes time to navigate a more challenging relationship with our kids, with new rules of engagement. As those stakes get higher, we tend to forget to look away. We overfocus more than ever because we fear the consequences more viscerally. So, I assert that the most challenging friendship to navigate may be the burgeoning one that is possible between a parent and their adult child. The beauty inherent in that challenge is that it identifies the extent one will go to in order to sustain a relationship when its landscape changes so profoundly; how far the heart will stretch and the mind expand to accommodate those changes. For if the relationship between parent and adult child does not evolve into a form of friendship, then it often cannot sustain its closeness. If the dynamic of power doesn't shift from giver / receiver to a more balanced kind of loving, a young adult may resent and push against the parents' clearly defined role as provider.

We see this necessary shift in dynamic play out in the formation of man and woman after God separates the first human into its separate male and female parts — Adam and Chava. In Genesis we learn of the directive to Adam that "he shall leave his mother and his father and cleave to his wife"! But Adam had no earthly parents. What dynamic is God referring to as He commands this shifting of emotional and behavioral "households"?

Consider the words of Rebbetzin Tziporah Heller: "The normal relationship between parents and children is that parents give and children receive. The love that grows between them is surprisingly unbalanced. *Parents love their children far more than most children love their parents. There is a flaw inherent in the relationship that causes this misbalance. Love is never the result of taking. It is the result of giving. The more we give, the more we love. The more we love, the more we are beloved.*"[26]

This is reenforced by the great *mussar* giant Rabbi Eliyahu Dessler, who, in his epic book *Strive for Truth!*,[27] teaches that love and giving always come together. Is the giving a consequence of the love, or is perhaps the reverse true: Is the love a result of the giving? We usually think it is love that causes giving because we observe that a person showers gifts and favors on the beloved. But there is another side to the argument. Giving may bring about love for the same reason a person loves what he has created or nurtured: He recognizes in it part of himself. Whether it is a child he has brought into the world, an animal he has reared, a

---

26   Rebbetzin Tziporah Heller, "Getting and Giving the Love You Need," https://aish.com/48898307/, emphasis added.

27   Rabbi Eliyahu E. Dessler, *Michtav Me'Eliyahu* (*Strive for Truth!*), Kuntres HaHesed (section on Kindness).

plant he has tended, or even a thing he has made or a house he has built — a person is bound in love to the work of his hands, for in it he finds himself.

For Adam to love his wife properly he would need to leave behind the childhood model of being exclusively the receiver or the giver. The lines between giver and receiver are blurred as a true oneness of mutual vulnerability and reciprocity is allowed to flourish.

We are not 50/50 but rather 100/100. And that creates the glorious intimate friendship possible between couples.

We have a model for that relationship. It is not encumbered by confusing feelings of lust or even by expectations. It has a chemistry, but not one that is dependent on physical attraction. It is called platonic friendship. It is the thing that causes the Talmud to say, "Either a friend or death"[28] and Sefer Hamidot LehaMeiri to say, "A person without a friend is like a left hand without a right one." Pirkei Avot 1:6 teaches that friendship is so vital we should be willing to pay for it! *"Acquire* a friend" (even if it costs money!!) — because there are costs involved in sustaining friendships. And while not all those costs are financial, there are investments of time and patience and loyalty and sometimes the discomfort of tolerating the seemingly intolerable. But the cost is worth it. Because friendship is a relationship's greatest glue.

When our children developmentally need to stop needing us, many parents feel as though their very position is threatened. Their attachment to the position of giver and its inherent emotional rewards feels shaky and tenuous. What does it mean to not be needed? Does it mean I have been successful — or I have failed? Can or will my child love me and want to be near me if they don't need me?

The fifth commandment tells us to honor our father and mother, and this commandment has no statute of limitations. But note that it does not say "love your parents" or even "enjoy spending time" with them! Closer examination of this commandment gives us guidelines on the standards of treatment and of comportment required regarding our treatment of our parents. What we can and cannot say. What we need or don't need to provide. It is behaviorally driven, not emotionally driven. It teaches us to act in gratitude for the gift of life we were provided. And it is the bridge we traverse that teaches us how to have gratitude for God!

If one wants a relationship with one's adult children, then the spirit of friendship must be acquired as well. The work in this is mostly on the parents in the recognition of the autonomy of their child. In the respect and honor afforded their decisions and choices, even when they are in conflict with ours. In a

---

28   Babylonian Talmud Bava Batra 16b.

celebration — not just a tolerance — of their differences from us. In an acceptance and even admiration of their unique perspectives. In the space between us. In the boundaries required in all respectful relationships. This requires more, not less, looking away.

The love I felt for my children hit me like a freight train. I never imagined I could experience such a depth and breadth of feeling. My desire to give was unbounded. I understood what Rabbi Akiva meant when he said, "More than the calf desires to suck, the mother wishes to suckle." My desire to "feed" my children spilled over into every aspect of their lives. I wanted to be the font of all wisdom. The source of all love. The place of all nourishment. And then they became teens. I remember the first shut doors — first to the bathroom, then to their bedrooms. I remember the sound of the car door shutting without me behind the wheel. I remember the sound of the door of the dorm building clicking shut behind me ("Don't let it hit you as you leave, Ma!"). I remember the doors of communications slamming shut. Those doors that I had helped seal with my refusal to relinquish control over their lives. By the magnified looking I could not stop engaging in. And I had plenty of rationalization for my actions: "I am STILL the parent!" "I cannot allow them to DESTROY THEIR OWN LIVES." "This is still my job!"

In agony I went to my dearest friend. She spoke to me as only she can.

A true friend does not collude with you! They do not defend your feelings at the risk of the truth. She had watched this power struggle unfold before my unseeing eyes and gently helped me understand what needed to occur. She and I are very, very different. We practice different religions. We have different interests. We look different. We think differently. We enjoy different foods and music and even people. But our celebration of one another's differences has been the fertile ground for my most enduring relationship. She asked the poignant question: Why am I charmed by her differences and not by those of my children? Why do I thrill to our disagreements and yearn to focus on what unites us rather than what divides us? Why do I not worry about her when she does not act like / think like / behave like me? The answer was a painful one to be sure: "Because you are my friend, not my child!" I declared. "Lucky me," she replied. Ouch.

I would never assume to know what is ultimately right for my best friend. I trust that she will do that work. I know that when she needs to process, sometimes she seeks my opinion and sometimes she seeks my ability to listen. I recognize both our autonomy and our interconnectedness. I respect her boundaries and know her limitations. And she knows mine. I know when to stand back and when to dive in. I know this because, over 40 years, I have learned to watch, wait, and wonder. To read her signals. To tread gently but passionately. To adjust my step to fall into hers.

Perhaps it was time to make friends with my adult kids!

Friendship is both acquired and bestowed upon us. We can find it by proximity. We can nurture it across miles. It feels so good because it is that unconditional form of love that we crave. It makes us feel seen and heard and understood by someone who has no skin in the game. At a certain point, all parents will need to reach out to their children with a gift of this friendship. It is deeply vulnerable to be needy when you are an adult. Many kids push away all reminders of their dependency — because the cost of showing their vulnerability is to be shoved back into the role of receiver. To be infantilized.

But when we offer friendship to our adult children, we give them permission to need us once again. And we give ourselves permission to enjoy them not as reflections of ourselves, but as the souls we had the gift of nurturing as they made their own personal journeys through this transmigration.

I have had to pull back in order to get closer. And in this seeming dichotomy lies the essence of friendship — a foundation of any relationship, romantic or platonic. I acquired friendship with my adult children by modeling it upon my already mature friendships with peers. And now I have two more friends. Who want to be with me again. Who want my wisdom of years again. Who love me unconditionally again.

It took me analyzing and micromanaging less. And looking away more.

Just look away. You will find yourself closer than you ever thought possible.

Fostering and Maintaining Intimate Friendship and Love

Hedy Schleifer

Hedy Shleifer, a master couples' therapist, co-founded Encounter-centered Couples Therapy and Encounter-centered Transformation (EcT). Hedy, who speaks seven languages, has taught and provided her approach to relationships in more than 39 countries. Revered by students and clients all over the world, she is the subject of the documentary "Hedy and Yumi Crossing the Bridge," which tells the story of her life's work through the lens of her relationship with her husband and professional partner, Yumi, and won Best Documentary at the 2009 LA Femme Film Festival in Hollywood. Her talk at TEDxTelAviv on The Power of Connection *is not to be missed.*

Through connection we have the power to transform ourselves. Connection is our essence. It is humanity's superpower. It requires us to share kindness and to develop compassion, generosity of spirit, unconditional patience, respect, and honor — all of which enable us to gradually grow into who we truly are, in all our full, essential humanity. We are conceived in connection and then we spend nine months ensconced within the safety of our mother's wombs. Ideally, we are born into the welcoming embrace of loving parents who — if they know how important it is for us to feel connected — smile at us, soothe us, and sing to us. Their delighted facial expressions convey to us the message: "We are so glad that you came into this world to be with us!" Through this first loving connection with our family, we learn how to stay connected naturally to others — and the art of friendship is born.

Author Elif Shafak wrote, "Every true love is a story of unexpected transformation. If we are the same person before and after we loved, that means we haven't loved enough."[29]

---

29   Elif Shafak, *The Forty Rules of Love: A Novel of Rumi*, New York: Viking Penguin, 2010.

From Unconscious to Conscious Friendship

The year was 1964. I had just returned to my home town of Antwerp, Belgium, after experiencing a tragic boating accident on the River Parana in the Brazilian jungle, in which I lost my friend Luzzi. Yumi was in Europe on assignment from his American company. Twenty years earlier, on August 9, 1944, he had lost both his sisters when the refugee boat they were on was torpedoed on its way to Palestine, and the survivors machine-gunned. His understanding of the profound grief I felt was visceral. I was born on August 19, 1944, ten days after his sisters were killed. When we met, we felt not only friendship, but a strange kinship, almost like brother and sister.

"What am I to you?" asked Yumi.

"You are my best friend," I answered.

And so he said, "As your best friend, I recommend you marry me!"

We were married on April 13, 1965, in Tel Aviv, Israel. Unbeknownst to us, we were beginning a journey toward building a living laboratory for a passionately full marriage, in which we would foster and maintain a flourishing friendship. We did not yet know how to successfully combine and balance all the complex elements — friendship, romance, desire, and soulmate-ness — that comprise an intimate relationship. I must honestly say that Yumi and I were, at that time, Olympic champions of unconsciousness. We had no idea that there *was* such a thing as a conscious relationship, within which one makes the shift willingly from automatic reactivity to thoughtful intentionality. Moving from coping in isolation to living in connection.

Our saving grace was that we devised a way to welcome Shabbat in our own special way; a way that allowed us to deeply connect with each other. We made a commitment to never enter the sanctity of Shabbat with angry feelings. Inspired by the idea of water as transformative, as with the ritual of immersing in the *mikvah*, the ritual bath, we would talk things out while soaking in the tub together. It was a serious commitment. So much so that one day we overheard our son Yigal, who was then four years old, say, "No, my parents can't come to the phone right now. They're in the bathtub, and they'll be there for a long time."

Each week, when we were finally ready to drain the water out of the tub, our promise to each other would be to surrender to peace and forgiveness.

Over the years, Yumi and I became avid students of the power of connection. Our friendship deepened. William Blake wrote, "The bird a nest. The spider a web. Man friendship." Yes, indeed! Yumi and I learned to land increasingly within the safety and sanctity of true friendship.

The Three Invisible Connectors in Friendship

Yumi and I developed a core guiding principle, inspired by the Jewish philosopher Martin Buber. To foster and maintain our flourishing friendship, three invisible connectors had to be embraced within it:

- The relational space between us
- The bridge connecting our worlds
- The encounter of our souls

An idea that comes through Buber's teaching is that our relationship lives in the space between us. It doesn't live in one or the other of us, nor even in our dialogue. Our relationship lives in the space between us, which is sacred.

It was from the space between the two cherubs that God spoke to the Israelites in ancient time. Space is sacred, indeed; one of God's names is *HaMakom*, which means The Place.

Buber explains that "when two people relate to each other authentically and humanly, God is the electricity that surges between them."[30]

Yumi and I were influenced by Martin Buber because he based his relational philosophy on the deep and long friendship with his wife, Paula. With Paula, he viscerally and palpably experienced an encounter of souls, which he describes in his book *I and Thou*.

This profound form of encounter is not reserved only for romantic relationships; I also experienced it with my mother. By her nineties she was living in an old-age home outside of Tel Aviv. When I visited her, and looked at her frail and fragile body as she sat in her wheelchair, I was flooded with negative emotions: guilt, anger, resentment, and shame. My mother had been my friend and my hero, the fierce woman who crossed the Alps on foot while pregnant with me after a daring, brilliant escape from Rivesaltes, a Nazi transit camp in Vichy France. The story I grew up with is that, when she reached the Swiss border and found it closed to refugees, she hurled herself over a fenced border, survived, and recovered in a Swiss hospital before being sent to the refugee camp where I was born.

At first, all I could think of was that I could not bear to see my mother this way. But then, suddenly, I had a realization: I wasn't visiting my mother, I was polluting the space between us with my own emotions. I made the conscious decision to leave my own world and the neighborhood of mixed emotions, and to *cross the bridge* that connected our worlds in order to truly *be* with her. Once I made that decision, once I crossed, our eyes met.

---

30   Martin Buber, *I and Thou*, 1923.

She looked at me intently. And then, in Yiddish, she said, *"Di bisst mein tochter"* ("You are my daughter"). It had been months since she had recognized me. But, of course, I hadn't been with her in months. We both cried together.

The Little Prince, created by Antoine de Saint-Exupéry, speaks of being responsible for our friends. Yes! It was my responsibility to *truly* meet my mother, to give her my undivided, loving presence. To quiet the thoughts and chatter in my mind so I could cross over to her reality. Henry David Thoreau wrote, "The language of friendship is not words, but meanings." When I arrived in my mother's world, our language was made of the multi-layered meanings of our rich relationship as a mother and a daughter. That experience is the encounter of the souls.

In this encounter, two individuals, with their uniqueness and differences, enter together a dimension of oneness.

Gently close your eyes. Visualize yourself sitting across from a beloved — a partner, a friend, a parent, or a child. With your imagination, see, feel, and sense the quality of the relational space between you both. Imagine a bridge that connects your world to the world of the other person. Let yourself feel invited to cross this bridge to visit the other where they live right now. See how the space between the two of you fills with thankfulness and delight.

Friendship and the Brain

What Martin Buber could not know as a twentieth-century philosopher when he taught about the sacred space between us, and the encounter of the souls, is what the new brain science of the twenty-first century would teach us. The relatively new discipline of interpersonal neurobiology explores brain plasticity (or neuroplasticity) — the ability of our brains to change, adapt, and grow in response to our experiences. It turns out that our friendships and love connections change our brains to be able to respond more consciously and intentionally rather than get hijacked into automatic reactivity. Relationships change our brains — and good, deep relationships change our brains even more.

Amazingly, what interpersonal neurobiologists have discovered is that when we are in close physical proximity with someone we love, and we look into each other's eyes with soft eyes and we speak to each other in such a way that we feel felt, then our limbic systems, the structures in the brain that deal with emotions and memory, become resonant with each other. Scientists have called this limbic resonance between people in harmony the *brain-bridge*. A further discovery scientists have made is that once the brain-bridge is established between two people, their central nervous systems relax together. It turns out that the brain is the only human organ that does not regulate from within, the way, for example, our hearts, lungs, and kidneys do. The brain needs to be attuned to another brain to achieve full relaxation. We cannot regulate as deeply and fully alone as we can when we are together. Because calming down is more effective in relationship to another trusted person, rather than in isolation, it is counterproductive to say to a child who is acting out, "Go to your room until you have calmed down."

> *Choose a time to offer a child, spouse, or friend your full attention, with curiosity and openheartedness, without providing any advice, as you listen to them talk about what's on their mind.*

Friends Hold Each Other's Hands

"He held my hand in a way I didn't even know a hand could be held." This is how I begin the story of how my husband, Yumi, gave me support twenty-two years ago when I was diagnosed with breast cancer. We sat together, both terrified. Then Yumi said to me, "Hedy, how long shall we be terrified? Two hours? Three? After that, this is not a problem to be solved. It is an adventure to be lived." Yumi gave the adventure a name: Rallying around the Boob. Everyone who rallied became a member of the Boob Brigade.

Researcher Dr. James A. Coan, who studies the neuroscience of emotion and social relationships, wondered how the presence of a loved one might alter the brain's response to a threatening situation. He designed a unique test in which the subject knew there was a twenty percent chance of experiencing a slight electric shock to their ankle. Critically, during the test, some subjects had their hands held by their spouse, a boyfriend or girlfriend, or a stranger. Dr. Coan found that the neural regions of the brain associated with processing threat were significantly less active when someone was holding the participant's hand. The level of activity was even lower for those subjects whose hands were being held by their loved one.[31]

Even more remarkable were the findings when Dr. Coan decided to adapt the test to introduce the *threat* of the shock to the person holding the subject's hand. The subject's brain responded as if they themselves were in danger of

---

31   Jane Kelly, "'Shocking' New Research Finds Friendships Are Key to Good Health," *UVA Today*, May 26, 2017.

receiving the shock, to the point that it became impossible to tell which person was actually the recipient of the shock. Dr. Coan realized that we adapt to each other by sending brain signals that essentially say, "I am with you." Over time, this message transforms into, "I am you and you are me and we are here." There is a verse in Song of Songs that asserts: *"Ani le dodi ve dodi li,"*[32] "I am my beloved's and my beloved is mine." Connection to others is not only a survival skill — it gives us our humanity and our ability to flourish.

True Love Is a Story of Unexpected Transformation

Over the years, Yumi and I filled our relational space with treasures and now, in the new phase of life we have entered called Elderhood, we draw from it like a well-stocked bank account. Today, Yumi lives with a changed memory. It is now my turn to hold his hand "the way he didn't know a hand could be held." As a wife, I find myself dipping into the rich, fertile, relational soil that Yumi and I cultivated for over fifty-four years. In it I find the generosity of spirit, the calm patience, the openheartedness in which I am able to live every moment with my "new" husband. I call this new Yumi the twenty-ninth version of my husband in our long journey together through life. He has had the courage to transform many times. Over the years, I have decided to choose him as my beloved and best friend again and again. I do miss my previous Yumi, but yet again I welcome my new, transformed man. I realize that this twenty-ninth husband requires of me a new way to love my man. It is a kinder, sweeter, more affectionate, more present love, and an additional lesson in the deep meaning of giving unconditionally. That is why I am calling our new adventure Rallying around the Essence. Our essence is our core potential for full humanity, and it stays intact no matter what occurs. I do not accept the label of *caregiver.* Yumi and I are each other's *care-partners.* I care for him as deeply as I can, and he cares for me as deeply as he can. This way, our friendship continues to grow and thrive after all these years.

I have just lost my precious best friend and soul sister, Louise. She died on the third Shabbat of April 2020, after suffering progressive supranuclear palsy, an illness that systematically took away her agency. A group of women, good friends of Louise, created a Zoom funeral and a Zoom *shivah* for her. Friends and family gathered to honor our beloved Louise. I was in awe of the power of the stories that were told about her — stories we all had held onto as treasures in our souls. I learned from this experience that our friendships continue to blossom even after our deaths, when our friends share their treasured stories of us.

---

32   Song of Songs 6:3.

Martin Buber wrote that all of life is in the encounter. He pointed us toward the relational paradigm. Our Western culture looks at life through the prism of the individual paradigm. In it, our highest aspiration is to become independent, autonomous, and self-governed. The relational paradigm, on the other hand, posits that we are born in connection and that our highest purpose is to live in that connection and interdependence. Albert Einstein has said that our separation is an optical illusion of consciousness. In *I and Thou,* Buber wrote that a human being becomes whole not in virtue of a relation to himself, but rather in virtue of an authentic relation to another human being.

We are one web of humanity. Our friendships gift us with the opportunity to experience our true essence in connection, and through that connection we find our wholeness.

Tapping Jewish Learning and Wisdom to Cultivate Friendships

Dr. Orit Kent

Dr. Orit Kent is the founder and co-director of Pedagogy of Partnership (PoP), an innovative, research-based model that brings Jewish learning wisdom to bear on twenty-first-century education and communal life. Through PoP, powered by the Hadar Institute, Orit works to re-envision Jewish learning and teach core relational skills to cultivate the habits of wonder, empathy, and responsibility. A long-time educator, researcher, and writer, Orit has written widely about peer- and relationship-based learning. She is the co-author of the award-winning book A Philosophy of Havruta.

Nobody sees a flower really; it is so small. We haven't time, and to see takes time — like to have a friend takes time.
Georgia O'Keefe

I was walking back home from the train station after a long day at work, in a rush to get home to make dinner. I passed Jenny, a neighbor I had seen on multiple occasions but had never spoken to. I said hello and she responded accordingly. That could have been the end of the story. It often is. I happened to notice that Jenny was carrying a bag of berries and made a comment about how beautiful they looked. Jenny shared that she loves to stop at a market to get fresh berries for her children. My curiosity got the best of me, and so I inquired about her children — how old were they and what else did they like to eat and do. Thus began a friendship that has spanned close to two decades.

Within Jewish tradition, we have texts that discuss the value of friendship. We also have references to a Jewish learning practice called *havruta*, which creates a bridge between friendship and learning Torah together. The Aramaic term *havruta* contains within it the Hebrew letters for the word *haver,* friend. And while everyone who studies Torah together is not necessarily friends and every group of friends does not necessarily study Torah together, *havruta* offers a model of relationship that has enduring wisdom to teach us about friendship still today.

Havruta study is a Jewish learning tradition in which two people learn a text together, reading it aloud, discussing its meaning, and exploring its broader applications to their lives. It is an age-old mode of Torah study that, in the ideal, provides an opportunity for rich social, intellectual, ethical, and spiritual engagement.[33]

An understanding of the merits of studying with others seems to reach as far back as the Babylonian Talmud, edited in the sixth century. A number of talmudic stories call our attention to the importance of having a good study partner and the trauma that prevails when that study partner is no longer present. For example, we are told of the story of Rabbi Yohanan, one of the greatest rabbis in his time, who is despondent when his study partner Reish Lakish dies because his new study partner does not debate with him as Reish Lakish did. Importantly, this story calls our attention to the value of a sustained relationship with others who can speak to us directly, challenge our ideas, and help us see things in new ways.

In Tractate Taanit of the Talmud, we are told about Honi the Circle Maker,[34] who returns to the house of study after falling asleep for 70 years. When he returns, no one recognizes him or believes he is who he says he is. In reference to his situation, another sage explains: "Either *havruta* or death"; for Honi, life without people who truly know him is not worth living. This story emphasizes the centrality of friendship in our lives, and part of that centrality is having people who notice and recognize us for who we are.

How might we cultivate the type of relationship for which Honi longed? Our sages taught: "Make for yourself a teacher and acquire for yourself a friend."[35] Some commentators note that the connection of teaching and friendship is an indication of the role that learning together plays in friendship. In addition, the word *acquire* hints at the fact that intentionality is involved and that *havruta* friendship requires our attention and work.

---

33   The value of studying with others and specifically with a partner is highlighted as far back as in the Talmud. Scholars debate when *havruta* became a form of study practiced by students in *yeshivot*, institutions for Jewish learning. Sources suggest that *havruta* as a form of study practiced in *yeshivot* had its roots in the sixteenth century. It seems to have become widely used in *yeshivot* at some point in the nineteenth century. Today, *havruta* as a form of study is used in traditional *yeshivot* and in many modern and liberal Jewish contexts.

34   The Talmud tells stories of Honi drawing a circle as part of a ritual to bring rain during drought — hence his moniker, Honi the Circle Maker.

35   Pirkei Avot 1:6.

A commentary on this teaching further probes: "How does one acquire a friend? A person acquires a friend for themself by eating and drinking with their friend, by studying Torah with their friend, by lodging with their friend, by sharing their private thoughts about Torah and other parts of life."[36]

> *Reflect on a friendship you developed. What*
> *contributed to cultivating this friendship?*

We make friends by sharing in the most fundamental human experiences of life, which include our daily activities, for some the study of Torah, and the revealing of our inner thoughts to another person in mutual trust. We know that some people form friendships based on activities and others form friendships based on emotional closeness. Avot d'Rabbi Natan points out that we all need both. We acquire friends through both doing things together and sharing our inner selves. The kinds of engagement highlighted in the text intertwines us in one another's lives through regularly occurring activities like eating, lodging, and learning. These regular points of contact are so important because they bring us into each other's presence physically, emotionally, and spiritually. They create opportunities to attend to one another and be affected by one another.

Avot d'Rabbi Natan continues: "When one is engaged in Torah learning with their friend, and one of them makes a mistake in the *halachah* (Jewish law), their friend corrects them." One of the most important roles of a true friend, therefore, is to help us stay on the right path and seek to understand the correct way. Avot d'Rabbi Natan brings in the biblical wisdom that "two are better than one … For should they fall, one can raise up the other."[37] Friends who invest in their relationship serve to hold one another steady and true in matters of Torah and life. Our friends can fortify us to seek the good and help us be our best selves and we, in turn, can do this for our friends. This kind of friendship is truly a gift to be treasured.[38]

We know we enjoy and benefit from friends. And as Robert Waldinger and Marc Schulz document through their longitudinal research, "[T]he engine of the

---

36   Avot d'Rabbi Natan 8:3.

37   Ecclesiastes 4:9–10.

38   My thanks to my colleague Allison Cook with whom I explored this text in Avot d'Rabbi Natan and wrote about it in a blog: https://www.jewishchallenge.org/insights/2019/6/19/torah-and-friendshipfor-their-own-sake.

good life is not the self ... but rather our connections to others."[39] Their research and that of others highlight that relationships not only help improve our mental health but also help our physical well-being. As life is increasingly busy, it can sometimes feel hard to find the time to make friends, and even if we don't fall asleep for 70 years like Honi, it can also feel hard to keep friends.

Fast forward 15 years. Jenny and I have not spoken in a few months and, when we do, it is often in passing. Our kids are no longer so young that they run around in our backyards together, allowing Jenny and me built-in time to catch up. Between the schedules and needs of our now teenage children and our ailing parents and the demands of work, it's hard to find time for each other. As we have been less involved in each other's lives and we have less shared between us, we have unintentionally grown distant.

Turning to the Jewish learning practice of *havruta* can give us some guidance on this as well.

Introduce a Text to Your Friendship

While we often think of *havruta* as being about two partners in learning, there is actually a third partner — the Torah text.[40] It is through engaging with the Torah text that the partners come to better know the Torah and each other. When we apply this idea to friendship, we expand the notion of a text to mean any third thing (big or small) that both friends can engage with in some way. It could be a Torah text — and it could also be many other things, such as an image, story, poem, article, book, video, song, shared view or activity, etc. The "text" becomes a common focus through which friends can share an experience of engaging together. And through shared experience, the grounds of friendship are cultivated.

Tailor *Havruta* Practices to Cultivate Your Friendship

Breaking down *havruta* study into six core practices — listening, articulating,

---

39   Robert Waldinger, MD, and Marc Schulz, PhD, *The Good Life: Lessons from the World's Longest Study of Happiness*, New York, NY: Simon & Schuster, 2023, p. 52.

40   Elie Holzer and Orit Kent, *A Philosophy of Havruta: Understanding and Teaching the Art of Text Study in Pairs*, Boston: Academic Studies Press, 2013.

wondering, focusing, supporting, and challenging[41] — highlights the profound, far-reaching lessons we can bring to cultivate and grow our friendships. Here are a few of these practices as well as phrases to enact them.

Listening

Havruta study is predicated on active listening. When learners approach a Torah text for the first time, they put aside their preconceived notions and allow the text to speak to them on its own terms. They train themselves to be alert for the text's core ideas, its nuances, and its ambiguities. Plus, they must listen to each other. The practice of *havruta* study depends on each partner being willing to consider the opinions, viewpoints, assumptions, and ideas of the other, thereby fostering respect and honor that will generate success. That is the power of listening.

Listening can have a big impact on our friendships. It displays a generosity of spirit to those around us, indicating, "I want to stop the other things I'm doing and thinking about and take the time to hear what you have to say, to be present, to learn from you and be responsive." Listening to another conveys deep respect and encouragement. We need people who are sensitive, thoughtful, open-minded, and able to consider things from multiple angles. Imagine if more people were experienced in making space for each other's voices and perspectives.

Simply saying, "I'd love to hear more about that" and giving the other person an opportunity to speak can go a long way toward establishing and re-establishing our connections and friendships. Listening does take time — but more important than the quantity of time we spend listening is making sure there are moments of quality listening when we put devices and other things aside to really focus on our friend. Giving ourselves and our friends the gift of intentional listening, even if only for five minutes, can be meaningful and energizing.

Articulating

Articulating or sharing thoughts out loud within a *havruta* challenges people to go beyond staying quiet or jumping to state a final interpretation. The practice of articulating equips learners to ask questions and acknowledge

---

41   These practices are based in educational research. See Orit Kent, "A Theory of *Havruta* Learning," Journal of Jewish Education, 2010, 76(3), p. 215–245, https://doi.org/10.1080/152 44113.2010.501499.

their uncertainties, to think aloud together in order to explore and refine their thinking, and to check for understanding by restating the other's ideas. Distinct from other habits of speech, articulating is not about talking *over* others or a text, but talking *with* others and *with* a text in a cooperatively constructed conversation. More than a performance of self-expression, articulating empowers people as active participants and creates a respectful working relationship with another person and with the text itself.

This is key to developing and strengthening friendships. Through this kind of articulating, people explore their ideas by thinking aloud together, allowing one another into their thought process *before* ideas are fully formed and opening the possibility of building ideas together. One friend might say to another, "I think this might mean ... What do you think?" By sharing our thinking out loud, we invite our friends into our conversation, which helps them get to know us and invites their insights. This kind of back and forth opens up a friendship space filled with ideas, questions, silence, and laughter.

Wondering

Wondering occurs in *havruta* when learners' minds and hearts are actively engaged in listening to the text and to each other. They notice little quirks and opacities in what they hear and they begin to ask, "What does this mean?" Learners can build up their capacity to wonder and fuel the creative process of meaning-making and problem-solving with their observations and questions.

Friendship also benefits from our sense of curiosity and wonder. To connect with another person, we need to lean into this curiosity not for the sake of being a busybody but to really attend to the other person and the world together. Taking a few minutes to notice what is going on with a friend, what they are doing or even what they are carrying as I did with Jenny, can have far-reaching effect. We can say to one another, "I notice that you are ..." or "I was wondering how you were doing ..." or "I was wondering about what you said or did that time and would love to hear more ..." and give them space to respond. Noticing and wondering can also focus on things in our environments: "I noticed those new flowers growing in your garden" or "I wonder what this means or how this works?" A simple noticing or wondering can help build or rebuild a bridge of connection while also opening ourselves to the joy of seeing our world anew. No matter how long friends know each other, or how close they are, there is always room to discover new things to wonder about. This is part of what keeps friendships growing.

Be Content with Small Steps over Time

Havruta learning also helps us recognize the value and potential impact of small moves. In *havruta*, a single question that takes a minute to ask can change the whole course of thinking and the insights that are developed. And because *havruta* is based on a commitment to ongoing learning together, it's OK if we only have five minutes to ask a question and begin to consider the response, because we know we will continue to probe the text together at another time.

Small moves can be sustaining for friendship too. Sometimes, in friendships, we need to carve out more time for a heart to hear or for a longer activity together. Sometimes what we need is for our friend to ask a question that signals they care, or to take the time to share something so we can laugh together, nod together, and even sigh together. There are endless small moves to be made that help us weave together the threads of our friendships.

The True Benefit of Five Minutes

I text Jenny, "Do you have time for a five-minute walk?" She responds, "Sure." I go to her house and we walk around the block. I say, "I'd love to hear how you are doing." Inevitably, as she talks, I am amazed at all she is trying to do both at home and at work and the grace with which she's doing it. As we round the corner, we happen to look up and see a rainbow in the sky. This becomes the shared text for the last minute of our walk as we recount other rainbows we have seen and the significance of those moments. Our five minutes are up. We agree to walk again for five minutes the next week. I go back home feeling grounded and joyful.

> *For which friend might you carve out some time?*
> *How can you reach out?*

While there are many practical reasons we may seek out friends, at the end of the day the joy of being attuned to another and, in turn, recognized by them knows no limit. Our sources teach that when two people sit together and words of Torah are uttered between them, the *Shechinah* / Divine presence abides between them.[42] When we have a *havruta* friend for study and life, we open space for the unknown and infinite in our lives. Perhaps that is the true benefit of friendship.

---

42   Pirkei Avot 3:2.

Doing Our Inner Work for Friendship

Dr. Alan Morinis

Alan Morinis is an anthropologist, filmmaker, writer, student of spiritual traditions, and founder of The Mussar Institute. He is an active interpreter of the teachings and practices of the mussar *tradition and regularly gives lectures and workshops. Born and raised in a culturally Jewish but non-observant home, he studied anthropology at Oxford University on a Rhodes Scholarship. The author of* Everyday Holiness, Climbing Jacob's Ladder, Every Day Holy Day, *and* With Heart in Mind, *he is a producer of several feature films, television dramas, and documentaries.*

A World of Affectionate Friendship

Judaism is a religion of friendship. Traditional Jewish sources view our world, in its essence, as a place of closeness and intimacy. In Hebrew, this is called *olam ha'yedidut* — a world of affectionate friendship.

This perspective features prominently in the thought of Rabbi Shlomo Wolbe,[43] a great thinker who taught *mussar*, a Jewish spiritual tradition that focuses on personal self-development to overcome inner obstacles and achieve greater awareness, wisdom, and transformation. Rabbi Wolbe said, "If we wish to outline the Torah of Israel in great brevity, literally 'on one foot,'[44] we would call it: 'a world of *yedidut* [affectionate friendship].'"[45]

Rabbi Wolbe sees our world as having been established, from the moment of

---

43 Rabbi Shlomo Wolbe was a German-born, university-educated rabbi who studied in the pre-Holocaust Lithuanian *yeshivot*. He was the *menahel ruchani*, spiritual head, of the Be'er Yaakov *yeshivah* in Israel for more than thirty years.

44 Whether that "foot" is interpreted literally, as the length of time one could balance on one leg, or idiomatically, as a single foundational principle upon which everything else "stands."

45 This and subsequent quotes from Rabbi Wolbe (unless otherwise noted) are drawn from the essay "Psychiatria ve-Dat" ("Psychiatry and Religion") published in Bishvilei ha'Refu'ah (In the Paths of Medicine), vol. 5, Laniado Hospital, Kiryat Sanz, Sivan 5742, 1982, p. 57–60, as translated by Rabbi Micha Berger.

its creation, as a place of friendship. He points to the warmth and caring that the Torah tells us is the essence of the bond between God and humanity, citing Psalms: "You are close, O Lord."[46] As we pray in times of serenity and express gratitude in times of joy, we feel closeness and affection to God. We feel that same affection for the people around us.

Rabbi Wolbe sees the pull we feel to connect with other people and with God as the source of the cohesive energy that holds the world together. The pull we feel toward fond relationships is an essential aspect of our humanity, and the institutions of Jewish life are meant to validate that innate tendency and to give it form and durability in this world.

Balancing Affection and Estrangement

Rabbi Wolbe does not overlook the tremendous forces of cruelty and alienation that plague our world. When he examines these tendencies, he points out that the Torah repeatedly warns against submission to what is described in Hebrew as an *el zar*. This term is usually translated as strange god or foreign god, but it can also mean god of estrangement. In Rabbi Wolbe's view, the *el zar* is the force of disconnection and alienation in the world. He writes, "What a frightening force is the *el zar*, which transforms a person into being a stranger to himself, to others, and to his Creator — truly a stranger, without emotion, without understanding, without connection, without love!"[47]

Rabbi Wolbe uses the lens of *mussar* to help us see and understand the difference between the world of affection (*olam ha'yedidut*) and the world of estrangement (*olam ha'zarut*). *Mussar* focuses on cultivating our *middot* — our inner traits — as the pathway to spiritual growth in general, but it is easy to see how the same methodology will have an impact on building relationships and bringing about the realization of *olam ha'yedidut*. *Mussar* teachers tell us that our *middot* can either aid or detract from our spiritual advancement and from our participation in *olam ha'yedidut*.

To a *mussar* teacher, there are no negative traits — not even anger, envy, impatience, selfishness, judgment, or pride. Even those traits have the potential to play a positive role in life. Anger might be an appropriate response to seeing injustice in the world and a motivator to respond to that injustice; envy can be a positive stimulus for accomplishing one's own goals; pride can instill self-esteem.

---

46 Psalm 119:151.

47 Alei Shur, vol. 2, Jerusalem: Hotsa'at Bet HaMussar, 1986, p. 83.

But if traits such as these become the strongest forces in a person's inner life, they can erect barriers between people that damage relationships and expel a person from *olam ha'yedidut.*

> *Choose a trait that irritates you, your own or a trait of someone close to you, and practice reframing it in a positive way.*

Experiencing a Whole Friendship

In the Torah, David and Jonathan's extraordinary friendship defies everyday explanation. Their souls are described as being knit together — *nikshar.*[48] This framework has guided my closest friendships and my view of friendship in general. When you are truly friends with someone, your separateness is transcended. Your love for that person grows from "I like you, I care about you" to become "you are a part of me."

Friendship also comes with challenges, and two souls knitted together can quickly become unraveled. Several years ago, a colleague and close friend was handling a tremendous amount of work. I wanted to help them, but my many efforts to step up were dismissed or scorned.

It wasn't until after our friendship and our professional relationship fell apart that I began to understand their point of view. To my friend, my efforts to support them weren't seen as helpful at all. When I offered help, I was undermining their leadership. When I spoke up with suggestions, I was revealing my lack of confidence in their ability to do their work.

Yes, the Torah shows us a moment of David and Jonathan's friendship when they are bonded so deeply their souls are knit together. But what about the moments we don't see? The same traits that bond us deeply to one another inevitably cause misunderstandings, frustrations, and annoyances in our relationships. Those less-than-perfect moments are part of the whole too.

In the Tomer Devorah, a work from the sixteenth century by Rabbi Moses Cordovero, he expounds upon the thirteen *middot harachamim*, traits of God. The first two traits are traditionally translated from the Hebrew as compassion before a person misses the mark and compassion after a person misses the mark. Rabbi Cordovero brings this to our earthly level, saying, this trait is tolerance —

---

48   1 Samuel 18:1.

and it's so important it is listed twice. First, tolerate your friend, and then tolerate them again. If you love someone as a true friend, and you have tolerance, you can weather the moments of frustration and miscommunication that inevitably come up. If we don't have tolerance, our relationships disintegrate and our souls unravel.

Working on Ourselves

When we examine the list of traits that disrupt relationships, we can see that they are all tied to the forces of ego. A person who *consistently* feels impatience, intolerance, envy, anger, judgment, and the like self-situates at the center of their world; they see everyone else as somehow lower, wrong, inept, or failing in some way. This is the defining difference between *olam ha'yedidut* and *olam ha'zarut.* When a person's inner world is dominated by a self-centered force, they are confined to the world of estrangement and they will find themselves disconnected consistently in their relationships — whether with God, with other people, or with themselves.

Anger is a good example of an ego-based force that disrupts relationships. Nowhere in the *mussar* literature is anger condemned. Rather, anger is seen as a trait that has its time, place, and measure. Yet, when anger dominates a person's dealings with others, friendly relationships become impossible. If a person were to recognize that their anger was destroying their relationships and wanted to do something about it, the *mussar* teachers would not guide that person to strive to be calmer and more accommodating, as we might expect. Instead, they counsel that person to cultivate the trait of humility.

This fix may not immediately make logical sense, but it comes directly from the teachings of the Ramban,[49] who said, "Once you have distanced yourself from anger, the quality of humility will enter your heart." His insight is that there is an inverse relationship between humility and anger — the two cannot co-exist in your heart. If you are angry, you are not humble. And if you are angry, that form of self-centeredness will cause your relationships to suffer.

When a person's inner life is characterized by humility, generosity, calmness, compassion, and the like, when they live by traits that are not self-serving, that facilitate relationship, the result will be that the person lives in *olam ha'yedidut* — the world of affectionate friendship. In my teaching of *mussar* students, I saw a very simple demonstration of this principle at work. There is a teaching in Pirkei

---

49   Rabbi Moshe ben Nachman, Nachmanides, in Iggeret ha'Ramban, a letter he wrote to his son.

Avot[50] that says, "Greet everyone with a friendly countenance." Based on that "first principle," I assigned *mussar* students the practice of smiling at whomever they encountered over the course of their day. Our role model in this practice was the talmudic sage Rabban Yochanan ben Zakkai, about whom it was said that "no one ever greeted him first, not even a gentile in the marketplace."[51]

When the students reported back on their assignment, they were surprised to discover that they had all had the same experience. When they smiled at someone, that person almost invariably smiled back at them. Whereas previously, many of them had been moving through a world of grim faces, downturned lips, and averted eyes, now their world was populated with bright eyes, smiles, and even warm words of greeting. Having taken up this simple practice of smiling, they had transferred themselves from a self-imposed *olam ha'zarut* to a much more enjoyable *olam ha'yedidut.*

The forces of estrangement are vanquished by developing the sorts of character traits that build caring and closeness to others.[52] In other words, the world may have been founded on a principle of affection and it may feature bondedness as its deepest human principle, but it is in our hands to cultivate the traits that will help us develop into the type of person with whom others find it easy and satisfying to connect. When Rabban Yochanan ben Zakkai directed his students to "Go forth and see what is the right path to which a person should adhere," Rabbi Yehoshua came back and answered, "Be a good friend."[53]

That the onus is on us to develop the traits that facilitate being a good friend is pointed out by another great *mussar* teacher, Rabbi Avraham Grodzinski. Rabbi Grodzinski wrote, "A good friend is not only something to find, but more importantly something to become. Being a good friend implies intrinsic growth within the person, independent of the relationship."[54] In other words, from a *mussar* perspective, our task is to work on ourselves not with the goal of winning relationships but in order to realize our human potential. When we do that, what we will see is that focusing on our own growth produces better relationships and deeper friendships. This is something Rabbi Grodzinski not only preached,

---

50   Pirkei Avot 1:15.

51   Berachot 17a.

52   An important caveat: We are only addressing relationships that are, at their core, healthy, or have the potential to be healthy. Nothing said here pertains to dealing with abusive, oppressive, or exploitative relationships, which unfortunately do exist.

53   Pirkei Avot 2:9, according to the interpretation of Rabbeinu Yonah.

54   Avraham Grodzinski, *Torat Avraham*, Bene Brak, Israel: Yeshivat Kotel Avreichim, 1977-1978, p. 465–466. Rabbi Grodzinski was Rabbi Wolbe's father-in-law.

but practiced. His son described how his father spent two *years* perfecting the attribute of "greet every person with a pleasant countenance," including practicing a warm smile in front of a mirror.

Friendship is a perfect mirror of the inner life. If you undertake an examination of your friendships, what you will see reflected back is an image of yourself, and that image will reveal the work that needs to be done for you to reach your full human and spiritual potential. When you undertake to do the work and make the changes that will actually bring you closer to fulfilling your potential, then you will have made it possible to have positive relationships with good friends who will guide you, be honest in their feedback, and pick you up when you fall.

Finding Strength in Friendship

This accounts for the rabbinic advice to "cling to friends."[55] We gain so much from having friends accompanying us as we — and they — navigate the challenges of life. The journey is not always smooth; there are bound to be bumps, detours, and even dead ends along the way. We will stumble and fall. The help and support we receive from our friends gives us strength, reminds us of our purpose, and helps us continue in the pursuit of our goals.

A dear friend, Seymour, passed recently. Seymour was a California psychiatrist with whom I had studied *mussar* for many years. When he received a terminal diagnosis, he called to let me know.

He wanted to thank me for our years of friendship, and to say goodbye.

"What's the prognosis?" I asked him.

"I'm pretty stable," he replied. "I'm on chemo, but it won't work for long."

"So," I said. "I'll speak to you next week."

We continued to speak regularly until he passed. As I mourn him, I cannot stop thinking about how he reached out to me, to keep me in his heart as he dealt with his diagnosis, and how my only recourse was to keep reaching out to him in return.

Life is not without its challenges. It will never be all calm seas and smooth sailing — but friendship is a boat through those churning waters. The modern philosopher Ram Dass coined a beautiful phrase, "walking each other home." I am comforted by the image of Seymour and me strolling in step together, side by side, enjoying each other's company as he walked home.

The emphasis on the individual in modern culture can lead people to cut

---

55   Pirkei Avot 6:6.

themselves off from others. We judge others and recoil or, maybe even more often, we judge ourselves and withdraw. Either way, we impose the punishment of solitary confinement on ourselves. This is not the Jewish way. Jewish tradition sees bonding ourselves to worthy companions as an essential feature of a life well-lived.

Ultimately, we can see that we live in two parallel worlds operating simultaneously. The world of friendship, *olam ha'yedidut*, is characterized by love, joy, tranquility, optimism, harmony, generosity, confidence, and faithfulness. The other world — the world of estrangement, *olam ha'zarut* — is characterized by animosity, anger, blame, resentment, criticism, anxiety, sadness, loneliness, and fear. The lesson of the *mussar* teachers is that if we do the work to transform ourselves we will also transform the world in which we live, for ourselves and for others.

RAISING RESILIENT
AND SPIRITUAL
CHILDREN

In a rapidly changing and sometimes confusing world, our children's ability to develop the capacity for good relationships is not something we should take for granted. The quality of our parenting has a foundational influence on our children's ability to have healthy relationships.

Parenting experts Dr. Daniel Siegel and Dr. Tina Payne Bryson note that "when kids feel safe, seen, soothed, and secure, they build a strong foundation for emotional resilience and healthy relationships throughout their lives."[56]

Dr. Richard Schwartz, the founder of Internal Family Systems therapy, elaborates: "The family is the primary system where we learn resilience. It's in the family that we develop the tools to navigate challenges, build relationships, and cultivate a sense of belonging."[57]

When we raise resilient and spiritual children who can access their inner guidance, who can delve into the wisdom of their soul, we find that they can not only handle the world but also make positive contributions to their communities. Four acclaimed parenting experts offer direction in this chapter. Nili Couzens playfully frames the big picture of the parenting adventure, offers stories and values that strengthen us as parents, and teaches us how to interpret and reframe messages and situations to help raise wonderful people. Researcher and author Dr. Lisa Miller draws on rigorous scientific studies that demonstrate that spirituality is one of the roots of wellness in the first two decades of life; she teaches us how to leverage this often untapped resource for developing our children's resilience, health, and healing. Resilience expert, physician, and media personality Dr. Deborah Gilboa explains resilience in ways that help parents teach it through practical skills we can use for raising resilient children. Author Dasee Berkovitz dovetails Jewish wisdom and stories of her own parenting to elevate our journey toward becoming soulful parents.

---

56   Daniel J. Siegel, MD, and Tina Payne Bryson, PhD, *The Power of Showing Up: How Parental Presence Shapes Who Our Kids Become and How Their Brains Get Wired*, New York: Ballantine Books, 2020, p. 10.

57   Richard C. Schwartz, PhD, *Introduction to the Internal Family Systems Model*, 1995.

Raising Good Adults

Nili Couzens

Nili Couzens is an international motivational speaker who has been inspiring audiences around the world for almost two decades. Nili has lectured in Israel, South Africa, Greece, England, Belgium, Central America, and more than 35 cities across the United States and Canada, including universities such as Penn, Tufts, Brandeis, and Northwestern. She is a trip educator for Momentum and founding director of Jewish Life Seminars, an educational organization in the Greater Philadelphia area, where she spearheaded women's educational initiatives and taught for 17 years.

What is the purpose of childhood? The goal of raising good kids is not to have good kids. The goal of raising good kids is to, one day, have good adults. Kids misbehave because they don't know the rules yet. They grab, they fight, they don't share. They don't say *please* or *thank you*. They gloat when they win, and sulk when they lose. They're kids. They're supposed to misbehave — that's what kids do. Ancient Jewish wisdom teaches that each of us is a soul sent to planet Earth with a mission to accomplish; children are simply the newest recruits. Rather than let these new souls flounder around while they try — and probably fail, repeatedly — to figure life out on their own, they have been apprenticed to older souls to show them how life works. We call this apprenticeship *childhood*. We call the older souls to whom they have been apprenticed *parents*. That's you.

The big mistake parents make is to be proud of our kids when they excel in their areas of natural expertise, and to get upset when they misbehave. Every child usually has an area where they naturally excel, whether it is being naturally organized, kind, charming, athletic, smart, patient, or artistic. These are their innate skill areas, where they're leading the pack. As parents, we naturally take pride in our children's accomplishments: "My daughter is valedictorian! I don't even know when she studies, she's just naturally brilliant!" "My son makes dinner from start to finish, I can't even boil water! I don't know how he does it." There's absolutely nothing wrong with being proud of your kids, but you may not have actually done much to contribute to their success in those particular areas. Their talents, whatever they are, were included in their "hard drive," so to speak.

Where we as parents can really guide our children is when they *don't* know what to do. We can guide the child who needs to gain confidence, the son who struggles at school, the daughter who can't keep her room neat. Whatever areas our children are struggling with should be seen as a cosmic "wink" from God, steering us toward what is expected of us as parents. Too often, instead of saying, "That's my cue!" and getting to work, we can get frustrated or angry that our kids don't have it all together. Which, on the one hand we know is ridiculous — they're kids, of course they make mistakes. And yet, we've all been there. "How many tests do you have to fail before you actually just study?!" "I can't find anything in this room, clean up this pigsty!!" You get the idea.

> *Consider one of your children. What is a challenge or growth opportunity for them that you might see as a "wink" inviting you to offer them fitting support?*

What our children really need when they keep failing in a particular arena is love and repeated, repeated, (repeated) instruction. Think about your own failures for a minute: How many times do you need to be reminded to (fill in the blank)? More than once, I'm sure. The goal of raising kids is not to have good kids. The goal of raising kids is to one day have good adults. It bears repeating. This is a mantra that can get us through our busiest, hardest parenting days.

Business Is Booming

Imagine you're opening a restaurant. You have agonized over every item on the menu, the decor, the paint colors, the dishes — endless details that needed to be decided. And finally, finally, everything is finished. It's opening night, and your restaurant is neat, gorgeous, perfect. Ready for a crowd. You open your doors — and no one's there. Throughout the evening, everything stays neat, gorgeous, perfect. And silent and empty. Is that why you opened your restaurant? Of course not. Silent perfection is not the goal of a restaurant. Crowds and noise and dirty pots and used dishes — that is the goal of a restaurant. You want action and mess and traffic! That's when you know business is booming! Every night after you close the restaurant, of course you clean up. You have to. But only so you can mess it all up again tomorrow. The goal of the restaurant is not achieved by the cleaning crew. The goal of the restaurant is achieved in the chaos of a packed night, in the lines around the corner, in trying to keep up with the orders.

Life goals are not achieved in the calm. Life goals are achieved in the chaos.

We know this in every other area. The ER doctor knows she's doing her job when the ER is full of sick, injured patients. She's not frustrated that her ER is cluttered with the sick and the injured — sickness and injury are the reason she became a doctor in the first place. A busy ER means she's able to help people. Business is booming. The teacher knows he's doing his job because the class hasn't learned everything yet. He's not frustrated with his students for being ignorant on the topic. Ignorance is the reason he became a teacher in the first place. Business is booming. The goal of family life is not a constantly clean, perfect, quiet house. The goal of family life is to prepare our children for adult life — which involves fighting, bonding, trust, communication, making up, making a mess, teaching, loving, and laughing. That's what a healthy family looks like. All that noise and mess and chaos — we call that *life*.

The next time life gets crazy, just try and smile to yourself. Business is booming. The natural unfolding of life, with all its noise and mess and chaos, builds the greatest skill our children will need to successfully navigate life on planet Earth: resilience. The dictionary defines *resilience* as the capacity to recover quickly from difficulties; toughness. We all know life here on Earth is peppered with difficulty. Our capacity to recover quickly and get back in the ring develops through the practice of resilience. Resilience is not innate. It is not a gift that can be given. It is a skill developed through experiencing the drip irrigation of failure, through our phoenix-like survival of setbacks, over and over and over again. There is no shortcut to resilience. You cannot cram for resilience any more than you can cram for a harvest. You have to prepare the land, plant at the right time, water the seeds, pray for success — and wait. You wait for the miracle of growth, and you pray to God that you did things well enough. You won't really know until something sprouts.

Raising children is a lot like that. You can't force resilience — or anything else — into your children. You can't make your children kind. Or thoughtful. Or hard working. You can — and should — model all those things for them. You can present them with the opportunity to pantomime all the skills and values they will need for a successful life. But you can't actually give your values to your children. Values must be chosen. So you plant your seeds, nurture them, pray for success, and wait. The rains of failure that shape children into grown-ups will come. They're inescapable. Sometimes a drizzle; sometimes a flood. The tiny, adorable pains of first days of school and first lost teeth quickly morph into first dates and first broken heart. Being picked for the team but left out of the party; being the high school valedictorian but getting rejected from the first-choice college. The heartbreak that coaxes resilience is a script we would never write for our children, but nevertheless it is a play they must perform. And they must perform it alone. Parents can be the coaches; we can play the supporting roles and the adoring fans — but we are never the directors, the writers, or the understudies. This is the performance of a life. Our job is to prepare them, and step aside. Yes, they'll get bumped around, and fail, and cry. But they'll be fine. May we be blessed to learn that our children are not as fragile as we think they are.

Becoming Antifragile: Going Beyond Resilience

The dictionary defines *fragile* as easily broken or destroyed, like a crystal vase or a light bulb. But how many of us have successfully filled a vase or changed a light bulb with nary a mishap? I would venture to say all of us. We handle these "fragile" items almost daily, and nothing spontaneously explodes in our hands. *Fragile* doesn't really mean easily broken. *Fragile* might be better defined as easily broken when treated roughly.

The dictionary suggests that the opposite of fragile is *strong*, like a boulder. But imagine dropping a boulder from the top of a hundred-story building. It would still break. *Strong* doesn't mean unbreakable; it means difficult to break. That doesn't fully capture the opposite of *fragile*. If something being fragile means it breaks easily when treated roughly, then the polar opposite of that would be something that gets stronger when treated roughly. There is no word for that in English, but a man named Nassim Nicholas Taleb created a word, and wrote a book about it. He called it *Antifragile*.

Taleb explains, "Antifragility is beyond resilience or robustness. The resilient resists shocks and stays the same; the antifragile gets better."[58] Your muscles are antifragile, because muscles get stronger from being stressed. In fact, if you don't use your muscles, they'll atrophy and become fragile. Bones are antifragile, because bone density increases from exercises that stress them. If you don't stress your bones, you ultimately weaken them. Once you look for it, there are examples of antifragility everywhere. Plant regrowth is stronger after a forest fire. A pearl is just a grain of sand that aggravated an oyster. If a butterfly doesn't struggle to leave the cocoon, it will never fly.

"What doesn't kill you makes you stronger" can actually be true and demonstrable. The German Blitz of London during World War II was intended to break the British, but had the opposite effect; famously, the Blitz of London

---

58   Nassim Nicholas Taleb, *Antifragile: Things That Gain from Disorder*, New York: Random House,, 2012.

emboldened the nation and stiffened their resolve. Terror attacks often cause citizens to double down on their right to freedom. New recruits morph into soldiers after the tough treatment of basic training. The mindset of a nation is antifragile. People are antifragile. And most importantly, your children are antifragile. Don't "fragilize" them — it will only backfire. No one will pave the way for them in adulthood. Letting our kids fail ultimately puts them on the only path to success. Helicopter parenting won't prepare our kids for real life. Dissolving with guilt, or cushioning every blow, or taking their pain on as our own won't prepare them for real life.

> *Bring to mind a story that you can share with your children about a challenge that made you stronger. How might you share this story to bring the term* antifragile *to your family?*

What will? Believing in them enough to stand on the sidelines while they figure it out.

Although the Olympic coach will choreograph grueling workouts and relentless hours of training, he knows that when that well-prepared athlete finally steps into the arena, she steps in alone. There is no other way to compete, to win or to lose. The parents are the coaches. The child is the athlete. The bad news is: Your child might fail. The good news is: She's antifragile. She'll just get better. There is a famous saying in Proverbs: "The *tzadik* (righteous person) falls seven times and gets up."[59] People usually take that to mean that the *tzadik* is strong because, although he falls like everyone else, he gets up and tries again. And because he always gets up, he is strong despite his failings.

Rabbi Yitzchak Hutner, a venerated sage of the twentieth century, explained the verse differently. He wrote: "Fools believe that the intent of the verse is to teach something remarkable — that the righteous person falls seven times and, despite this, he rises. But the knowledgeable are aware that the essence of the righteous man's rising again is because of his seven falls."[60] The righteous person is not righteous despite his seven falls. He is righteous because of them. Because the *tzadik* is antifragile.

---

59   Proverbs 24:16.

60   Pachad Yitzchak: Igrot u'ketavim 128.

Jewish Values

As parents, it's our job to identify what values are important to us, and to then strive to impart those values to the next generation. That's universal for all parents on earth. As Jews, we don't need to search too far to find those values. We don't need to reinvent the wheel. Jewish values have changed the world more than once. We have been at this thing called *life* for thousands of years, and our Book of Values not only reveals what our values should be, but even tells us how to transmit them. We are charged with talking about Jewish values — always: when we're sitting at home and when we're walking on the road; when we get up in the morning and when we go to bed at night.[61] Tell stories that illustrate your values. Talk about your failures. Tell your children how you built your own resilience. Tell them God gives partial credit and second chances. Explain that God believes in us and loves us not because we're perfect, but just because we are. God doesn't need us to be perfect, God already is perfection. God wants us to be flawed and to fail, but also to apologize, and be accountable, and to make ourselves get up and try again. God wants us to be resilient. That's why God made us antifragile.

Jewish history tells the story of our greatest heroes and heroines, who faced hardship and failure and continued to strive for greatness. Abraham faced ten tests from which no one could rescue him; he had to face them alone. Sarah, Rebecca, and Rachel all faced childlessness. Moses never made it to the Promised Land. Aharon the High Priest watched in silence as two of his sons died on the most important day of his life. These are the stories of our ancestors. They are not sugar-coated. Our tales are not of perfect men, of people free from mistakes; our tales are told of people who admitted their flaws, who apologized, and who forgave. Our stories are stories of consequence because we matter, and our actions matter. Every year we sit at the Passover Seder for the express purpose of telling our children our story. The main commandment of the night is *"V'higad'ta l'vincha,"* "And you will tell your children." How else will they know if you, the parents, don't tell them? Tell your children that we were slaves in Egypt. That we were beaten, and starved, and humiliated. Tell your children we never gave up hope, and we cried out to God. Tell your children that oppression happens in every generation, so it may happen to them too, one day, but they'll be OK. Tell your children that the Jewish People will always survive, because *Am Yisrael chai.* The People of Israel lives, because God will always save us. Tell your children that the Jewish nation is not just resilient. Tell them that we are antifragile.

---

61   Deuteronomy 6:7.

Strengthening Your Family's Spiritual Core

Dr. Lisa Miller

Lisa Miller, PhD, is the New York Times-*bestselling author of* The Spiritual Child: The New Science on Parenting for Health and Lifelong Thriving *and* The Awakened Brain: The New Science of Spirituality and Our Quest for an Inspired Life. *She is a professor in the Clinical Psychology Program at Teachers College, Columbia University, and founder and director of the Spirituality Mind Body Institute, the first Ivy League graduate program and research institute in spirituality and psychology. She has held more than a decade of joint appointments in the Department of Psychiatry at Columbia University Medical School and her innovative research has been published in more than one hundred peer-reviewed articles in leading journals. She is editor of* The Oxford Handbook of Psychology and Spirituality.

Twenty years ago, there was no science on spirituality and mental health to speak of — all you might come across was a handful of articles on adults asserting that, if you attend religious services, you'll be more likely to have social support. What we have discovered since then is that is only the tip of the iceberg. There is now an ever-growing scientific body of research examining the connection between spirituality, mental health, and thriving that speaks to the importance of developing a spiritual life for our children and ourselves. Science doesn't validate spiritual experience but measured spiritual experience is a form of data, and it allows those who are skeptical to open up to the idea that spiritual awareness is a powerful tool for living our best lives. Logic, reason, inspiration, and intuition can all work together. How do we define spirituality? None of the scientists considering this over the past decades have come up with a universally agreed-upon definition, but what scientists do have are tools to identify common threads within the spiritual life. They have ascertained that these common threads carry vast implications for the rest of our lives: for our mental health, wellness, relationships, teamwork, decision-making, and fitness. They can even identify how those common spiritual threads correlate to certain aspects of our biology. They have found that there is a foundational capacity for spiritual awareness with which we are all endowed. The rich array of diverse, beautiful faith traditions present in our world are all essentially different expressions of this common capacity.

There are four major elements concerning the development of the spiritual life that are universal:

1. We are born spiritual. Every single one of us is endowed with the capacity for transcendent awareness, for spiritual life. We all have the capacity to perceive and to feel a dynamic connection to a higher power, whether we name it God, Hashem, Allah, the Universe, or any higher life force. This relationship can take different forms: It can be dualistic, "I talk to God and I hear God answer." It can be monist, "I am of the universe, I am part of the oneness." It can be, as in many rich indigenous traditions, a pure awareness of God's presence and spirit within and throughout all of creation. We know that this capacity is innate, and heritable, due to the gold standard in science — twin studies. Scientists look at twins raised together and twins raised apart, and factor the degree of commonality as a function of shared genes. IQ, for example, is about half heritable and half environmentally shaped, and temperament is roughly the same. Research has shown that the capacity we have to experience the transcendent, the sacred, is one-third heritable and two-thirds socialized. This means that, while every one of us is born with an innate capacity for spiritual life, how we are shaped by our families, our cultures, our communities, our schools really does have a great impact on the formation and depth of our spirituality, our spiritual core.

2. With the onset of puberty a biological clock goes off, and there comes a surge in this capacity for connection. With this surge comes a hunger for transcendence, a nagging in the mind and heart.

3. This surge can be supported by clergy, by elders, by those who have walked the path already. Conversely, we know that if this surge is not supported, a young person can go looking for their own answers — the danger of which is that they can find false mentors, insincere guides. The more we show up for young people, for our children, the more we can help them in their natural development. It is clear that humanity has always understood this. Biological puberty, fertility, is almost always marked as a time of augmented spiritual awareness and spiritual contribution within the community. Whether you're talking about confirmation, bar and bat mitzvah, or *inípi*, it's present in just about every culture through time.

4. If this process is supported, the science of the past twenty years has shown that there is nothing in the clinical or social sciences as profoundly protective against the most prevalent forms of pathology, addiction, depression, or risk-taking as having a personal spirituality. Children who are

raised with religion — particularly one that is multi-generational, passed down within the family — are eighty percent less likely to become involved in substance dependence and abuse, are sixty percent less likely to develop a major depressive disorder, and are fifty percent less likely to attempt suicide. Girls are seventy percent less likely to become involved in sexual risk-taking. If we examine demographics and family constellation and all the things that social science and clinical scientists look at, a familial religion and spirituality is the most powerful protection a teen can have against these various forms of inner suffering and outer risk-taking.

What does this personal spiritual life look like? With the formation of the spiritual core being one-third heritable and two-thirds socialized, there are universal features common to all spiritual traditions:

- A deep sense of interconnectedness and unity with others; belief in a common foundation of being
- Love seen as a transformative, relational force, not simply as an emotion like happiness
- The practice of some form of meditation or prayer as a means of transcendent connection
- An understanding that morality is not relative; that there is an absolute standard derived from our relationship to an ultimate reality
- The belief that altruism, giving to others, *tikun olam* (repairing the world), is sacred; a form of service to the Higher Power

Above all, the universal common denominator is having a sense of connection to the transcendent and the sacred. In the Jewish tradition, this might correlate to: "I turn to God for guidance in times of difficulty." It might be feeling a profound sense of connection with Jewish history and peoplehood. Some feel it when immersing themselves in nature, some feel it in the presence of their family, some feel it in the synagogue and at prayer, some feel it through dedicating themselves to charitable endeavors, some feel it when studying sacred texts, some feel it when perpetuating holy traditions such as a participating in a Passover Seder or building a sukkah. Connecting to the sacred and transcendent, however we do it, changes our lives. It even physically changes our brains. Findings from a study at Columbia showed that middle-aged people who had a sustained spiritual life displayed increased cortical thickness in the parietal, precuneus, and occipital regions of the brain.[62] Notably, about eighty percent of people with recurrent depression show cortical thinness in these areas. These findings suggest that spirituality is connected to mental health and recovery. The fact that the sustained use of spirituality will actually change a person's brain structure means that someone who is spiritually "developed" might have the same job, the same friendships and relationships, and live in the same house as someone who is not, and yet see and experience their life — through the lens of their spiritually developed brain — in a completely different way. Another study was done at Yale on younger people between the ages of eighteen and twenty-five.[63] While the study of older people showed structural differences — greater strength — in the cortex's processing power, the study of younger people examined function. Functional MRIs measure changes in blood flow due to brain activity, and the fMRIs of young people with spiritually engaged lives showed the usage of many of the same regions that, in older people with spiritual lives, had become thicker structurally. How we use the spiritual "muscle" does in fact affect the nature of its strength, and daily spiritual awareness and practice have a long-standing impact on our capacity to effectively develop a "spiritual" brain.

Consider a regular spiritual practice with which you can enrich your family. What can you do now to implement this practice? What will you need to do in the future to stay accountable to this practice?

How does developing a "spiritual brain" affect our mental health, our wellness, our relationships? Consider helpful character traits that would enable a person to have a successful, happy life: grit, optimism, forgiveness, commitment, resilience, and persistence. These traits tend to be linked; they are not sprinkled across humanity evenly, but cluster within the same people. In a sampling of six

---

62 Lisa Miller, PhD; Ravi Bansal, PhD; Priya Wickramaratne, PhD; Xuejun Hao, PhD; Craig E. Tenke, PhD; Myrna M. Weissman, PhD; Bradley S. Peterson, MD, Neuroanatomical Correlates of Religiosity and Spirituality: A Study in Adults at High and Low Familial Risk for Depression, JAMA Psychiatry, 2014;71(2), p. 128–135, doi:10.1001/jamapsychiatry.2013.3067..

63 Lisa Miller, Iris M. Balodis, Clayton H. McClintock, Jiansong Xu, Cheryl M. Lacadie, Rajita Sinha, Marc N. Potenza, Neural Correlates of Personalized Spiritual Experiences, Cerebral Cortex, Volume 29, Issue 6, June 2019, p. 2331–2338, https://academic.oup.com/cercor/article/29/6/2331/5017785?login=false.

thousand college students, forty percent of the group scored high in forgiveness, gratitude, optimism, grit, and living a life of meaning, while thirty percent of the group scored low in all these traits. Looking at this through a scientific lens, these virtues or character traits that we see as separate can be regarded as a singular character strength — and this singular character strength correlated with the students' levels of daily spiritual awareness. Daily spiritual awareness, however it manifests in an individual, is foundational to developing these character strengths and virtues. When we examine the lives of middle and high school students, we see that the strength of their daily spiritual awareness predicts growth in these positive character traits. Why is this? The developing adolescent engages with fundamental questions and self-assessment. The adolescent asks: Who am I? What is my meaning, my purpose in life? What are relationships about, and what should they be about? What is the very nature of reality?

When these questions are asked by an adolescent without the benefit of a spiritual core, the answers they arrive at can be harsh. Who are they? Only their parts and pieces. I am great at math / I'm not so good at math. I'm a terrific athlete / I'm a terrible athlete. I have lots of money / I'm poor. They are only the sum of their attributes — their gains and losses. What happens when one of these adolescents is faced with disappointment? When a star student gets a C, a beauty queen loses their crown, an athlete is injured and can no longer play, a rich kid discovers their family has lost its money? We live in a world of measurement, and these people are deeply vulnerable to the commodification of who they are. They feel that their very being has been demoted. What is left when performance or possessions dwindle? Not much, if all they are is a basket of parts and pieces.

When these questions are asked by an adolescent with a strong spiritual core, the answers are very different. That adolescent knows themself to be a soul of infinite worth, a child of God. When that is the case, what is the significance of their particular attributes? If they are, for example, good at math, then perhaps their skill has been bestowed upon them so they can carve out their purpose in life, their calling and contribution to the world. But skill in math is not at the deep core of who they are, nor are any of their other outward attributes. Being wealthy or poor, a great or mediocre athlete, popular or unpopular, successful or struggling, happy or dissatisfied with their physical appearance — none of this is foundationally who they are. It cannot define them, because they are a child of God, a soul on earth and, therefore, whatever their skills, they are beings of infinite worth. They will be able to sustain themselves through disappointment because they do not define themselves by their attributes. Any particular disappointment could be devastating, could be a loss, could be the last thing they wanted to have happen, but still it has not changed the essence of who they are. In fact, this loss, whatever it is, might even turn out to be the beginning of a new opportunity, a new phase. It actually is part of their path. All pieces of their path are intrinsic to it — the ones they like and the ones that, at first, they don't like, or may never like — they are still an opening to the next chapter.

An adolescent — and an adult — with a strong, cultivated spiritual core will view relationships through a very different lens than one who has not developed a strong spiritual core. To a person with a strong spiritual core, if they are a soul on Earth then so are all others souls on Earth. Relationships are therefore about interest, about support, about entering each other's lives at particular moments, in a meaningful confluence of events. On a harsh day, relationships are about forgiveness; and on a good day, they are about celebrating showing up in each other's lives. That is relational spirituality. To an adolescent without a strong spiritual core, relationships — like attributes — are nothing but a measurement contest. They may be surrounded by people but feel totally alone because there is no opportunity for real connection, only competition. Who is this person? Well, it looks to me like they only got an 86, but I got a 92. Or ooh, vice versa, I got the 86 and they got the 92. This is my competitor. This is the person in the world of measurement against whom I measure myself. That is a very lonely attitude, and a lonely way to sit in a classroom.

We have a choice in the development of our children's spirituality. There is always a choice as to how we cultivate their spiritual socialization to complement and enhance the one-third innate spiritual inclination they have inherited. It doesn't land only on us. Parents, grandparents, community, tradition all play their part. We can find external support — through communities of faith, communities of service, communities of practice. And we can support internal development by teaching and encouraging the use of meditation and prayer, by walking in nature and being attentive, and by remembering that we shape our own socialization increasingly as we get older. This is our work and this is our choice. It concerns every human being on earth. We are all spiritual beings. We affect each other. We are souls on earth, working in design, in tandem with one another. And when we see that and live that truth, we realize our potentials to live bigger lives, happier lives, healthier lives — lives lived on spiritual ground.

Resilience & Growth

Dr. Deborah Gilboa

Resilience expert Deborah Gilboa, MD (aka "Dr. G"), works with families, educators, executives, and businesses to identify the mindset and strategies to turn stress to an advantage. A leading media personality seen regularly on TODAY *and* Good Morning America *and the resilience expert for* The Doctors, *she is also featured frequently in* The Washington Post, The New York Times, Huffington Post, *and countless other digital and print outlets. Dr. G is a board-certified attending family physician and a Momentum trip educator. She is the author of* Get the Behavior You Want ... Without Being the Parent You Hate *and* From Stressed to Resilient.

If it were possible to protect our children from every struggle, to cocoon them against any and all possibilities of illness, job losses, relationship conflict, financial trial, difficult bosses, injury and infirmity, we would give almost anything to do that, wouldn't we? But it's not possible, and we know it. Therefore, we are obligated not to *shelter* our children from adversity, but to *prepare* them for it. Our job as parents is to strengthen our children so they can face whatever life throws at them — and the trait that will see them through the hard times, and strengthen them, is resilience.

What is resilience? Resilience is the ability to handle hard experiences, navigate them, and continue to pursue positive goals. Or, as the American Psychological Association defines it, "Resilience is the process of *adapting well* in the face of adversity, trauma, tragedy, threats or significant sources of stress."

Who needs resilience? Everyone. Intelligence doesn't supersede it, wealth doesn't preclude it, and faith doesn't replace it. Bad things happen to everyone. Rabbi Jonathan Sacks put it this way: "This is how to deal with crisis. Wrestle with it, refusing to let it go until it blesses you, until you emerge stronger, better or wiser than you were before. To be a Jew is not to accept defeat."[64]

Who has resilience? Everyone is born with some resilience, and everyone has the ability to develop more. It's harder for some people to be naturally resilient

---

64   Rabbi Lord Jonathan Sacks, *Letters to the Next Generation: Reflections on Jewish Life*, The Office of Rabbi Sacks, 2019.

than for others, for a thousand or more reasons. Think of your own children: Some of them got hurt, or disappointed, or mad, and figured out how to get over it quickly, while others stayed upset for hours or days at a time. You likely know adults who are the same. Each person has an innate amount of resilience with which they begin life, and the capacity to build more.

Can one really learn resilience? Yes. Think of your own life: Picture the stress you were managing ten years ago. If that was all of the stress you had to manage today, would it feel as challenging as it did then? Probably not. That's because you've trained up since then, building your own resilience by practicing old and new ways to manage difficulty and keep finding joy.

Can you teach it? Absolutely. The best education is experiential, which means we can't just tell our children to be resilient and expect success. The hardest part of teaching resilience is that it means allowing our children to go through something difficult in the first place. Many parents, no matter how resilient they may be, struggle to take that necessary step back to allow their children to learn resilience. Furthermore, even if you yourself are great at something — especially a trait as invisible as resilience — that doesn't mean it's easy for you to teach someone else how to develop that same trait.

According to studies by the American College Health Association, as well as research conducted at many universities from USC to Harvard, young people are struggling with having enough resilience. A recent article on resilience in Inc.com related that a nationwide study of college freshmen undertaken in 2015 revealed that sixty percent felt "emotionally unprepared for college life." According to the National Alliance on Mental Illness, one in four college students is diagnosed with or treated for a mental health condition every year. Eight in ten students felt "overwhelmed" and forty-five percent felt that "things were hopeless." Unfortunately, it's that very obstacle — mental illness — that keeps many parents from giving their children the opportunity to struggle. Parents face so many troubling uncertainties about the causes and exacerbation of mental distress that they are afraid of any experience that might push their child or teen beyond their ability to cope. And parents struggle with their own coping. No matter how well an adult handles their own trials and tribulations, it is far more difficult to watch a child struggle, especially if the adult could step in and fix — or even prevent — the problem in the first place.

It's easy to forget that something that is uncomfortable is not necessarily unsafe, and that discomfort is necessary for learning and growth. Societal pressures are making all of this worse. We're often judged, and taught to judge ourselves, according to the measure of our child's happiness at any given moment. That is a terrible metric; if we are doing our job as parents, then it's more than likely that, at any given moment, *we* are the cause of our child's unhappiness! I was the mother who said, "No, you can't have the firetruck back because you hit your brother in the head with it." I was the mother who turned off the Wi-Fi because chores were not being done. I was the mother who insisted on the consequence that if one of my children spoke disrespectfully to an adult, he didn't get to go to a friend's house.

Years ago, I got a call from the principal. My son had drummed on the bottom of another student after first grade circle time. She told him to stop, but some of the other kids laughed so he *did it again.* When my son got home from school that day and learned he could not go to the neighborhood carnival with the rest of the family, but instead needed to stay with a babysitter and write a letter of apology to his classmate's parents, he promptly burst into tears. Seeing that my eyes were also filling with tears, he asked me, "Why are you sad??" I told him that I was disappointed not to be going to the carnival as a family, and he quickly responded, "So, change your mind!" I asked him if he thought it was more important to me to have our family tradition uninterrupted, or to raise him to be a man of integrity. My six-year-old dropped his shoulders, gave me a look of profound disappointment, and replied, "the integrity thing."

Often, as parents, we have to choose between our child's happiness — and our own — or their progress toward being a good person. We've learned a lot in the past two generations about the importance of keeping kids emotionally safe. Protecting kids from trauma is a big part of our responsibility. Because we're worried about their growing anxiety, depression, and self-harm, we've put ourselves solely in charge of preventing those outcomes. In this effort, we forget that kids also need practice in preventing and navigating their own mental distress. Instead of working to anticipate, prevent, or solve every obstacle our children might face, our job is most often to take one step back — with empathy — and support their efforts to navigate struggle on their own.

How do we build resilience? By teaching our children what they can do when they hit an obstacle. There are three skills everyone should develop in order to become more resilient: the ability to explain what's happening to them in a way that will help others feel empathy; the ability to solve problems; and the ability to know how and when to reach out for help. We all worry about the short- and long-term effects of struggle. That's smart. Building resilience through the three skills I've mentioned won't protect our children from ever feeling sadness, anger, shame, or loneliness. These three skills will, however, act as a firewall between those feelings and acts of self-harm. Teens and adults who suffer from mental distress (everyone) or mental illness (eighteen percent of people) are less likely to self-harm when they understand and can demonstrate these three skills.

Storytelling

Every child — and adult — needs to know how to explain, to themselves and to others, what is happening to them. It might seem strange to stress the importance of teaching children to tell their side of the story, because they often do this well — and loudly — from a very young age. However, children and teenagers need to understand what works, and what doesn't work, in getting others to really hear and believe them. We must teach our children how to talk about what they've experienced:

1. Their stories must be truthful. Lying or exaggerating may make the listener feel bad for them, but it won't build their resilience. And it makes it much harder for people to believe them the next time they want to share their story.

2. Their stories must be only theirs. Teach your children to stick to what they experienced and felt, and not focus on what anyone else involved was thinking or feeling — it's too easy to be wrong.

3. The stories must include their feelings. Expressing and describing true emotions — even the hard ones like anger, sadness, and shame — without lashing out or behaving badly is a crucial part of strengthening resilience and building empathy for them.

Problem-Solving

One November day, my son the kindergartner came up to me holding one of my kitchen strainers and asked, "Ima, how do you clean this?"

It looked entirely clean, so I — a mom of four boys — was of course immediately suspicious. "Why do you need to clean it?" I asked.

"Oh!" He held up my kitchen utensil proudly. "My favorite Lego fell in the toilet. But Ms. DeWitt says I'm a problem-solver!"

As adults, we are expert problem-solvers. What I learned from my son's kindergarten teacher was that we have to stop being the problem-solvers for our children sooner than we think. Instead, we must start encouraging them to solve their own problems. Even though they're often terrible at it. So how do we do this? Let them practice! When your child comes to you with a problem, try not to solve it for them, unless they are actually in danger. As long as they are safe, this is an opportunity for them to build a crucial skill:

1. Show them how to try. Walk them through the steps they should take to solve a problem:

A.   Name the problem (my head hurts).

B.   Think of what might have caused it (I'm tired, hungry, dehydrated, upset).

C.   Choose a goal now (get rid of my headache).

D.   Think of ways to achieve that goal (take a nap, drink water, eat a snack, rub my head, talk about my feelings, take medicine).

E.   Pick the solution that seems best.

F.   See if it works.

G.   Try another solution, if the first one doesn't help.

2. If they are hesitant, encourage them by reminding them of their prior problem-solving experiences. Ask them about problems they've solved in the past — how they felt beforehand, what they tried, what didn't work and what did. They have some skills already!

Reaching Out for Help

Asking for help can be tricky for kids; doing it too often gets in the way of learning how to handle problems yourself, but not asking for help when you're in over your head can rapidly make problems worse. Acknowledge this conflict with your children, and talk about the questions they can ask themselves to figure out whether and when it's time to ask for help:

Is anyone in danger? Kids and teens need clear guidelines about when to ask for help, because they can find themselves in situations with very high stakes, very quickly. Teach them to get help immediately if they feel they or someone else might be in danger. Have you tried to solve this problem yourself? If they're not in danger, but they are uncomfortable or feel stuck, have they tried anything to solve the issue? If they have already tried a couple of solutions that didn't work, then it's OK to ask for help. Where can you go for help? Ask your children — at a time when they're not in distress — to make a list of supports and resources. Brainstorm with them to work out who has the experience and the empathy to help them, and who they can trust to protect them.

Don't be afraid of a certain amount of stress in your child's life. It will — with your coaching and support — make them stronger, just like exercise makes their body stronger. With the strategies I have outlined above, you can use the challenges your child faces to help them build their resilience so they can handle each individual challenge as it appears, and become better able to manage whatever difficulties they will face in the future. When you see that your child is unhappy, ask yourself: Are they in immediate danger? If the answer is no, as it will be the vast majority of the time, take an empathy-filled step back and support them as they navigate this opportunity to grow their resilience.

Reflect on things your parents did or did not do that helped you become a resilient person. How might you offer your parents appreciation? Imagine your child, years from now, reflecting on your parenting. What would you hope they recall? How might that inspire your parenting in the coming days and months?

Soulful Parenting

Dasee Berkowitz

Dasee Berkowitz is a facilitator, educator, and author of Becoming a Soulful Parent: A Path to the Wisdom Within. *She has guided hundreds of leaders, volunteers, and parents to find their own genius so they can lead their organizations, communities, and families with integrity and love.*

Embracing Struggle

A friend once asked me what I wanted most for my children. When I told her that I wanted them to struggle, she gave me a puzzled look. She views me as someone who nurtures and supports their kids and wants what's best for them — and she is right. All of these things are true. So why would I want them to struggle? "Every struggle is an opportunity for growth," I told her. In a culture that lauds beauty, achievement, and happy endings, struggles, setbacks, and loss seem to have little place. However, just as muscles stretch when torn, and over time heal and even become stronger, the small tears that may challenge our children in the short term will build up their muscles for the long term. Mothers know this truth intuitively, from the very event through which we claimed our titles in the first place. This remains true for those of us who did not give birth physically, who may have faced prolonged waiting for our adopted child, or have known the worry that accompanies surrogacy. While the process of bringing children into our lives involves pain, the rewards are immeasurable.

Reflecting this truth, in Judaism the image of a woman enduring birth pangs is used as a metaphor for the nation approaching redemption: "Like a woman with child approaching childbirth, screaming in her pangs, so have we become."[65] The time of redemption, the mythical and mystical end of time, when all things become one and whole, is uneasy to say the least. A redemptive time, according to the Talmud, is not quick and simple, but contains different kinds of pain, similar to the pains a pregnant woman feels at the time of giving birth.[66] When I rush to make things better for my kids, and intervene automatically when they struggle,

---

65   Isaiah 26:17.

66   Sanhedrin 98b.

I don't allow them to experience the process through which they will tear their muscles and then experience the regeneration of those muscles — a process that allows them to develop the stamina necessary to meet all the inevitable challenges of life.

> *Before you step in to help your child, stop and take a*
> *breath to slow down your reaction. What new insight is*
> *born in that space that will better help your child move*
> *through the struggle?*

Broken Hearts: A Lesson for Our Children — and for Us

The Hasidic master the Kotzker Rebbe famously said, "There's nothing so whole as a broken heart." The phrase is enigmatic. What could be whole about something broken? The wisdom of the statement is found when we understand that wholeness must be multi-dimensional. The physical realm is limited to two or three dimensions, while a fourth dimension lets in elements that aren't perceived by the untrained eye. When I experience heartbreak or loss, when I know sadness or pain, the brokenness I feel opens up a world of emotions that might otherwise be suppressed or kept within. True wholeness only comes about when we can experience the whole range of human emotions, not merely the pleasant ones. Touching our own brokenness can also connect us to others more readily, enabling us to recognize what might be broken in them. A point of connection opens.

This lesson is just as true for our children, and should be remembered when we try to parent them toward inhabiting their lives wholly. Brené Brown, the speaker, writer, and researcher who teaches about shame and vulnerability, writes about wholehearted living from a slightly different angle: "Wholehearted living is about engaging with our lives from a place of worthiness. It means cultivating the courage, compassion and connection to wake up in the morning and think, 'No matter what gets done and how much is left undone, I am enough.'"[67] When I read these words, I hear an echo of the Jewish concept of *tzelem Elohim* — the idea that every human being is created in the image of God. Each one of us, unique. Each one of us, worthy. How might we cultivate that

---

67   Brené Brown, *The Gifts of Imperfection: Let Go of Who You Think You're Supposed to Be and Embrace Who You Are*, Center City, MN: Hazelden Publishing, 2010.

awareness in our children? How might we cultivate that awareness in ourselves? In Pirkei Avot the rabbis tell us: "Beloved is a human being for being created in the image of God. Still greater was God's love, in that God gave to the human being the knowledge of being so created."[68] Our worth as human beings does not come only from being created in the image of God; what is remarkable is that we have been given the ability to be aware that we are created in God's image. We are valuable and more than enough not because of what we do, how good we look, or how successful we are — but simply because we are. Carrying this awareness of our God-given souls with us as we live and parent can help us become more soulful parents. Without this awareness it is easy to perceive any struggle as completely negative — to ask, when faced with a problem, "Why me? Everyone else seems to be going about their lives just fine." At first glance, it is easy to assume that everyone else seems to be figuring out how to balance their home life and work life. How to balance leisure time with time volunteering. How to answer their kids when they ask hard questions about sexuality, religion, or politics. "Just look at those happy and composed Facebook feeds! Why am I struggling so much?"

While the movement is gradual, by adding the lens of soulful parenting, "Why me?" can gently turn into, "This is exactly meant for me." The motivational phrase, "You got this!" can turn us toward a more subtle, internal prayer, "I can move through this."

> *The next time a challenge comes your way, shift from asking, "Why me?" to, "How can I shift my perspective to help me move through this?"*

How Can We Raise Resilient Children? Let's Start with Our Own Practice

I could spend all day writing about how important it is to teach our children to be resilient. After all, they have to bounce back from difficult situations all the time. To be a child, as Brené Brown writes, is to be "hardwired for struggle." Children's brains are still developing. They are put in situations day after day in which they have to learn new skills, whether that is needing to adapt to a mean kid at school, to a teacher who doesn't know how to reach them, or to a sibling

---

68   Pirkei Avot 3:14.

who constantly takes their stuff without asking. They could probably teach us a thing or two about resilience. As parents, our competencies and habits protect us from challenges on a daily basis: We delegate tasks to others who are more capable at completing them than we are, we use Waze to prevent us from getting lost, we invite friends over for dinner who make us feel good, we avoid people who bring us down. So many of us move through our lives with a modicum of control. Until of course things get out of control, which, for many parents occurs in relation to us and our children.

Instead of focusing only on how we might raise resilient children, let's also focus on how to become more resilient while parenting our children. We have all had those moments. There was a time when one of my children was very disruptive at school. An afternoon of crying and angry outbursts on his part was met with some tough love and vigilant attending on mine. Other parents may have children who are sinking further within themselves, weighed down by the heaviness of not understanding the lessons taught at school, or of not being included by their peers. Every child struggles, and all parents struggle with supporting them. Their suffering coupled with our desire to help leads us to ask, "What now?" It is too easy, and too common, to react to our children's difficulties with anger, defensiveness, or even despair. How can we avoid these reactions? How can we respond while holding on to a sense of resilience and a deep awareness that we will be able to move through this period?

Opening ourselves up to teachings from our wisdom tradition can help. In the Torah's first chapter, light and darkness are introduced. "There was evening, there was morning, one day."[69] I love this juxtaposition. Yes, there is shadow, and yes, in the morning there will be light. It's all one. We can't have only light, happiness, and joy. There will be darkness as well. Rabbi Abraham Isaac HaKohen Kook, the mystic who served as the first chief rabbi of British Mandate Palestine, taught that not only is darkness a part of the natural rhythm of each day, but that it is good, just as light is good. He said, "And the day and night together complete each other to form time. And if it weren't for darkness, which is the expression of a brokenness and a lack of unity, there would be no urgency to become better, which is the basis for completing everything, until [there will be a time when] there is nothing lacking in reality."[70] Brokenness and discord are necessary. When my child is behaving in a difficult way, it is a part of the fabric of the universe. It is there to teach him something, and to teach me something too. It opens up the possibility that I will grow.

---

69   Genesis 1:5.

70   Rabbi Abraham Isaac HaKohen Kook, *Shemonah Kevatzim* 7:63.

Rav Kook continues, "It comes out that this limitation of darkness is the catalyst for renewal, and thus is also good, just like good is completely good." Resilience is not only having the ability to bounce back from our challenges; it is also about moving through to something new. Resilience is how we respond to challenge. It is good because we are good. Becoming resilient requires faith. It's a faith born of a process. It's the still, small voice that says, "I can move through this. This too shall pass." It's my son, who is a skateboarder, saying, "I can do this," when he encounters a difficult trick. It's my daughter, who is beginning to read, sounding out the words, saying to me, "Don't tell me, I've got this."

Our Role As Storytellers

Becoming resilient is not something that happens through grand moments. It develops slowly. We are resilient when we decide to lean into discomfort, to stay in a conversation instead of bolting, to look someone in the eye instead of looking away. Only we know when we are flexing our resilience muscles. Only our children will know when they are flexing theirs. But kids being kids, they may also forget those moments. As their parents, we serve as a living archive in which their expressions are housed and can be retrieved when they are needed most. On Passover we are invited to become storytellers with the Hagaddah's famous dictum: "And you shall tell your children on this day." Moreover, we are told that the more we expand and expound on the telling, the more praiseworthy it is. We must extend this into our daily lives, through retelling the stories of our children's lives to them.

During the COVID-19 pandemic, we had to shelter in place for Passover so our seder was limited to our family of five. Our children became very grumpy at this prospect, chanting in unison, "This is going to be terrible!" My heart sank. We were trying to make the best of a bad situation, but they said it like it is — as all children do. But then, at a certain point, our eldest changed the mood, exhorting his siblings, "Come on guys, let's make this good!" His decision inspired his siblings to get it together too and make the best of seder night. I remembered this recently when my son was having a hard time at school. I reminded him of his decision to switch perspectives. "You know you can just decide to make things better." A recollection from his mom of an earlier time in which he'd made that choice helped him make the mental shift to follow through on a commitment. It made all the difference.

In addition to appreciating the next time your child shows resilience, hold on to the moment so you can replay it when they need a boost of encouragement.

Pomegranate Trees

As I was walking home the other day, I noticed the blossoms on the pomegranate trees that dot the edges of my Jerusalem street. The fruit that bursts on to the scene on Rosh Hashanah, the holiday of renewal, begins to flower during the three weeks between 17 Tammuz and 9 Av, the darkest period of the Jewish calendar. Each year I am struck by the asynchronicity. At the moment when, in our collective memory, we are in a place of descent, nature reminds us: The month of Elul is around the corner, as it is every year. I'm still here, there is time for reconciliation, there is time to mend, there will be time to rebuild. It will come. You just need to be open and ready for a new season to begin.

When things feel dark, unclear, or murky for you, what phrase or mantra can you repeat to yourself in order to keep faith, to know that a new season is around the corner?

CARING FOR
PARENTS

As our parents age, we often find ourselves taking on more and more responsibility for their well-being. While this is an end in itself, it can also make us stronger and better people. Caring for parents can strengthen our empathy and compassion and reinforce connections within the family. When we care for parents, we also serve as a role model for our own children. As Mother Teresa said, "Not all of us can do great things, but we can do small things with great love."[71]

The challenges inherent in caring for aging parents often foster resilience, patience, and problem-solving. In the process we may confront the inevitability of aging and death, leading us to deeper appreciation for relationships, life, and the time we have with loved ones.

The authors in this section have a deep understanding of how difficult caring for parents can be, and they help us see that the challenge also comes with remarkable gifts and opportunities. Lori Palatnik shares personal accounts that can guide us to make the most of the parenting we received and the opportunity to care for our parents. Rabbi Dr. Binyamin Lau tells a personal story of caring for his aging father and shows how their bond strengthened and grew. Citing teachings from the Talmud and true anecdotes, he delves into Jewish wisdom's practicalities and priorities in caring for elderly parents. Jane Isay relays years of research and humorous stories around the changing relationship between parents and adult children, and the ways in which "Honor your father and your mother"[72] takes on different meaning and behaviors throughout life's various phases. She gives us a peek into the perspective of an elder, drawing on her personal experience and the stories she has collected, which can help us to look at our parents' aging years with compassion during their later years.

---

71   Mother Teresa, *No Greater Love,* Novato, CA: New World Library, 1997.

72   Exodus 20:11.

Caring for Parents — Great, Greater, and Greatest

Lori Palatnik

Lori Palatnik is founding director of Momentum Unlimited (formerly JWRP). A world-renowned Jewish educator, speaker, media personality, and author, in 2020 she was selected to light the diaspora torch at the national ceremony for Israel's seventy-second Independence Day.

Great

I was a brand new mother, overwhelmed and exhausted caring for baby Shoshana. One day, blurry eyed after being up with her all night and caring for her all morning, I suddenly had an epiphany. Without hesitating, I picked up the phone to call my husband at his office. The receptionist said he and the other rabbis were in a meeting, but I told her it was important and to please interrupt him and ask him to come to the phone.

"What's wrong?" he asked breathlessly.

"Nothing's wrong," I reassured him. "Yakov, you know how much we love Shoshana?"

"Yes ..."

"We love her so much we can't believe it. We've never felt such love. We would do anything for her, throw ourselves in front of a truck for her — right?"

"Um, Lori, you got me out of a meeting ..."

"Yakov, I realized today that *our parents love us like we love Shoshana!*"

I continued sharing my epiphany. This explained *everything* — why our parents constantly worry about us even once we are grown, why they tell us to wear sweaters when they are cold, why they insist we call them when we get home so they'll know we are safe.

Suffice to say that my husband wasn't as blown away by my epiphany as I was. He mumbled something and returned to his meeting. But later that night we spoke about it again, laughing at my insistence on sharing it immediately but agreeing that no one truly appreciates their parents' love until they become parents themselves.

Greater

In 2007 I had the incredible opportunity to donate my kidney to a woman I had never met before. It was the greatest experience of my life. People are often critical when I say that, often countering my claim with a variation on, "The greatest experience of your life? What about having children?"

It was the greatest experience of my life because, through it, God gave me the purest opportunity to give. The initial desire to have children is actually selfish; we *want* to have them. But after a baby arrives, we quickly realize that having children is not about what *we* want. Parenting is a constant, 24/7 act of giving. (Our rabbi used to say, "If you want to have children for what they will do for you, get a butler — they're cheaper.") The other criticism I hear concerns the fact that I gave my kidney to a stranger. They say, "I can imagine giving a kidney to my child, my parent, perhaps a sibling, but to someone I don't know?" I always explain that I was much happier giving it to someone I didn't know. I'm happy no one I know needed a kidney — but more importantly, if I had given it to someone I knew, it would have created an imbalanced relationship. What if, for example, I had given it to my friend and neighbor Robin, and then six months later I had called her and explained that I was going to give a talk in LA the following week, could she please cover my carpool? And she had replied, "Sorry but I'm busy next week, no can do." What would I be thinking? "I gave you my kidney, and you can't cover my carpool?" There would be a constant feeling of "you owe me" in the air. That's not a good feeling, and certainly does not create healthy relationships.

But somehow we seem to have that very attitude with our parents: "I didn't ask to be born, but now that I am here I expect you to feed me, clothe me, put me through school, pay for my wedding, set my spouse up in business, help with a down payment on our home ...." Everything our parents do for us should be seen in this context — as acts of giving. And that means that we, as children, need to be in a constant state of gratitude. Judaism reflects this. The fifth of the Ten Commandments does not talk about honoring our children, but honoring our parents. The Talmud, too, explores not what we owe our children, but rather what we owe our parents.[73] How do we reconcile this with all of the harm *some* parents do to their children? The Torah in no way condones abuse, and for the sake of this discussion we are focusing on the families where there is no abuse but plenty of parenting mistakes. Our parents were not perfect and we are not perfect parents ourselves, so how should we process their, and our, mistakes in the proper way? Imagine you are sixteen years old and your parents come home

73   Babylonian Talmud, Kiddushin 31b.

and say to you, excited, "Happy Birthday! Take a look at your gift, it's in the driveway — a brand new car!!!" You rush out, thrilled, but when you see the car, it's on cement blocks — there are no wheels! At this point you have two choices. You can yell, "Thanks for nothing!" turn around, march back into the house, slam the door to your room, and let the car sit in the driveway and rust. Or you can thank them for the car, find a job, make enough money to buy wheels for your car, and go somewhere in life. All of our parents gave us cars with missing parts. We have a choice: We can focus on their mistakes, blame them for the failings in our lives, or we can take what they gave us, work hard, fill in the missing parts, and create a fulfilling, productive, and meaningful life.

> *List three strengths you have worked hard to cultivate*
> *on your own. Consider how the "missing parts" from*
> *the way you were parented have helped to make your*
> *car stronger, faster, and more reliable.*

Why do we owe our parents everything? Because even with their mistakes they gave us the greatest gift anyone could ever give — life. How can we ever truly repay our parents? Well, time goes on, and parents age, and suddenly the opportunity to truly show our gratitude is placed in front of us. The tables turn, and those who once cared for us need us to care for them. My grandmother, of blessed memory, whom we called Bubby, used to say, "One mother can care for five children, but five children can't care for one mother." My mother was one of five, and I am one of four, and my mother now quotes her mother as my siblings and I learn to navigate this most challenging time during which our parents age, are in need, and, yes, pass away. I have learned much from this new stage of life, with Judaism as my guide:

People are different; not everyone will react like you. When faced with a crisis, some siblings step up and some run away. After my father had a stroke, I initially resented various family members' reactions, but then I came to realize that people really are different; it is not a lack of caring or love that sometimes paralyzes a person — it is simply how they cope (or don't cope) in a crisis. Some spring into action; others freeze. No matter how difficult it is for us, we need to be patient with how others process pain and fear.

Consider a family dynamic when you need to stretch to find empathy for the response of another family member. What keeps you from getting there? What can help you get there?

Working as a team is best for everyone. It does not help the aging or infirm parent to see their kids in conflict when trying to support them. Doctors and other health providers do not need inquiries or direction from multiple sources. Caring for parents is a team sport, and every player should take on a specific role. Supporting our aged mother after our father's passing has not been easy, but it went smoother and became easier once everyone found their roles. We created a shared sibling WhatsApp channel to post thoughts, concerns, and plans of action. One sibling communicates with our mother's doctor; we can all express our concerns to that sibling, and they in turn pass them on. None of us live in the city of our birth, where our mother is in an assisted-living facility, so one of us is assigned the task of placing the Amazon orders for anything our mother needs. Of course, every sibling team will need to develop different roles depending on the particular needs of their parent or parents.

The cycle of life is awesome. In God's infinite wisdom, we were created in such a way that we have no memory of our first years of life. If we did remember the countless diaper changes, our parents' sleepless nights, and all the new emotions and fears they and we grappled with, it might well be traumatic! But as our parents age, this cycle returns, in reverse. Some of us may discover that now our parents need us to change their diapers, stay up all night with them, soothe their fears and emotions. We must strive to see this as our chance to truly give back, in return for all our parents did for us — even if we don't remember it.

Our relationships with our parents are complicated; use this time to work through them. The Talmud says that honoring one's parents is the hardest mitzvah in the Torah.[74] Ask any teenager to express their feelings for their parents and you may be able to squeeze out admission of a love–hate relationship. Parents are the ones who love us and yet discipline us. Their judgment is often guided by, and clouded by, how they themselves were raised. There are many reasons why Judaism mandates official mourning for most loved ones for thirty days after their passing, but mandates mourning for a parent for eleven months. It

---

74   Jerusalem Talmud Peah 1:1.

takes time to properly process this complex relationship. Caring for aged parents while they are still here is a way of healing what is strained or difficult in the relationship before it is too late, so that loving closure can be achieved.

> *Consider an area in your relationship with a parent or parental figure that can use attention or healthful closure. What support can you seek that will be helpful to you during this process?*

Remember, your kids are watching. One day, you too will be elderly and perhaps in need. How you treat your aging parents now is setting an example for your children for the future. I sat at my father's bedside and wondered, "Who will step up for me when it's my turn?" We really have no idea how each of our grown children — together with their future partners — will react in our final years. All we can do is be the best role models possible.

> *What behaviors of caring for elders and parents did you witness as a young person? And now what behaviors of caring for elders and parents can children in your family and environment witness? What role can you take in this process?*

Consult with the wise. There are times when siblings may find themselves in conflict about how to care for a parent, including end-of-life issues. Find someone you can turn to together for guidance in navigating what can often become a minefield. Siblings may not only have different personalities and perspectives, but also may be guided by different values or levels of Jewish observance. Those who are wise, and expert in medical ethics, can help find what is right in your situation, based on your family dynamics — knowing that what parents ultimately want is for their children to remain loving and close to each other long after they are gone.

Greatest

Two years after donating my kidney, the woman who received it invited me to her daughter's wedding. Of course, I traveled to the wedding. Imagine how I felt at the *chuppah*, sitting with the other guests, watching the ceremony. When it ended, music played, people clapped and cheered, the bride and groom left the *chuppah*, and the mother of the bride ran into my arms, crying, thanking me for letting her live to see that day. There are no words for the pleasure I felt at that moment. I wouldn't have traded it for all the money in the world; it was truly priceless.

What act of generosity has given you great pleasure?
To whom might you direct a next act of generosity?
Schedule a time for your next act of generosity.

Our rabbi was blessed with twelve children. He told us that on their birthdays, his children give their *mother* a gift, to thank her for giving them life. The Torah tells us that the reward for honoring our parents is long life.[75] The question our sages then ask is: long life in this world, or in the next?[76] It may be one and it may be both, but either way your life will change for the good if you see caring for elderly parents not as a burden, but as a tremendous opportunity to give, to heal, and to show gratitude for all they did for us — even if there were some missing parts.

---

75   Exodus 20:12; Deuteronomy 5:16.

76   Chayei Adam 67:3; Babylonian Talmud Kiddushin 31b.

Honoring Our Parents in Their Golden Years

Rabbi Dr. Binyamin Lau

Rabbi Dr. Binyamin Lau leads the team behind 929, an Israeli social initiative aimed at creating discourse among all sectors of society based on the revival and relevance of the 929 chapters of the Tanach. He served as senior rabbi of the Ramban Synagogue in Jerusalem and, in collaboration with social justice NGO Ma'aglei Tzedek, founded the Beit Midrash for Social Justice at Beit Morasha. A noted author, he has published scores of books and research articles on Jewish heritage. His prolific writings focus on Jewish philosophy, issues of halachah and society, and the connection between biblical, mishnaic, and talmudic sources and contemporary social and political realities.

O n my father's eightieth birthday, he said to us, his children, "I pray that I will never fall on your hands." A few days later, he experienced a terrible fall. This was when my siblings and I were truly given the opportunity to fulfill one of the Ten Commandments, "Honor your father and mother." This commandment, of honoring your father and mother, becomes especially relevant in parents' old age, and it also becomes extremely challenging, because it entails a complete role reversal. As their children, we may want our parents to continue caring for us — but now, instead, we must care for them. There is no one perfect way to honor our parents. When we are with our children, we may think we should spend more time with our parents. When we are with our parents, we may think we should spend more time with our grandchildren. But whether we have the opportunity to be with our parents, our children, or our grandchildren, we should try to be fully present. Fortunately, Jewish wisdom gives us guidance on how to honor and care for our aging parents.

Dedicate Time

In the past, reaching retirement was seen as an achievement and a privilege, yet today this period of time is often difficult, characterized by reduced income and soaring expenses. People are living much longer. Of course, there are many benefits to living longer; individuals can see not only their children, but their grandchildren and even their great-grandchildren grow up, and they can play an active part in their lives. This is a phenomenon that was rarely seen in previous generations. According to our sages, "One does not express grievance upon a bounty of goodness."[77] However, the particular bounty of being blessed with longer lives can also lead to financial and social challenges. Today, adult children in their thirties, forties, and fifties are called the *sandwich generation*; they have become sandwiched between the responsibility for bringing up their own children, giving them emotional, physical, and financial support, and the responsibility of caring for their aging parents. At the stage when their parents begin to need their support, these adults of the sandwich generation are usually at the height of their professional careers, working long, tiring hours while also caring for their own children in a myriad of ways. Suddenly — or gradually — they also become responsible for their parents, often being expected to step in and assist their parents in maintaining a healthy lifestyle, a duty that can usurp both their time and resources. Who will finance their elderly parents' medical and supplementary expenses? According to our sages, an adult child does not necessarily need to contribute financially in order to honor their parents.[78] If the parents have resources, those are used first, the Talmud[79] teaches, and clarifies that adult children can dedicate their time and efforts to help their parents. Time, after all, is our most precious resource.

A former colleague who was an only child lived in Jerusalem while his parents lived in Tel Aviv. Every other day, he received an urgent phone call from his parents. He was constantly taking time off from work to drive to Tel Aviv to help them. It was extremely difficult. One day, he joked, "Where is my sister when I need her the most?" As an only child, the responsibility of caring for his parents rested on his shoulders alone.

While sharing the responsibility with other siblings may lighten the load, we know that children cannot possibly dedicate themselves to their parents in the same way that their parents dedicated themselves to them when they were growing up. Still, we can do our best to fulfill our various responsibilities.

---

77   Mishnah Taanit.

78   Kiddushin 32a.

79   Kiddushin 32a.

Escorting Parents

Jewish wisdom teaches us the importance of escorting our parents. The Talmud speaks of "bring them in and take them out."[80] It is up to adult children to help older parents find meaningful, enjoyable settings where they will feel active, important, wanted, and dignified. We must help our parents feel like they can continue growing and giving.

Should we help our parents continue to live in their homes? If they cannot, should they live with us, or should they live in a nursing home? One friend's parents are in their eighties and have been together for sixty years. His father has Alzheimer's and has recently become aggressive, including toward his wife. Obviously, this causes her great suffering. My friend found himself tortured with the quandary of whether to move his father to a nursing home or help him stay at home. In discussing this with my friend, I evoked the Talmud's description of "bring them in and take them out." I told him that in this case, honoring his parents involved taking his father out. In a nursing home, his father would be able to receive the care and security he needs, which would also allow his mother to live her final years in dignity. Sometimes, the right thing to do is take elderly parents out of their homes, and sometimes the right thing to do is to bring them into your own home. Sometimes a nursing home is best. Each situation is unique, with its own set of circumstances.

Help Parents Find Meaning

At some point, senior citizens leave the workforce. After experiencing long — and hopefully fulfilling — careers, they can find themselves, suddenly, with very little to do. Jewish wisdom believes that old age is a distinct time of life during which we are still able to find meaning and enjoy living. The Talmud explains that when older people feel important, needed, and capable, they will continue to experience the will to live.[81] Conversely, when they feel superfluous, or overly dependent on others, they may begin to deteriorate emotionally. If older adults reach the tragic point at which they feel they have nothing left to live for, they may become emotionally shattered. King Solomon captured this concern when he warned, "Days of sorrow can come, and years arrive in which you will say, 'I have no desire in them.'"[82]

---

80   Kiddushin 31b.

81   Shabbat 152a.

82   Ecclesiastes 12:1.

As their adult children, it is our responsibility to help our parents continue to find meaning and purpose in their lives. We can do so in the following ways:

1. Invite them to share their stories. Even while senior citizens' short-term memories may be failing them, their long-term memories often remain clear or even improve. Ask your parents about their youth and engage their grandchildren and great-grandchildren to do the same. Sharing their stories not only brings meaning to their lives and helps them reminisce and feel relevant, it helps us retain and pass on family stories too. Transmitting family stories is a gift not only to the elders but also to the children.

When my father had reached old age, I would take him to synagogue in his wheelchair. Along the way, people would look me in the eye and wish me, "Shabbat Shalom."

I would reply warmly, "Say Shabbat Shalom to my father too!"

Sometimes people simply stop interacting with those over a certain age. They may speak over them and about them, instead of to them. This is wrong. We need to be careful to include the senior citizens in our lives in conversations. Even if they are mostly quiet themselves, because of hearing issues or dementia or any reason, we must speak directly to our loved ones. Ask them questions, ask their opinions. Request that they share their stories.

> *Imagine an elder whom you can help engage to share their story. Is there a practical and creative way to do this? Can you imagine helping grandchildren or other family members take part in the process? How could the stories be gathered and shared? What would help make it practical and doable?*

2. Be flexible in making room for their contributions. We may need to be creative in connecting our elders with continued opportunities to be contributing members of their communities. A sixty-five-year-old woman called me in tears. Her father, a Kohen, had reached eighty-seven years old and, in all his long life, since his bar mitzvah, had never once missed reciting the priestly blessing for the congregation in synagogue during Shabbat services.[83] Recently, her father

---

83   In Israel, the priestly blessing (Birkat Kohanim) is recited in synagogues every Shabbat and festival; in the rest of the world, it is only recited during festival services.

had begun using a wheelchair. When he went to synagogue and prepared to say the blessing, a member of the congregation approached him and said he could not recite the blessing from the wheelchair because the Torah states that the priests stood while offering their blessing. This member believed this was a literal requirement according to Jewish law.

The man left the synagogue devastated. He told his daughter, "You can kill me now. If I cannot say this blessing, and there is no blessing left in me, what do I have left in my life?" I told his daughter to invite him to my synagogue, where he could continue saying the blessing. I later wrote a *responsa*, a rabbinic decision, affirming that individuals in wheelchairs can recite the priestly blessing. Seniors are a valuable — and often underutilized — segment of our communities. They are rich with life experience. Some communities have created multi-generational mentorship programs. A nonprofit organization in Jerusalem, Yad LaKashish, empowers low-income elderly through meaningful work opportunities and promotes positive attitudes toward seniors through inter-generational connections.

3. Help them engage with technology. Today, technology plays a big part in how we communicate, and we need to ensure the older generation is not left out. Older people can use Zoom and WhatsApp, but they may need to be repeatedly walked through the process. Explain how to use the relevant technology respectfully and patiently; doing so will guarantee your loved ones are included in today's conversations. During the pandemic, my mother enjoyed joining as many virtual Torah classes as she possibly could. She is ninety-one years old, and will often ask for my assistance when signing on to Zoom. Sometimes her calls are time consuming and require a good measure of patience, but I know that one day I will miss her calls. One day I will dream of hearing from her just one more time.

Seize the Time You Have Together

In Hebrew, there is a term for missing an opportunity — *hachmatza*. It is related to the word for *fermenting* (like *chametz*, leavened grain that is avoided on Passover). Think of a missed opportunity when a dough over-ferments and spoils. It's a terrible feeling to know that we had the chance to honor our parents and did not do so while they were alive. We should all wake up to this reality before it's too late and seize the moment while we can. When we honor our elderly parents — dedicating our time and effort to them, helping them find meaning, treating them with dignity, and embracing our time together — we also set a positive example for our children. They see what it means to honor parents. I pray that my children will never need to fulfill the commandment of honoring me to the fullest extent that can become necessary. But if they do, I hope they will do so with compassion and respect, enabling my physical and emotional longevity to feel *joie de vivre* — joy in living — in my old age.

The time we have together is precious and limited. Consider an elder who has impacted your life. Write and send a note of appreciation to them or give them a call to express your gratitude.

Whom Do We Honor?

Jane Isay

Jane Isay has been an editor for more than forty years. She discovered Mary Pipher's Reviving Ophelia, *commissioned Patricia O'Connor's bestselling* Woe Is I *and Rachel Simmons's* Odd Girl Out, *and edited such nonfiction classics as* Praying for Sheetrock *and* Friday Night Lights. *She's written several books of her own, including* Secrets and Lies, Mom Still Likes You Best, *and* Walking on Eggshells. *She lives in New York City, not too far from her children and grandchildren.*

When I was a child, sitting with my family in temple on the High Holy Days, there always came a moment in the liturgy when we were instructed, "Honor your father and your mother." My mother would always look over to catch my eye at that point. She would nod, and shake her finger at me, and smile from ear to ear. I would nod back at her. I was a good girl, so this was an inside joke between us. I listened to my parents and did my best to oblige. Their approval meant everything to me.

It became more difficult to obey that commandment once I became a teenager. I was, child of my times, critical of everything. How my mother dressed. What she ate. What she had to say. Her friends. How she treated my brother and me. I don't remember whether my mother continued our High Holy Day pantomime when I was an adolescent. Of course, when I grew up and went away to college, and got married, all of that went away. I might honor my parents once I had grown to adulthood, but I didn't have to obey them anymore, and "obey your mother and father" had been the subtext of the commandment in my family.

Perhaps you can see where I am going. In every generation, in every life stage, that commandment takes on a different meaning. So follow me now, through the ways in which "Honor your father and your mother" takes on different meanings and demands different behavior as the years go on. When I began to write books about family interactions, my first effort concerned trying to understand the relationship between parents and their grown children. I knew there was a problem, because I was suffering from my ignorance. All my friends with children in their twenties and thirties were experiencing similar problems. They weren't honoring us. They weren't even returning our phone calls! I was the mother of two grown sons. We had raised them to build their own lives, to go out into the world with energy and confidence, which was wonderful. However, that also meant that we had, like so many parents, moved from the center of their lives to the periphery. It hurt. This was back in the day of the landline. At one point, my younger son was running a senatorial campaign, hard fought and difficult. I left him a message: "Hi, Josh, it's Mom. Give me a call." No returned call. Second message: "Hi, it's your mother. Call me." Nothing. Third message: "Hello there, son, are you OK?" Silence. Finally, I left him this message: "Hi, Josh, it's your mom. If you don't call me today, I am going to vote for the other candidate." Moments later, the phone rang. It was Josh.

As I interviewed both generations for that book, which I titled *Walking on Eggshells*, I came to realize that, as much as they love us, grown children need to separate from us again, just as they did when they were two years old and when they were teenagers. The young adults I interviewed told me how much they love their parents, even when they weren't speaking, even when they were deep in conflict. Still, they needed to accomplish a major task vis à vis their parents: to separate enough — and grow up enough — that they could see us, their parents, as people. Not giants, not judges in full robes, not angels or devils. When our adult children begin to see us as complicated, loving, imperfect human beings, that perception can become the foundation of a lasting, mature relationship. "Honor your father and your mother," at that stage, translates to the necessity of accepting parents' faults, quirks, and annoying habits. It's a difficult transition. We are still authority figures to them. Our advice, which we have offered them all their lives, is often heard as criticism. A shrug of the shoulders or a funny look from us, and they are hurt and angry — just as they were as teens. They can tell what we are thinking, even when we say nothing — they learned to read our expressions when they were small. During this new stage, as they learn to honor us anew, differently, we must learn to honor our children too, by respecting their boundaries and sometimes biting our tongues. This can be annoying, but it has great purpose. It will grant us access to the next generation, when it arrives.

Rabbi Elimelech Bar-Shaul, the former chief rabbi of Rehovot, Israel, wrote, "Parents need to remember that their adult children need their maturity recognized, and no longer want to be seen as children."[84]

---

84   Rabbi Elimelech Bar-Shaul, *Reiach Mayim* (*Scent of Water*), Merkaz Shapira, 2014, p. 68.

*What is one thing you can do to treat a young adult in
your life with the dignity of maturity? What makes it
hard for parents to shift how they relate to their adult
children? What can help smooth this shift?*

The arrival of grandchildren marks another transition in the meaning of this commandment. The power relationship between the two adult generations begins to shift. Our grown children are now parents themselves, and they are the authority in their children's lives. They have the authority to invite us into their children's lives — or not. Once we become grandparents, we can honor our children by following the rules they set for their children, even if they seem foolish to us. We may chafe at the idea of restricting sweets, for example, wanting to indulge our beloved grandchildren. We may not want to defer to strict bedtimes our children ask us to enforce when we are babysitting. Respecting the decisions of our grown children may be easy in principle, but it's not always so easy to hold back our instinctive protests on a day-to-day basis: "No sweets? But he loves cookies!" "We were having too much fun to put him to bed at the time you said. It's so early!" We may reason that we raised our children by our rules and they turned out OK. What we need to remember is that times have changed and they are now in charge. If we don't abide by their wishes, they may interpret our behavior as lack of respect. And they may be right.

We may feel dishonored when our kids set rules of conduct for us toward their children, but there is a harder stage even than that. Imagine how much worse it will feel to be told by adult children that it is time to relinquish our car keys; it's no longer safe for us to drive. Many of us entered this stage sooner than expected during the COVID-19 pandemic, when suddenly advice started ricocheting around the country. Parents of a certain age, nowhere near frailty or senility, were suddenly being given instructions on how to behave by their adult children. My first experience of this happened on March 11, 2020. The pandemic was creeping through New York. I can see Mount Sinai Hospital from my windows; I knew we were in trouble, but I had no plan. My younger son called. "Mom, you need to cancel your dinner tonight. You can't go out with friends anymore, it's not safe. Mom, you have to be careful. No more supermarkets, no more restaurants, no more dinner parties until this is over." I didn't like this at all. The tone of his voice was stern. Had I given him advice in that tone when he was young? I hoped I hadn't, but of course I had. I remembered giving him instructions about where to stand in the subway while waiting for a train late at night. Same tone. Reminding him to wear a helmet while riding his bike. Same tone.

Bring to mind the last time you needed to be firm with your children. Were you able to do so without engendering antagonism or resentment? Is there something you'd like to do differently next time?

My friends received the same treatment from their grown children. "I'm sorry, but you can't see the grandchildren. They may be vectors." *What? How dare you tell me how to behave. I am still the captain of my ship!* "I'll pick you up this afternoon, you're coming to the country with me." *No! I make my decisions.* "You don't have a choice, Dad. You're doing what I say." How can such authoritarian behavior fulfill the commandment of honoring your father and your mother? It is one thing to follow rules about the grandchildren — we do that for many reasons. But surely, asking us to give up control over our own lives shows lack of respect on their part, doesn't it? On further consideration, I came to see that our grown children were taking the risk of making us resentful and angry in order to act in our best interests. They were protecting us. Maybe it was partly satisfying to exert control over an elderly parent, to use a tone they remembered from their own childhood and adolescence. But still. Those instructions were acts of love.

I think what we experienced during the pandemic foreshadowed the time in our lives that may arrive when our children will kindly, but firmly, take away our car keys, telling us we're no longer safe on the road. Or recommend, in no uncertain terms, that it's time to move to a "facility." How must our children follow the biblical commandment to honor us, their parents, when the time arrives when they must take charge of us? With humility. With tenderness. With patience. With memory. Care must be taken with tone. After all, we are still old enough to be their parents. We *are* their parents. We have lived a long time and we know a lot. They must remember that. If you have reached this stage with your parents, let me give you some advice: Giving up our independence in order to be safe, or well, feels like a humiliation. We may be too proud to show it, but you need to understand that that is how we are feeling. So be kind — kinder than you feel. We know you have other things to do, pressing responsibilities; don't remind us. Leave enough time for these conversations. You may feel impatient. And you're probably right. But remember how much patience it took to raise you. We are stubborn and proud; we may need more than one conversation to agree to some new restriction, some required change. And always, always, we need reassurance of your love. Elders don't get a lot of respect in this world; remember how certain politicians were ready to sacrifice our lives for the economy? We need it from you.

Consider our lives while we are still alive. Don't wait for Yizkor. As you take over the reins on our behalf, prepare yourselves by thinking of what we have done, for you, for the family, and for others. What we came from, and what we accomplished in our lives. Feel free to remember all your resentments too. Recall every mistake we have made, how badly we behaved and how we hurt you. And then remember how much we love you.

> *Make a list of ways your parents or a parental figure express love for you. How does this list reflect who they are, where they come from, and what they have accomplished?*

I know it is going to be hard. Taking care of elderly parents while raising a new generation, and working, and trying to make a life under trying circumstances is hard. You will fail, you will lose your temper, you will cut corners. Your parents did the same when they raised you. And you are probably not the perfect parent to your children and grandchildren either. Honoring your father and your mother means accepting, respecting, loving, and caring for them. Easier said than done, friends. But there are ways to approach the ideal. And that's all we can ask of ourselves and our children.

מֵצַר

—PSALMS 59:17

—PSALMS 119:143

FROM NARROW STRAITS, I CALLED GOD. GOD ANSWERED ME, BRINGING EXPANSIVE RELIEF —PSALMS 118:5

WHEN THE JEWISH PEOPLE ARE IN ANY STRAITS, GOD IS IN STRAITS —ISAIAH 63:9

WHEN I FIND MYSELF IN STRAITS AND DISTRESS, YOUR COMMANDMENTS ARE MY DELIGHT

I WILL SING OF YOUR STRENGTH AND EXULT YOUR KINDNESS FOR YOU HAVE BEEN MY HAVEN WHEN I HAVE BEEN IN STRAITS

NAVIGATING THROUGH
CHALLENGING
STRAITS

We must bear in mind that living wondrously does not mean that we never stumble or blunder. A smooth sea, Franklin D. Roosevelt was reputed to have said, never made a skilled sailor. Or to quote Disney's retelling of the legend of *Mulan*, "The flower that blooms in adversity is the rarest and most beautiful of all!"[85] Learning to live wondrously requires acknowledgment and acceptance that we will necessarily encounter challenges in our lives — challenges of all shapes and sizes, grueling conversations to managing the competing demands of work and family, the inevitable seasons of loss and mental health issues. As Jews we define greatness not by what happens to us, but by who we are in the face of what happens to us.

Judaism offers an operating system that addresses both the joys and the oys of life. When it comes to challenges and opportunities, our sages teach: "According to the effort is the reward."[86] The loftiest reward for our efforts is in the form of our learning and growth. Weathering tragedies, disasters, and pain can — with time — reveal to us deepened aspects of who we are. These experiences nurture and shape our resilience, revealing the potential of whom we can become, even and especially in the face of our grievous setbacks.

The Jewish morning prayers include an enigmatic blessing that is often translated as: "Blessed are you *Adonai* our God, Majesty of the world, who has provided me with all I need." On the surface, the phrase appears to imply that all our needs are met and we are offering thanks for the abundance of that goodness. However, one surprising interpretation asserts that we are actually offering thanks to God for giving us needs. In this reading, we acknowledge that our needs and our deficiencies are invaluable and instructive. This is not to say that we seek out challenges. We still labor to avoid them. But when they inevitably arise, we can encounter them and honor them as the source of our very greatness. They are the place where the soul meets its potential.

Rabbi Jonathan Sacks puts it this way:

---

85   *Mulan*, directed by Tony Bancroft and Barry Cook, Walt Disney Feature Animation, 1998.

86   Pirkei Avot 5:23.

Suffering is bad. Judaism makes no attempt to hide this fact. The Talmud gives an account of various sages who fell ill. When asked, "Are your sufferings precious to you?" they replied, "Neither they nor their reward."[87] When they befall us or someone close to us, they can lead us to despair. Alternatively, we can respond stoically. We can practice the attribute of *gevurah*, strength in adversity. But there is a third possibility. We can respond ... with compassion, kindness and love. We can become like the olive which, when crushed, produces the pure oil that fuels the light of holiness.[88]

And, in fact, the sages compared the Jewish people to olives: "Rabbi Joshua ben Levi asked: Why is Israel likened to an olive? To teach us that just as the leaves of an olive tree do not fall off, neither in the summer nor in the rainy season, so too Israel will not be destroyed, neither in this world nor in the World that is Coming. And Rabbi Yochanan says: It is to tell you that just as an olive yields its oil by being crushed, so too Israel fulfils [its potential] through [pressure and] suffering."[89]

How often have you witnessed the emergence of distinctive inner resolve emerge in the face of difficulty? That was certainly the case across Israel in the aftermath of the October 7 attack in 2023. We beheld a remarkable volunteerism across the country and throughout the global Jewish world, for example, to support the families of the hostages, among others. Living wondrously can mean engaging with challenges in order to extract the soul's sweetest oil. We can then use that singular oil as a balm as we attend to what most pains and troubles the world.

It seems like a tall order. How can we take the initial steps down this path? Rabbi Nachman of Breslov offers guidance on releasing our painful emotions in ways that boost our energy to navigate through narrow straits. He suggests focusing on one's broken heart each day for a limited amount of time, such as an hour. Indeed,

---

87   Babylonian Talmud Brachot 5b.

88   Rabbi Jonathan Sacks, "Covenant & Conversation: Crushed for the Light," Tetzaveh, The Rabbi Sacks Legacy, 5778, https://rabbisacks.org/covenant-conversation/tetzaveh/crushed-for-the-light/.

89   Talmud Menachot 53b.

Shelly Shem-Tov, whose son, Omer, is one of the hostages kidnapped by Hamas from the Nova Festival, described her approach to a Momentum gathering over four hundred days after her son was kidnapped. Every morning, she said, she spends a set time experiencing heaviness, thinking of her son and others who have not seen daylight for so long, tasting breakfast in agony, knowing that her son is hungry. Connecting with God in that way gives her strength. Only then does she shift to envision her son coming home and to taste its joy, turning to leadership and activism among the families of other hostages.[90]

Rabbi Nachman recommends speaking with God in one's own words about one's broken heart. Then, to avoid shifting from broken heartedness (which is helpful) to depression (which is not), to transition to deliberate joy for the remainder of the day.[91] Why? Because joy sustains resilience and provides the energy to effectively navigate through challenging straits.[92]

With this in mind, may we all seek and find the proper words, the appropriate balance, the mental clarity, and the wisdom to achieve our fullest, most wondrous potential.

The following four chapters explore: engaging in difficult conversations, managing work and family, wisdom in times of loss, and facing mental health challenges.

90   Shelly Shem-Tov is one of the founders of the Hostage Forum.

91   Rabbi Nachman of Breslov, *Likutei Moharan II, 24*.

90   M.M. Tugade and B.L. Fredrickson, "Resilient individuals use positive emotions to bounce back from negative emotional experiences," Journal of Personality and Social Psychology, 86(2), 2004, p. 320–333. B.L. Fredrickson and T. Joiner, "Positive emotions trigger upward spirals toward emotional wellbeing," Psychological Science, 13(2), 2002, p. 172–175. M.D. Seery, E.A. Holman, and R.C. Silver, "Whatever does not kill us: Cumulative lifetime adversity, vulnerability, and resilience," Journal of Personality and Social Psychology, 99(6), 2010, p. 1025–1041.

DRAWING ON WISDOM FOR

TIMES OF LOSS

When someone dear to us is torn away, life can feel like a forever-altered abyss of pain — whether we have lost a beloved individual or, as in the aftermath of October 7, face a tragedy of national and international proportions. How does Jewish wisdom guide us in such cases?

Grief is often treacherously isolating. It can mark us with an overpowering sense of loneliness. In response to that isolating sense, Jewish tradition directs us to show up: Show up for those in grief. Show up to the funeral. Show up during the seven days of *shivah* mourning. Show up after *shivah*. Be tangibly present with those in grief. We are directed not to give advice or create undue distraction, but rather to simply be present fully, in order to help bear a bit of the heavy burden of the bereaved.[93]

What should we actually do or say? How can our presence offer some consolation to a mourner who is broken hearted?

The Hebrew word for *consolation* — *nechama* — provides some insight. This word also has a second meaning in Hebrew. The first time this word appears in the Torah is in Genesis, at the beginning of the story of the flood: "God regretted (*va'yinachem*) creating humans on Earth."[94] In English *consolation* and *regret* may not seem related to each other at all, but in biblical Hebrew it is the same word! What can we learn from this? On this phrase in Genesis, the famous medieval commentator Rashi brings several biblical verses with the word *nechama* and concludes that it always implies "a change in mind — *machshava acheret*."

Being present with a mourner with compassion and the intent to bear a measure of their painful burden can with time *change their outlook*. People's minds change not so much as a result of what we say or do, but because of *how* we are with them. When we are fully present and attentive, we create a compassionate shared space that generates movement. Over time a mourner can feel less lost and isolated. Very gradually, their mindset can begin to shift.

---

93   Psalm 91:15.

94   Genesis 6:6.

Consolation and comfort result from this slow reshaping of the mourner's outlook, this slight but essential "change of mind."

The change in mind also involves emerging from the fog of grief with recognition of what is and isn't gone. My husband, David, attended a workshop years ago with the famous psychologist Dr. Harry Levinson,[95] about the importance of the mourning process. What stayed with David all these years has been Levinson's explanation that mourning entails not only being present with feelings as they arise, but also the important process of sifting through what has been lost to find what to bring forth into one's future — memories, lessons, or convictions. As we sit with mourners and listen to them, this metaphorical sorting process starts taking place; with time, it offers mourners a recalibration. In the face of the new absence, they can both honor the painful loss and acknowledge what will live on in and through them.

In this chapter, Rabbi David Aaron explores the journey of loss through questions — both the helpful and unhelpful — that we tend to ask. He shares personal accounts, explains the wisdom behind Jewish mourning practices, and provides metaphors that foster hope. Dr. Arielle Lehmann shares personal reflections on losing her beloved mother, poignantly contemplating prayer, uncertainty, her mother's last words, and the seven days of *shivah*. Harry Rothenberg offers guidance for the grief process from his experience as a personal injury lawyer as well as insights into grief gleaned from the experience of two Jewish patriarchs.

---

95   Harry Levinson (1922-2012) served as chair of The Levinson Institute and clinical professor of psychology emeritus in the Department of Psychiatry, Harvard Medical School.

Wisdom in Times of Loss

Rabbi David Aaron

Spiritual leader and educator Rabbi David Aaron delves fearlessly into life's biggest questions and shares the transformational wisdom of Torah with people of all ages. He is the dean and founder of Isralight, an international organization; and Yeshivat Orayta, a program for high school graduates. The author of eight books, including The God-Powered Life: Awakening to Your Divine Purpose, *he received his rabbinic ordination from Yeshivat Itri.*

In times of pain and loss, people often ask rabbis: Why is this happening to me? As a rabbi myself, I'm flattered that they think I know, but the truth is it is an impossible question to answer. I cannot tell you why this is happening: why you have lost a loved one, why your body is failing you, why your heart is broken. I simply do not know. What I can tell you is this: *Why is this happening to me?* is the wrong question.

We cannot understand God. We cannot even begin to try. It would be like trying to play a CD on a cassette player — impossible. This is the meaning of the verse in Isaiah: "For My thoughts are not your thoughts, neither are your ways My ways, declares the Lord."[96] Instead, we must ask: What is this pain I am experiencing *asking of me*? How can I give this pain meaning? How can I weather this storm and emerge from it a better person?

In Pain, with God

Months before my wife was due to give birth to our first child, we took Lamaze classes together. I thought I was prepared to help and support her, to guide her calmly through this beautiful process. But when the day came, and I could see the pain of labor on her face with each contraction, I couldn't handle it. I was more of a *schlimaz*[97] than a Lamaze master. I was beside myself. I tried to help her practice the deep breaths we had learned, but I began to hyperventilate.

In between two contractions, she leveled her gaze at me and said, "Could you

---

96   Isaiah 55:8.

97   *Shlimazel* is a Yiddish word that means consistently unlucky and connotes clumsiness.

please calm down? Although I am in excruciating pain, I'm not suffering." Another contraction rose and fell. In the same even tone, she spoke again: "Suffering is pain without purpose. This is the most purposeful pain I could ever hope to experience."

I was floored. Amid the most pain she had ever experienced, my wife found a way to face it head-on. She turned her pain into power by remaining mindful of its purpose: to bring our child into the world.

Judaism teaches us that we are all souls, and our souls are a part of God. Most people think of God as distant or aloof. They think God is somewhere up there, watching us down here as we suffer alone. That image, that feeling, causes even more pain — and it is not what Judaism teaches. When our souls feel pain, God feels it too. A passage in the Talmud explains that when a person is sick, the Divine Presence stands right by their head.[98] Even when a person is just in pain, God says, "Oy, *my* head hurts. *My* limbs hurt."[99] As my wife labored to bring our child into the world, God was beside her, feeling her pain with her. This concept is everywhere in our texts. In Psalms, there is a famous verse: "Though I walk through the valley of the shadow of death, I will not fear evil because you are with me."[100] The Zohar, the central work of Jewish mysticism, adds one word of commentary on this verse: *Mamash*, really! God is really, literally with us when we are walking in the valley of the shadow of death.

Some might counter with: This can't be true. Where was God during the Holocaust? Where was God when the Jews were in the gas chambers? The answer is the same: God was in the gas chambers with us. We will never know why it happened to us, but we know God was there, feeling our pain. God shares our pain, literally.

Once, when I was at a seminar, I met a man who was the son of two survivors. He had made the Holocaust his life. He was very angry at Judaism, and very angry at God. At that seminar, I gave a talk on how God cries with us, how God feels our suffering. The man came up to me afterward and told me, "Now I can begin to believe in God. I can only believe in a God who suffers with us."

We do not know *why* we are in pain, *why* we have been subjected to injustice, *why* we have lost our loved ones. But if God is willing to go through our pain with us, then there must be a divine purpose in it — even if we do not know what it is, even if we *cannot* know what it is. Pain without purpose is suffering. Pain *with* purpose is power. Even when we don't know the specific purpose of our pain, we

---

98   Babylonian Talmud Shabbat 12b.

99   Babylonian Talmud Sanhedrin 46b.

100   Psalm 23:4.

can draw strength and empowerment from this understanding. We know we are not abandoned at this moment. We do not walk alone.

I Am Not a Judge

When we hear that someone has passed away, or when we see someone going through something very difficult, there is a short prayer that Jewish people say: *Baruch dayan Ha'Emet*, Blessed is God, the true judge. When I first heard this phrase many years ago, I was bothered by it. What a strange, horrible thing to say about — or to — someone in pain! If a person has lost their beloved, am I saying that God has judged and decided their beloved deserved to die? If I see someone with an illness or a handicap that has disrupted their life, must I really believe God has judged that is what this person deserves? After much thought, I began to understand the true meaning of the statement. When we see others in pain, we might judge them in our hearts, thinking they must have deserved what has happened to them. To *stop* ourselves from passing judgment, we say *Baruch dayan Ha'Emet*, Blessed is the true judge — which we most certainly are not. It is a reminder to ourselves that we are *not* the true judge, so we must never judge what anyone else is going through. We should never presume to know why anyone must endure pain and loss. We must reserve our judgment, our curiosity, and simply offer our compassion.

What can we do when others are in pain? If there is no answer to the *why* question, what can we possibly say? Well, I can tell you what *not* to say. My friend's son was killed in a car accident when he was a young man. At his funeral, the rabbi said in Yiddish, "*Mensch tracht, und Gott lacht*" ("Man plans, and God laughs"). I was furious. What an utterly inappropriate thing for someone to say at a funeral where parents had lost their son! Were my friends' dreams for their son pointless? Was God really laughing at their grief?

Others describe life as a grand tapestry: Humans only see the back of the tapestry, the messy side that makes no sense, with knots and frayed threads — while God sees the other side, which is a perfect work of art. I never liked that one either. Why would God keep us from the joy of seeing the beautiful tapestry?

It is probably best to stay away from these simplistic approaches entirely. In fact, it is probably best to stay away from speaking too much at all. When people are in pain, they are not looking for answers. In the midst of the haze of pain or grief, the last thing anyone needs is well-intentioned advice, flowery metaphors, or overly philosophical musings about God that hurt far more than they help.

I heard a story from a rabbi who gave a talk on faith after the Holocaust. At the end of his talk, a man stood up and spoke. "Rabbi, I cannot accept anything you've said in this class," he said in a thick Polish accent. "I am a survivor of Auschwitz, and nothing you say is satisfactory."

The rabbi replied, "Please share with me four points I've made in this class." The man thought for a moment, but he could not recall a single thing the rabbi had said. "Sir, I want to apologize," the rabbi said to the man. "This is a class of philosophy. You have experienced a pain that we cannot imagine. You don't need academic philosophizing. When we suffer, what we need is empathy, not philosophy."

The Power of Sitting *Shivah*

I lost both my parents within nine months of each other. Though Jewish tradition dictates that we sit *shivah*, a seven-day period after the deceased is buried when their family receives visitors, the last thing I wanted to do was have anyone in my home. What I wanted to do was lock myself in my room and never come out. I didn't want to think or talk about my parents, because it would only remind me of their inconceivable absence.

But Judaism tells us to open the door. It tells us that the way to heal from our grief is *by grieving*. To pass through the pain, it must be felt. To begin to grapple with my parents' loss, I needed to sit with my family and friends, no matter how much it hurt. I needed to receive phone calls and letters and flowers from faraway loved ones. I needed the people in my life to acknowledge the loss I had experienced, the chest-constricting pain I was feeling. Empathy, acknowledgment, and compassion are the only ways to help yourself and others in times of pain and loss. All we can do is sit *shivah*.

Reflect on a time you experienced someone sitting with pain and discomfort without trying to fix it or distract away from it. When someone was able to simply be there, quietly, with it. Next time someone you know is faced with grief, loneliness, or distress, try sitting with them for five to fifteen minutes, simply being present. Hold back advice, wisdom, or jokes. Just hold the intention of your presence helping to contradict the isolation. Lean in to the act of sharing the burden of their grief, even if only a little.

In a *shivah* house, you don't start the conversation. The mourners talk when they are able and, when they do, you listen compassionately. Your role in these moments is to share their grief. You might share a memory, "I remember a time when your mother did something amazing for me. Can I tell you about it, or write it down for you to read later?"

One night during the *shivah* for one of my parents, as I said goodbye to my guests and got ready for bed, I had a startling thought. I realized I was feeling a profound inner joy. Under the layers of grief and exhaustion, I was happy that I knew how to be sad. I was happy that I had a tradition that gave me real, honest ways to acknowledge, feel, and work through my grief.

Happiness at that moment wasn't found in smiling, or dancing, or telling a joke — or in avoiding pain. It was found in the knowledge that I was doing what I was supposed to be doing. I was supposed to be crying, telling stories, looking at old photos — addressing my pain head-on, not suppressing and avoiding it.

Moving Forward

Judaism offers wise rituals that guide us through an entire year of mourning the loss of a parent.[101] These practices allow us to feel our grief, carry it with us, and give in to it, all while showing us a way through it and beyond it.

The mourning begins with the *kriah*, when mourners tear their clothing or a symbolic piece of fabric over their hearts, as a primal release of emotion after the funeral. There is a tradition that during the *shivah* we cover every mirror in the house, so our vanity about our appearance doesn't distract us or make us self-conscious about the grief we feel. There is a tradition of not shaving or getting a haircut for the first thirty days of mourning, and of not attending public gatherings during the year of mourning.

This year of mourning tells us: Though you might want to, do not push away the pain. Do not try to avoid it or forget it. Allow this wisdom, these guidelines, to move you through the pain until you reach the other side, changed forever, but able to continue on.

---

101   The formal mourning period for other relatives ends with the thirty days following the funeral, called the *sheloshim.*

From Darkness, We Grow

Imagine you are a seed, but you do not know that you are a seed. When your turn comes to be planted in the earth, all you feel is that you are being buried alive. You know nothing else. From your perspective, is there anything more evil than what has just been done to you? You've been buried, and sure enough you will die. You are disintegrating into the ground, evolving into something you do not understand. Would you believe it if someone were to lean down and whisper in your ear, "You are not dying. You are growing roots. You are sprouting. And soon you will blossom." Never. You would never see the blessing in the tragedy. But knowing that God is with us in our pain, someday we might be able to look back and know that we were seeds, lost in the darkness, buried not so we would die but so we could grow into something we did not yet understand.

I cannot tell you why you are in pain, why you have lost someone, why this has happened to you. I cannot give you advice that will make your pain go away. But what I can do is encourage you to discover the traditions that will guide you through the pain and what this experience might mean for you. And though the purpose of your pain might not be apparent for a long time, or ever, when you consider that your pain does *have* a purpose you can turn your pain into power. With that wisdom, you can weather your grief and perhaps, someday, heal.

Lost and Found: A Personal Account of a Substantial Loss

Dr. Arielle Lehmann

Arielle Lehmann, PhD, is an Israeli social psychologist and writer. She heads the Reichman Sheba National Resilience Program, a partnership between the Reichman University School of Psychology and Sheba Medical Center, which trains mental health professionals to support patients post-trauma and nurture post-traumatic growth. As an expert group facilitator, she wrote the Israeli Open University textbook about group processes. She co-founded and managed a London-based start-up company developing software for group communications, and is a partner at Psifas, a leading Israeli consultancy for medical teamwork. Arielle and her husband live in Israel, where they are raising their four children. Her most recent book, Beyond Belief: Inspiring Stories of Extraordinary Israelis, *documents Israeli society through the powerful stories of 18 inspiring people, depicting a diverse portrait of life in Israel.*

Prologue

The year 2020 was a year of loss. It began with Elli. Elli is my cousin; emotionally she is my sister. Our mothers are sisters of a Jewish Italian origin, which means Elli and I grew up together with a deep sense of "La Famiglia." We celebrated the holidays together at the house of Nona, our grandmother, in Jerusalem. We traveled abroad together for the first time in our life when I was ten years old and Elli was twelve, and then again before my military service and just after Elli finished hers. Elli was a part of each junction and decision of mine and participated in all my celebrations. From the moment I remember myself, Elli has walked with me through the journey of Life. In February 2020 Elli went into surgery to treat a congenital heart condition. The surgeon made a tragic mistake and ruptured her aorta. Elli survived but was left with severe brain damage. She lost the ability to talk, walk, and see. I felt I lost my precious cousin-sister-friend, when she is still alive needing constant company and help.

In the next paragraphs I will tell my story of the year 2020. As the world was facing a threatening new pandemic, I was coping with personal losses. While the world's scientists were racing to find a new vaccine, I had to find my own emotional immunization. Looking for ways to sustain and support myself, I turned to my family — La Famiglia, again — as well as to my culture and professional background. I will share some of the experiences and insights I gathered along the way.

I have organized my story into seven sections, a literary structure I explored and adopted in my two recent books in which I interviewed and told the stories of inspiring Israelis. The structure of seven, *shivah*, which is the ancient Jewish tradition of mourning, seemed fitting to tell my own story of loss.

Prayer

A few days before Rosh Hashanah, around three in the morning, my phone rang. *Mom* flashed on the screen. Due to the unusual hour, I got worried. At the tender age of seventy-nine my mother was still working full time as a legal adviser, with the dual expertise of a lawyer as well as a clinical criminologist. She was very bright with unique traits that may sound contradictory but in fact blended into a charming, powerful presence. She was elegant and aristocratic yet friendly and accessible, focused and professional as well as funny and playful, an eloquent speaker and a rare listener. After my father passed away, my mother met a man who was younger than me and they formed a special friendship. She made us all forget her age, and yet there she was calling me in the middle of the night, saying repeatedly in a strangely detached voice that something about her "went wrong." We called an ambulance and rushed to her house to meet the medical team there. My mother collapsed on the way to the hospital with what I believed at the time to be a stroke. I thought of my cousin Elli: By then I had half a year of a close encounter with her brain damage. In the scary moments on the way to the hospital with my mother I found myself reviewing the situation: A group of more than fifteen relatives and close friends, including myself, was taking care of Elli day and night. It was a huge effort that required ongoing teamwork and coordination. My mother was much older. It would be left to me, my brother, and my sister to look after her. I found myself praying in the ambulance: "Please God if I cannot have my mom back then take her away, just do not do it halfway. I wish to be here for Elli. I cannot look after my mom too."

Until that moment I had prayed for the death of someone only once in my life. I was in my twenties and I found myself in the midst of a terrorist attack in the heart of Jerusalem. I was caught in the crossfire between the terrorists and the

Israeli police. I remember myself trembling in my hiding place and praying the first words that came to my mind: "Please God let them die and let me live." In the ambulance I found myself for the second time in my life praying for death, this time for someone so dear and beloved. It was too awkward. I didn't know what to make of it.

Uncertainty

My mom did not have a stroke. For six weeks she was hospitalized in the neurology ward without a diagnosis. During that time she suffered from recurrent seizures that left clear marks on her body and her mind. We lost her day by day, hour after hour without knowing why. The doctors ruled out all the evils they knew — the blood vessels were fine (hence it was not a stroke), the blood tests were good, repeated CT and MRI scans did not find anything. Yet my mother's brain was under severe attack from an unknown source. During the six weeks of hospitalization the doctors hoped and believed my mother would be saved. However, my brother, sister, and I felt differently. Day after day we saw how she was changing; it was as if she was running out of herself. I felt I was facing something even more challenging than loss — I was plunged into uncertainty. As a social psychologist I learned that families of Israeli soldiers who were killed managed to cope better than families of soldiers who went missing. The in-between is harder to bear, it does not let you mourn. We need a farewell in order to be able to carry on. My prayer from the ambulance resonated with me. I did not judge myself for wishing my mother to die. I accepted my inner truth: I did not want mom to stay alive without being herself.

COVID-19

My mother did not have Corona but she was hospitalized during the pandemic. Staying at hospital during the pandemic was difficult. Patients lay in their beds breathing heavily through face masks. They did not know who took care of them, everybody looked the same in uniform and covered faces. Doctors and nurses who deal regularly with work overload found themselves even more exhausted than usual. When someone coughed or cleared their throat it sounded like an alarm. Worst of all, each patient was allowed one visitor only. Patients were deprived of most of their social support when they needed it most. In our case the pandemic regulations meant only one of us would be allowed to stay with our mother when she was dying.

I will always remain grateful to the medical staff for ignoring the strict regulations and letting me, my brother, and sister stay together with mom in the last weeks of her life. Israelis are not very obedient — they often say that rules are meant to be broken. This approach does not always sit well with me, but during the last weeks of my mother's life it became a blessing.

Last Words

Mom is lying in bed in the ICU. She developed a lung infection and does not breath well. Her doctor comes to see her and prescribes antibiotics. He thinks she is likely to get stronger and to move to rehab. I find it hard to believe. I see how my mother's strength is draining out of her; by now she barely communicates with us and lies most of the time with her eyes closed. Suddenly, without opening her eyes, she is asking me, "Will they move me to rehab tomorrow?" "Yes," I lie, I see no point in correcting her now. She turns her head toward me, "Are there white angels there?" "Sure," I say, "there's anything you'd like. We will look after you just like you have always looked after us." Mom is smiling, her eyes are closed. She looks peaceful, even happy. "Cherish this moment," I tell myself. "Cherish this moment and let her go."

There were very few happy moments at the hospital. I am glad that in her last seconds Mom had angels on her mind and a smile on her face.

Shivah

The funeral took place in Rehovot, where my brother lives. Under COVID-19 regulations only twenty people were allowed to participate. Afterward we went to my mother's house. We did not expect a proper *shivah*, as people were not allowed to gather, but we took the plastic chairs out of the storage just in case.

My mother left an impact wherever she went. She had numerous relatives, friends, and colleagues who loved her dearly. For all these people she vanished without a warning; they wanted to come to say goodbye. Guests started arriving to the *shivah* despite the pandemic. It was the month of October and Israel's pleasant climate came to our help — we divided the visitors by putting most of the chairs outdoors, under the building. It was *shivah* in bubbles, so I am not sure who was there. I do know that plenty of people came, far more than we expected, and I ate more cookies during this week than ever before. The spirit of the *shivah* won over the pandemic — we were supported, nurtured, and embraced. The house became so full we were distracted from its emptiness.

Epilogue

Elli my cousin is now at home. She has lost so much — the ability to see, walk, talk, eat, or even swallow. She has not lost her mind or her memory though — she is fully present and aware of the situation. More importantly, she maintained her ability to love and be loved. Elli is surrounded by family members and friends who learn to communicate with her in her forced silence. La Famiglia is still there to support and comfort.

I am writing this chapter eight months after my mother passed away. I like to think about my mother as a source of life and light on Earth before passing away to a different dimension.

The Jewish faith is very thorough about the timeline of loss: *aninut,* the fragile time from the moment of death until the burial; *shivah*; *shloshim,* the thirty days following burial (which include the *shivah*), when mourning is expressed by avoiding public entertainment and celebrations; the first year.

The milestones of grief consider our vulnerability and pace it. A loss cannot be taken all at once, it is absorbed bit by bit. There are moments when it is odd and inconceivable, others when it is sharp and gripping. Like the waves of the ocean, the waves of sorrow are unpredictable. There is no point in fighting them, instead it is better to let them be. The more you accept these waves, the better your chance of getting back to shore safely.

> *What did getting back to shore safely mean to you at a time when you faced a big change that involved grief and mourning?*

If you had told me that in the span of one year I would lose my mother; Elli would lose her ability to see, talk, and walk; and the world would face a new type of virus imposing social distancing and locking me up, I would have said, "This is too much." Yet all this happened and somehow I still woke up in the morning with an appetite for life. Alongside the losses I realized that life is bigger and stronger than I am. There was a lot to do and deal with; I constantly needed to take care of my family as well as myself. My priorities became clearer than ever. I was in pain but I was not confused.

Between the lockdowns my husband and I managed to make the time and celebrate the bat mitzvah of Daria, our daughter. My mom and Elli were both hospitalized, several other guests were quarantined and could not make it, we had to party in face covers. It was not the bat mitzvah I had in mind. Yet it was a beautiful evening in Jaffa with sea views, golden sunset, and loving guests who made the effort to come and celebrate with us despite everything. For a few hours we put aside the worries and had an unforgettable time surrounded by family and friends. I felt we have taught Daria the most important lesson for life.

One month later I was asked to phrase the writing on my mother's grave. It was not easy to sum up seventy-nine intense years in one stone. I chose my words carefully:

Beloved mother, grandmother, sister, and friend
Dina Lehmann Jarash 1942-2020
Filled the world with life, wisdom, and beauty

THANK YOU

Looking to Our Forefathers for Guidance Through Grief

Harry Rothenberg, Esq.

Harry Rothenberg, Esq., a partner at The Rothenberg Law Firm (injurylawyer.com) and magna cum laude graduate of Harvard Law School, is best known for his successes in the courtroom on behalf of victims of catastrophic injury. His firm is one of the leading personal injury law firms in the United States. Harry is equally passionate about speaking on Jewish topics. A sought-after lecturer for his crowd-pleasing talks, Harry's favorite project is Beyond the Letter of the Law, *his popular weekly video series about Jewish holidays and the Torah portion of the week.*

A number of years ago, a client of mine lost her twelve-year-old son in indescribably gruesome fashion. Her son did not die immediately, but rather was comatose for a day and half before passing away. While her son was clinging to life, she told her other children that their brother had "one foot on Earth and one foot in Heaven. And if Heaven decides to call him up, we can never question God's decision."

Toward the very end, when her son's vital signs were plummeting, the doctors at the hospital told her and her husband that it was time to say goodbye. A family friend who was present and witnessed the scene later detailed it for me. The friend told me my client entered the room and spoke clearly to her son.

"I know you can still hear me," she said. "The Torah says, 'Honor your father and your mother.' I am your mother! And I am telling you, when you get up to Heaven, to make sure to pray for us. Pray for your grandparents. For me and your father. For your brothers and sisters. And your friends and community. I know that God will listen to you."

Rather than railing at God over the seeming injustice of her situation, she accepted what was happening and spoke words of comfort to her son, following in the stoic steps of Aaron, the high priest, and his brother, Moses.

One of the central prayers in the liturgy of the High Holy Days is designed to command our attention. In *Unetaneh Tokef,* we listen to the many ways God will mete out judgment in the coming year. *Who will live and who will die? Who will live a long life and who will die before their time?* And in case that is not enough of a wake-up call, we then delineate how those who are destined to pass away during the coming year will meet their end.

As we chant each phrase, I cannot help but think of clients who have met their end in similar fashions. As a plaintiff's personal injury attorney, I have represented survivors who have lost loved ones of every possible family relationship — grandparents, parents, spouses, siblings, and in the most tragic cases, children. I have also represented clients who are still-living victims of loss — amputees, paraplegics, brain injury victims, people who have lost senses or limbs or whose lives and bodies have been otherwise stunted or impaired.

Who by water? I think of those whose estates I have represented who drowned.
Who by fire? I think of those who were burned to death.
Who by sword? Fatal assaults.
Who by beast? Attacks by improperly guarded animals.
Who by storm? People killed during storms due to negligent construction.
Who by plague? In a world with COVID-19, we can all relate to that one.
Who by strangling? Had that case too.

The death cases in my office almost always contain one or sometimes two additional factors that magnify the pain of the loss: the suddenness, leaving the surviving family members no time to say goodbye or make amends; and the witnessing of the tragedy by family members. In addition to being a lawyer to those surviving family members, I often provide grief counseling, empathy, and a sympathetic ear. No matter how many times I go through that process, it never gets easier. Perhaps funeral directors and pathologists are able to immunize their feelings, but I have not yet been able to despite my nearly thirty years in this profession.

I am sometimes asked how can I do this kind of work without losing my faith in God. As an attorney my approach to a question begins with reviewing the relevant texts, so let's take a look at two biblical examples of dealing with loss that deeply affect me.

Perhaps the most iconic example of maintaining faith in the face of terrible loss is Aaron's reaction to the deaths of his sons. Aaron, the high priest of the Jewish people, sees that his eldest two sons have been killed by a fire from Heaven for bringing an unauthorized offering of incense to the Tabernacle. His younger brother, Moses, immediately offers him words of comfort — but Aaron remains completely silent.[102]

---

102 Leviticus 10:1-3.

Compare Aaron's reaction with an earlier scene in the Torah — the story of the patriarch Jacob and his son Joseph. When Jacob is presented with false evidence indicating the death of his beloved son Joseph, he cries out, "My son's garment. An evil beast has devoured him! Joseph has been torn apart!" Jacob begins a period of mourning — and does not stop for twenty-two years. He is eventually reunited with Joseph, who was actually alive in Egypt the entire time. During those twenty-two years, the many members of Jacob's large family tried to offer him words of comfort but he refused to be consoled, explaining that he will "go down to the grave mourning" for his son.[103]

Even a cursory comparison of those two scenes begs the question: Why was Jacob so emotional while Aaron remained silent and withdrawn? Was Jacob, despite his saintly stature and rock-solid faith in God, somehow less equipped to deal with tragedy than Aaron?

With some additional context, we can see that is not the case. Rather, each acted appropriately given their different circumstances. Aaron knew that the eyes of his fellow Jews were on him, waiting to see how he would act in the face of sudden, unspeakable tragedy occurring so soon after the dedication of the Tabernacle. Moses realized this as well, so he rushed in to offer Aaron the support he would need to steel himself. With Moses' words of comfort, Aaron was able to restrain himself — as difficult as it must have been.[104] For some, his stoic response is a reminder that it is possible (for most people, with time) to hold tight to a spiritual mindset that both the good and the (seemingly) bad come from God, and to accept God's action in both cases.[105]

Jacob was in a very different situation, with a different audience. He knew that the eyes of his sons were on him — sons whom he may have suspected had somehow been involved in the disappearance of their half-brother, Joseph, with whom they had long been at odds. His continued refusal to accept consolation was meant to discomfit his sons, to make them uncomfortable until they repented. His plan worked; years later the brothers openly expressed their regret at how they had treated Joseph, and showed they had learned from their actions, when they refused to leave their brother Benjamin behind in Egypt as a slave.[106]

---

103 Genesis 37:33-35.

104 One commentator points out that Aaron did initially begin to cry, but with Moses' assistance was able to collect himself.

105 The Torah hints at this point by using the exact same phraseology to describe the fire that descended from Heaven to consume the inaugural offerings in the Mishkan and the fire that descended from Heaven to kill Aaron's sons (Leviticus 9:24 and 10:2).

106 Genesis 42:21-22 and 44:18-34.

So how should we respond to tragedy? Perhaps by adopting both of these approaches.

Aaron's Method

It is not the pain that haunts us after a tragedy. Rather, it is the contradiction. As Jews, we can handle pain because we carry with us the collective memory of our ancestors, a history of an oft-persecuted people. Pain can be a catalyst for growth, but contradiction can be faith-rending. Why did such a bad thing happen to such a good person? Or to such a young, blameless person?

Rabbi Samson Raphael Hirsch explains that God has answers for everything He does. But God does not always share them with us. Asking God *madua*, why, means we are dragging God down into the human courtroom, where He does not belong and which has no jurisdiction over Him,[107] rather than God dragging us into the Courtroom of Heaven, where we do belong.

Most of the time in our lives, God so to speak pays us in cash. The things that God does — blessing us with the ability to live, breathe, eat, sleep, marry, have and raise children, earn a livelihood, learn, teach, help others — make sense. But in times of tragedy, God asks us to in a sense take his credit card, to trust Him by showing that we still live faithfully, even when things do not make sense. Someday they will, but not now.

That is Aaron's gift to us. Of course, he was heartbroken at the loss of two of his sons. But he did not allow that hole in his heart to reduce his love for and worship of God. He understood that no one — not our parents, spouses, children, or friends — loves us more than God. God exults in our triumphs and sympathizes with our losses. And after every bad day, my experience is that when we turn our pillows over to look for the cooler side, there is a virtual note underneath, written on extraterrestrial paper, with our name engraved on the envelope:

I know you had a difficult day. I just want to remind you how much I love you.

– God

Another client of mine was walking home one evening and saw a commotion on the other side of the street. He crossed to see the aftermath of an accident —

---

107 Decades ago, back in law school, in a lighter moment, a professor assigned us a case involving a lawsuit that a claimant brought in federal court against the Devil, blaming the defendant for many woes that had befallen the plaintiff. Without reaching the merits of the case, the court dismissed it by explaining that it did not have jurisdiction over the defendant.

someone had been hit by a car and was lying in the street, injured and bloodied to the point of unrecognizability. There was a scarf wrapped around his neck and face.

"Someone needs to move the scarf," said my client to the people around him. "He's going to suffocate."

"The paramedics aren't here yet," an onlooker replied. "I don't think we're supposed to touch anything."

Though he wasn't a doctor or a medical professional, he knew the least they could do was give the person some room to breathe, so he deftly lifted the scarf from the victim's face. Then off he went.

When he arrived at his house, his wife let him know that their son wasn't home yet. Like a bolt of lightning, he knew who the person in the street had been.

When I met my client and his wife in my office, I confessed that I was amazed he wasn't in a puddle of tears on the floor. How was he able to stay so silent, like Aaron? How was he so composed?

He told me something that has stayed with me since: He was able to withstand the tide of grief because he knew he had done everything he was able to for his son. He wasn't an EMT, so he couldn't have saved him. He wasn't a cop, so he couldn't solve the hit-and-run. God's judgment had been passed, and there was nothing he could do. But with one act of *chesed*, kindness, he may have been able to help his son breathe a little more easily for a little while longer.

"I'm thankful God gave me the opportunity," he said to me.

Jacob's Method

Tragedy should make us uncomfortable. Rather than asking God *madua*, why, which demands an answer, let us instead use the other Hebrew word for why, *lamah*. *Lamah* can also be read differently, as *l'ma*, meaning for what. For what purpose might God have placed me into this tragic situation?

> *What event in your life prompts you to ask, 'l'ma, for what purpose?' What answers do you imagine in response?*

The same client I mentioned earlier channeled her pain into action. Her twelve-year-old son was not able to celebrate his upcoming bar mitzvah because he passed away before his thirteenth birthday. In his honor, his mother started a foundation that has now helped countless other twelve-year-olds who otherwise would not have had the financial means to properly celebrate their bar mitzvahs. Similarly, a father who suffered the inconceivable loss of his teenage son in a school shooting has worked tirelessly since his son's death to create a long overdue national clearinghouse and standards for school safety.[108]

These parents' grief was a catalyst for speaking up and making change. By refusing to be consoled, by refusing to fall back into the comfort zones they inhabited before tragedy struck, they followed in the footsteps of our forefather Jacob. That change can be external, as it was for these parents who suffered tragedies and now devote themselves to making a difference for others. It can also be internal, a change that benefits the soul of the deceased.

When we witness tragedy from a spectator's seat, our role is different. If a close friend or community member loses a loved one, we are not expected to say Kaddish, but we can provide immeasurable support to the mourner, be it emotional, physical, or financial. In Jewish communities, the listings of *chesed* organizations that provide assistance to those in need are mainstays in helping those around us. The *ad hoc* networks of neighbors and friends that spring up to cook and clean and carpool and babysit for the survivors of tragedy, while also offering support, consolation, and guidance, are beautiful indicators that we are at our best when we take action to help others.

Howie, a nineteen year old from Atlanta, whose father I know, volunteered along with seven friends to spend five-and-a-half months working on a kibbutz in Israel during their gap year between high school and college. They were told beforehand that they would get one week off for vacation. Work on their kibbutz was not a desk job; it involved manual labor, working in the fields. After three-and-a-half months of difficult work, they were more than ready for their week off. The eight of them booked an Airbnb and planned a week of fun and relaxation.

A few days later, they received a call from the kibbutz telling them that, because several people on the kibbutz had gotten sick, all eight of them would have to return immediately to pick lettuce. They were furious but felt responsible to help and agreed to return. When they contacted Airbnb, they were told they could not get a refund for the remaining few days of their rental. After picking lettuce, angry about their shortened vacation, they found out what had happened at the event they had planned to attend that weekend — the Supernova Festival. Their anger over their missed opportunity and lost money immediately changed to profound gratitude to God for having saved their lives, mixed with sadness for the many lives lost that day and commitment to grow and serve in their honor.

In my office, each day brings new tragedy. With that tragedy comes challenge.

---

108   In perhaps the most successful example of this type of activity after tragedy, Mothers Against Drunk Driving was created by a mother who lost her teenage daughter in a collision caused by a drunk driver.

The Art and Practice of Living Wondrously

Though God's judgment has been passed, it is up to us to choose how we will deal with our grief. Although the pain doesn't disappear, we aim to grow stronger every day. We choose how we will move forward, so we can choose to seek solace and inspiration from the choices of our ancestors. Do we remain stoic, trusting in the judgment of God, like Aaron? Do we channel our grief into change, like Jacob? Most likely, we find truth in elements of both. No matter what we choose, in the face of tragedy, we roll up our sleeves and get to work to help the survivors — and in so doing we also help the souls of the departed. Fortunately, Jewish tradition and community provide enormous wellsprings of emotional, financial, spiritual, and physical support for those suffering even the most tragic and incomprehensible losses.

ENGAGING IN

DIFFICULT
CONVERSATIONS

A difficult conversation is one you consider worthy of engaging in, though the emotions involved cause such unease that you may be inclined to avoid it altogether. Participants in such a conversation often have different perspectives or values, or one may give feedback that can be challenging for another to hear.

Not every difficult conversation needs to happen. Choosing our battles is an important skill. As Shakespeare famously put it, "The better part of valor is discretion."[109] But as our society becomes more polarized and social media elevates echo chambers and in-group thinking, it is increasingly important for parents to model and initiate healthy arguments and informed, civil conversations — even when these are not easy. After October 7, with the increase in divisiveness on campuses and in many communities, the ability to engage in thoughtful, challenging conversation is more important than ever. This chapter asks how this type of conversation can be conducted skillfully.

Dr. Bruce Powell, a leader in the field of eduation and revered mentor among Jewish day-school principals, along with his adult children, Rebecca Powell and Jonathan Powell, explore how to create a culture of conversation, deepen knowledge together as a family, and hone foundational values. They share a roadmap developed by Resetting the Table, an organization that helps people have courageous conversations in the face of strong differences. Dr. Mijal Bitton and Dr. Noam Weissman explore the challenge of talking to young adults about Israel and antisemitism. They describe a theory of differing parenting styles and offer insight into how it can promote conversations that strengthen rather than strain relationships. Abi Dauber Sterne recommends getting clear on your goals before entering a difficult conversation, offers rules of thumb and intentions for having a healthy argument, and discusses two inspiring metaphors from Jewish tradition.

---

109 *Henry IV, Part 1.*

Context Is Text: Creating a Culture for Conversation

Dr. Bruce J. Powell, Rebecca Powell, and Jonathan Powell

For over 50 years, Dr. Bruce Powell has dedicated his professional life to Jewish education. He has helped found and lead three Jewish high schools in Los Angeles, and has consulted on the founding of 23 schools around North America. Bruce is the dean of the Masor School for Jewish Education and Leadership at the American Jewish University in Los Angeles. Along with Dr. Ron Wolfson, he co-authored Raising A+ Human Beings: Crafting a Jewish School Culture of Academic Excellence and AP Kindness.

Rebecca Powell is program director at Resetting the Table. She formerly served as the student activities director at Harvard Hillel and as an educator at Roundabout Theater Company, Central Synagogue, Capital Camps, and other Jewish institutions.

Jonathan Powell is a veteran speechwriter and communications professional based in Washington, DC. He has advised and crafted remarks, op-eds, and press materials for top figures in the executive branch, on Capitol Hill, and in Los Angeles City government, as well as for CEOs and nonprofit leaders across the country.

Preamble

When Dr. Ronit Ziv-Kreger called to ask if I would write an article on having tough conversations with teens, I balked. I explained that I left such conversations to Debby (my wife of 50 years) to handle. Then I realized that perhaps I could assemble the two younger children who Debby raised (I did help with homework and bedtime stories and washed the dishes), now ages 33 and 41, to work with me on this article. Both Jonathan and Rebecca agreed and suddenly the Powell family had a writing team.

This article is truly a collaboration. You will notice that it is written in the first person. Please regard the *I* as meaning all of us. Needless to say, having a professional team of thinkers and writers, all of whom grew up in our home, has been a special joy for both Debby and me.

Talking with Teens

Talking with teens is already a tall task. The combination of angst and anxiety, rebellious impulses and contrarian instincts, the desire to be seen as an adult and the still-developing maturity to actually act like one — all of it makes for a roller-coaster ride anytime you try to engage someone in their teenage years. It's a reality confronted by parents, teachers, educators, counselors, and many, many more.

Now add a major, significant, painful, gut-wrenching current event like the October 7 attacks into the mix and the conversations — particularly with Jewish young people — become even more fraught, difficult, and sensitive.

In some respects, this moment in Jewish communal life feels new and different; for American Jewish kids growing up in an era of relative peace, prosperity, and security, this kind of unsettling context upends our perspectives and sense of safety and self.

Yet in other respects, this story is actually pretty familiar. We can look back to what isn't really ancient history to find analogous discussions: to 1968 and the assassinations of Robert F. Kennedy and Martin Luther King Jr.; to 1970 and the shootings of American students at Kent State by members of the U.S. National Guard, or at Jackson State University by the Jackson police and Mississippi Highway Patrol. One could argue that nothing much has changed; indeed, I can still recall, at age 20, waging yelling matches with my father — a United States Marine Corps veteran who fought at Guadalcanal in 1942 — surrounding the immorality of the Vietnam War and racism in America.

Nothing was ever solved, and I continued to revere and respect my parents. But I decided long ago that there had to be a better way to address the idealism of youth and the passions of the historical moment.

Over the past 50 years in Jewish education I have come to the conclusion that perhaps (yes, *perhaps*, since I am never absolutely sure about anything) the most effective way to engage in difficult conversations is to first build the infrastructure for having such conversations — what I call the *culture for conversation*. Second, I believe those conversations must also involve deep, foundational knowledge; we must provide opportunities for education that will ultimately deepen the conversations that are possible. Third, making your family values clear in everyday interactions will build shared understandings around concepts of freedom and democracy, justice and peace, and what it means to share a world with other human beings. And finally, we must find a way to address differences that arise constructively, keeping our families intact and learning from one another in the process.

Will using these pillars make talking to teens and young adults any easier? The jury is out and may remain so forever. But hopefully the following pillars can help change the way we have those conversations and maybe lead to more productive discussions and better outcomes along the way.

Building Cultures for Conversation

In the Jewish community, we have an advantage in constructing the infrastructure for a good conversation. Building that scaffolding is embedded in the fabric of our history and texts.

Judaism teaches us that the only conversations worth having are those within the context of *machloket l'shem Shamayim* (arguments for the sake of Heaven). Such discussions are predicated upon the belief by all parties that human beings are created *b'tselem Elohim*, in the image of God. This means that every person is of infinite importance; every person contains unique gifts and insights; and every person deserves to be treated with dignity, with seriousness, with attention, and with uninterrupted focus.

American civic tradition teaches us that we have rights to free speech. Judaism amends that concept and adds that we have obligations of speech. Not surprisingly, the Latin root of obligation is *lig*, meaning connection. Indeed, speech is a means for people to connect with one another. It is a means to create relationships. It is also a uniquely human means to communicate to others that: I regard you as created in the image of God; I treat you with dignity; you have my uninterrupted attention; I value what you say; and I take what you say seriously.

Relationships and connections are built over time and within time. It often takes years, starting at birth, to create a culture in which children know that their parents trust them unconditionally; in which their relationship is built upon mutual obligations, shared understandings of dignity, the infinite value of the human soul, and love that knows no bounds.

That said, there is often a mistaken notion that parents and children can create "quality time" together. My experience of raising four children and teaching thousands of other people's kids tells me that quality time is an unreachable goal. But forging opportunities for quality interactions to emerge? That's well within our gasp. That's consistent with what the great philosopher Martin Buber once described as "I-thou moments" — personal, real, mutual interactions imbued with meaning, with connection, with benefits to all parties, and with no strings attached.

Once we have built a context in which children are regarded as created in the image of God, in which everyone shares and understands their obligations of speech, in which we know that things take time and we can provide unencumbered time to listen, I believe we then have established a culture for conversation.

Building Knowledge

What do we mean when we talk about *knowledge*? Is it merely facts, figures, timelines, and test material? Is it something you can only find in a textbook, or does it come from newspapers, traditional and social media, the internet, and other sources?

Oftentimes, the path of least resistance is the simplest course: Just leave it to the schools. What students learn in the classroom, we like to think, should be enough to afford them the foundation for intelligent conversations or the tools for tough debates or the skills to enter the workforce and engage with broader society. But what that schooling looks like isn't always standard, nor are school systems necessarily up to the task.

Most children, in America and in nations around the world, spend a required number of years in school. The worldwide average is 8.7 years, with most developed nations requiring from eight to fourteen years. Parents expect that their children will acquire a good deal of knowledge and skills during their time in school. Generally, this is true. The literacy rate is quite high in places that schooling exceeds even six years.

In America, where the requirement ranges from twelve to fourteen years depending on the state, most parents believe this should be quite enough education for their children to be able to engage in conversations about history, politics, science, and the arts. In practice, some parents leave most or all their children's education to the school.

The challenge for schools — especially high schools — is that they do not have enough time to provide a wide range of knowledge on politics, religion, Israeli history, Middle Eastern history, Black history, Latino history, and so forth. What that often means is, when engaging in difficult conversations, many teens simply do not possess the requisite knowledge and facts to feel equipped for the toughest exchanges. Particularly when it comes to Israel, the feeling of "I don't know enough" is prevalent among teens and adults alike.

I propose that education must continue in the home over dinner, during carpool time, on family trips, and elsewhere in kids' day-to-day lives. It means engaging in political discussions; having tons of books, magazines, and newspapers scattered around the house; and providing lists of suggested websites to gain additional information. It also means that parents have to possess a balanced, nuanced collection of knowledge to impart to their children.

Crucially, the acquisition of knowledge and facts at home should begin at the earliest possible age, or at whatever age a child is able to conceptualize and respond to various topics. I have found five-year-olds to be very aware and insightful, not to mention elementary and high school students.

In our highly polarized world, the idea that the books, magazines, or even textbooks we encounter could be providing absolute truth from a neutral lens feels far-fetched. Therefore, it's imperative that we make the effort to provide multi-vocal, nonprescriptive education.

> *Take stock of your own biases and perception gaps and the political slant of the material you consume. Seek out the best versions of the arguments on both sides (yes, even the side you can't stand) and learn them together. Then find the ugliest versions of the arguments on both sides (yes, even your own) so you understand what you might encounter in a less-respectful environment. Be open to discovering where your own opinions might fall short. Offer multiple points of view and help kids process them with your guidance, but not your direction.*

Perhaps above all, show your children that you respect and trust them enough to process tough information. Feel confident that when they look back at their childhood, they'd be wrong to say, "You never told me." They may form opinions different from your own — but that's fine. Go toward those differences and explore them together. That's where the true conversation begins.

Developing Foundational Values

What we ask our kids when they come home from school indicates to them what we value. And that says a great deal about the kinds of conversations we want to have.

If the first thing you ask is, "How was your math class today?" the kids internalize that you believe math is the most important thing. What would happen, though, if the first thing you ask every day is, "Did you do a mitzvah today?" or "Did you invite a lonely child to sit with you at lunch?" or "Did you thank your teacher at the end of the day?" or "What questions did you ask in your history class?"

To put a spin on an old phrase: We are what we ask. Our kids are taking note, and they're quite astute at reading the tea leaves of what we say.

Every year, our family chose a day in December to make our annual gifts to charities. We brought out the 100 solicitations we received in the mail over the past year and asked the kids to prioritize what they believed to be most important, and then we decided what to give. We provided $1,000 for them to allocate. They all understand, to this day, that *tzedakah* (justice / charity) is a common value for our family.

> *Consider including your children in the process of your family's giving of* tzedakah *resources to causes that are meaningful to your family.*

Using the tools of asking questions and taking action, the children develop a sense of shared values with their parents. As the children mature, parents can impart more sophisticated values discussions, such as the rights and responsibilities of citizenship, our obligations to our neighbors, and, my favorite, all the aspirational values found in the preamble to the United States Constitution:

"We the People of the United States, in Order to form a more perfect Union, establish Justice, insure domestic Tranquility, provide for the common defense, promote the general Welfare, and secure the Blessings of Liberty to ourselves and our Posterity ..."

You may find that at some point, even with this shared foundation, you and your child have real differences. You may interpret a value differently, or apply it differently, or each prioritize a different one over another. Still, with a lifetime of shared understanding of what these values mean in your family, you have a head start in exploring those differences together.

Going Toward Your Differences

So you've built a culture of *machloket l'shem Shamayim*. You've provided knowledge. You've imparted your values. And still, somehow you find your teen has come to the opposite conclusion on an issue. How could this be?

A younger child will likely vote however you would in their school's mock election; that's particularly true in this current age when political parties can feel as core to our identity as ethnicity or religion. But teens and young adults are notorious for taking new identities for a test-drive. They have an instinctive need to push boundaries, especially if it gets on their parents' nerves. Plus they have more access to information and opinions outside the home than perhaps ever before. As a result, they may come to different conclusions or explore other avenues of thinking.

Dismissing these ideas as a phase or being internally (or obviously) horrified that somehow your child has joined the other side puts us at risk of damaging the I-thou relationship we have worked so hard to build.

Instead, here's a basic road map to a conversation across differences, with your teen or really anyone. This road map was developed by Resetting the Table and is just a taste of the skills and processes for these kinds of conversations.

Step 1: Invite your teen to share their opinion. Do your best to pause your own reactions and stop preparing your next argument. Listen.

Step 2: Shift from a leading to a following posture. Ask questions that follow what seems most meaningful to them — not questions that challenge, try to lead them to a different conclusion, or focus on your own interest. If they said something was frustrating but didn't say why, ask about it. If they keep using a word over and over again, ask about its importance. Try to uncover what matters most.

Step 3: Demonstrate that you have understood them as they wish to be understood. Go beyond saying "I hear you." *Prove* to them that you understood the heart of the matter — the points that are most important and the reasons they care. Do this over and over until they confirm you got it right.

Step 4: Share that you see this differently and tell them why. Give your opinion and offer a challenge. Then try to identify the primary difference in your viewpoints and how you each relate to that difference.

Step 5: Talk about that difference. You may be surprised that, when you identify your actual differences, you realize you are usually not diametrically opposed. You're not stuck in a pattern of us and them. You see something differently and you can explore that together.

Find a time when the culture of conversation in your home feels sufficiently nourished to explore this road map on a topic that is divisive in your family. For your first time choose a moderate issue, not your most challenging, so you can practice and build the skills. Keep in mind that research has found that we tend to overestimate the degree of polarization we will meet[110]

This process is hard. It takes work and dedication. But proving to your child that you have seen them as they wish in a world that so often dismisses young people's opinions will shift the tone of the conversation and allow you both to be heard.

Let's Talk

What I am proposing in this brief article is difficult to do. Parents must work daily, with intentionality, to build a culture of unconditional embrace and engender the foundation stone upon which tough conversations may occur.

We must all be ever vigilant and mindful to impart additional knowledge to our children. Tough conversations must be based on a broad understanding of history and the human condition, however difficult some of those facts may seem. Let's not leave education to the schools alone.

And finally, spending time discussing and showing what we value, what our family cherishes, and how we can apply those values helps reduce the ire and angst of future tough conversations.

No matter what, we can have conversations across differences on the basis of understanding.

No matter what, our love for each other is unconditional. Now, let's talk!

---

110 See for example a December 2023 study by State Policy Network, http://spn.org/wp-content/uploads/2024/07/PolarizationStudy-v5-web-single.pdf.

The Challenge of Talking to Young Adults About Israel and Antisemitism

Dr. Mijal Bitton and Dr. Noam Weissman

in conversation for the podcast *Wondering Jews With Mijal and Noam*, produced by Rivky Stern

Dr. Mijal Bitton is a spiritual leader, public intellectual, and sociologist. The rosh kehilla *(communal leader) of the Downtown Minyan in New York City and a scholar-in-residence at the Maimonides Fund, Mijal is a visiting researcher at the New York University Wagner Graduate School of Public Service, where she directs pioneering research on Sephardic and Mizrahi Jews in the United States. She is an alumna of the Wexner Graduate Fellowship, a New Pluralists Field Builder, and a Sacks Scholar. Mijal is committed to building a welcoming and vibrant Jewish life, leveraging renewed Jewish solidarity and commitment post-October 7. She co-hosts the podcast* Wondering Jews.

Dr. Noam Weissman is the executive vice president of OpenDor Media, where he leads the educational vision, with content reaching millions of young people globally through the Unpacked brand. As co-host of Wondering Jews *with Mijal and host of* Unpacking Israeli History, *Noam facilitates discussions on Israel, antisemitism, and Judaism for a broad audience. He also spearheads Unpacked for Educators, a platform utilized by more than 10,000 educators worldwide, and recently launched ConnectED, a landmark independent schools initiative. He is a former principal of Shalhevet High School in Los Angeles.*

Rivky Stern is the head of podcasts for Unpacked, a division of OpenDor Media.

*M*ijal: I would love to speak about the following question that friends and peers, especially those who have children who are young adults, are asking: What is the best advice for parents who are talking to young adults about Israel and antisemitism?

Let's tease it out. What are some of the reasons why parents are struggling or feeling they need good advice in talking to their young adult children about Israel and about antisemitism?

Noam: So here's one thought: American exceptionalism. For two thousand years, the Jewish people had experienced oppression, persecution, pogroms, antisemitism, even state-sanctioned antisemitism, Holocaust, massacres, and everything. But they thought that the United States would be radically different. And broadly speaking, it has been. This moment since October 7 has caught people by surprise, so people are questioning the concept of American exceptionalism. And that's scary for people.

Mijal: Some very basic assumptions about people's reality have shifted, and therefore parents need advice. But you also introduced two new points.

One point is that this affects parents as well as children. Parents had a certain vision and thought: Now we just need to advise our kids. But this is a big challenge that is confronting the parents as well. It's really difficult to actually parent and give guidance when you too are struggling.

You also used the word *fear.* Not only are parents confused, but some are afraid. And sometimes it's hard for us, as parents, when we're supposed to have the answers, when in reality we're afraid and we don't have answers.

Noam: I think that's true. And I want to add another layer. After October 7, two generations are experiencing trauma together. Parents are dealing with something unexpected. Often, when parents experience the trauma at the same time as their kids, they struggle to cope with it, which makes it even harder to parent through it.

Mijal: Right. And here's another thing I think is challenging for parents. Some parents, especially when it comes to Israel, are nervous that they don't have enough information. That their kids are going to ask them about things they read about or see on social media, and the parents are nervous to say: To be honest I don't know. I don't know exactly what happened in the Second Lebanon War. I don't really know about area A and B and C.

> *Check out OpenDorMedia.org for excellent resources designed to help you build knowledge along with your teen. Explore history, Jewish ideas, and stories through filmmaking on digital platforms.*

I think some parents can feel shame if they care deeply about Israel and they have an expectation that a commitment to Israel comes with in-depth expertise. Knowledge is valuable; with that, this expectation to have expertise is really not realistic for most parents, since this is one of the most complicated geopolitical conflicts in history.

And there are a few more layers here.

You spoke before about what happens when you have a dual trauma. How we have parents who are dealing with their own challenge, and then needing to help their children deal with their own challenge.

But what happens when you have dual trauma, dual struggles and tension, but there's also a tension between the views of the two generations? Let's be frank: Sometimes parents stand in one place when it comes to Israel and Zionism and even antisemitism. And their children are in a different place.

Parents can really struggle with how to show up. How to speak about the emotions and feelings that are coming up, how to be a parent and how to love your children, how to raise them and guide them, and also how to stand up for your principles.

Noam: Mijal, as you know, I'm often speaking and teaching at elite, private high schools. I recently met with a parent at one of these schools and she said, "My child is embarrassed about Israel, and I feel complicit."

Mijal: Complicit in what?

Noam: In the fact that her daughter feels embarrassed. Because, she said, she hasn't taught her a lot about Israel, about Zionism.

Mijal: Wow, that's heavy. What do you say to that?

Noam: Well, I listened. She wasn't looking to me for advice. She was more unloading, saying, "We have to figure out this problem, because my child has been learning about the world in school through a little bit of indoctrination, and I haven't mitigated that at home. I haven't given her the history of Israel, Zionism, the Jewish story, and this is the consequence." So that line, "I feel complicit," was heavy.

Mijal: So now I feel like we can summarize. There are three main reasons parents are struggling with this, why parents are looking for advice on this. One is because parents themselves are feeling destabilized. Second is because parents feel unprepared, like they lack the knowledge and skills to help their children with such a complex issue. And the third might be a certain misalignment that parents and children might not be in the same place, or in a similar place, when it comes to something so foundational.

So to me, these are the three main reasons parents are seeking help in having these conversations, especially post-October 7.

Let me turn to you. We both work a lot with young adults, but you also work a lot with parents. So based on our conversation up until this point, what's the best advice you would give to parents in terms of talking to their kids about Israel and antisemitism?

Understanding Parenting Styles

Noam: Let's start with a diagnosis about parenting. That'll help us think through, first as a parent in general and then as a parent with regard to Israel and antisemitism.

Mijal: Sure, but I feel more qualified to talk about Israel than parenting [*laughs*].

Noam: One of my favorite lines is: I was an expert in parenting until I became one.

Mijal: I'm going to borrow that.

Noam: There was a professor by the name of Diana Baumrind who posited several different parenting styles that exist in the world. I'll describe each of them, and as I do please keep in mind how this is going to relate to our question. I'm going to paraphrase somewhat, but these ideas ultimately come from her.

Approach number one is called the Neglectful Parent. This parent is basically not really around emotionally. Not particularly responsive. Not really demanding. No rules, no structure. You want to smoke weed, drink alcohol, go for it, whatever. That's one type of parenting. We might have friends who are like that. Maybe sometimes we're like that.

Number two is called the Permissive Parent. They're the cool parent, who will host the party and say there are no rules here. The difference between them and the Neglectful Parent is that they're much more warm and they're much more nurturing. But they don't have boundaries.

The third approach is called the Authoritarian Parent. This is the approach of the parent who says: My house, my rules. And the expectations are through the roof: This is what it means to live in this house. Did you just ask me why? There's no why with me. Cause I said so. Cause I'm your parent. Ever heard of the concept of respecting your father and mother? And that's the end. That's authoritarian. A lot of us grew up with that, or we've seen it, or we've done it.

The last style is called the Authoritative Parent approach. Naturally, Diana Baumrind views this as the best approach. It's somebody who's loving, who's warm, who's supportive. But they're also very demanding. And they have expectations.

The way they go about it is by saying to the child: Come with me. I want to listen to your viewpoints. I want to hear what you think and what you feel and what you have to say. And we're going to have a conversation about this. You're going to learn about my values and my reasoning, but I want you to ask the question *why*. I'm here to walk through together with you the reasons I have for my approach.

So those are the four different parenting styles.

Gentle Parenting and Its Challenges

Mijal: Yeah, it's interesting. Before we go into the Israel topic, I think it will be helpful to consider the recent debate about the gentle parenting approach.

Noam: Tell me about it.

Mijal: Well, I'm speaking not as an expert, but as a parent. I'm paraphrasing and generalizing here, but gentle parenting is the approach of a lot of very popular parenting gurus. It's an explicit move away from the kind of authoritarian parenting that these adults might have had with their own parents. A lot of it is about listening to your kids. It's almost therapeutic, talking to them, understanding them, not really putting your foot down with any kind of significant consequences.

Recently there's been a very strong pushback against gentle parenting, arguing that it's really moving too much toward the model of Permissive Parenting, but this pushback is not that these parents are partying with their kids. Instead, the argument is that gentle parents are letting their kids decide what their family life should look like and thinking that in doing so they are being very committed parents.

While keeping this in mind, I want to go into how you apply the four parenting types to Israel.

Noam: Great, let's connect the dots here. We have different reasons for why this is a difficult subject for these parents in the first place. And by the way, I want to stop saying *they* and *these parents* and start saying *we*. We, because that includes us, Mijal.

Engaging in Difficult Conversations

Noam: So here's how I view it. The subject is not the content. The subject is not Israel. The subject is the person you're talking to. Israel is just the conduit to having an important conversation. But it's not about Israel. It's about your relationship to your child.

This is my approach to education in general. We have to switch the lens. Stop thinking about the thing in between you and the person and start thinking about you and the person.

Mijal: OK, so in your opinion the end goal is not that the child in front of you learns X, but the end goal is a stronger relationship and the way you relate to the child in front of you.

Noam: And that the child relates to the content. It's not about them knowing everything on the piece of paper. It's about the fact that they are going to have a relationship in a certain way to whatever is on that piece of paper.

Mijal: So it's more relational as opposed to empirical information knowing.

Noam: Exactly. I'm very interested in their relationship. I'm not interested in considering learning as filling a blank slate. Here's the content and let's see how it lands on everyone.

So let's look how this lens relates to Israel and antisemitism. We approach the child with the question: Who are you? Understand who they are deeply and engage them in conversation with an authoritative parenting approach by asking follow-up questions to deeply understand their experience. You bring them into your experience by getting permission from them to share your experience, to have that conversation in a way that they're not just giving you one-word answers.

> *Consider a topic that you can explore with your child using this approach — it might be Israel or antisemitism, or you might experiment first with a different topic.*

One of the best ways to know whether the conversation with your child is not working is by the quality of their response. If they're giving you one-word answers or if they're avoiding you altogether, there's information in that.

And that happens very often with the parents I speak to — that their kids are not engaging with them, or when they do engage they're answering in one word because they don't really feel their parents are listening to them and understanding them and seeing them.

However, we can express a deep respect for your child, not implying that they know everything but that what they think matters, so the child can trust you as the parent. What that does is it opens up this doorway for genuine conversation and communication.

More than anything, the child craves two things: care and credibility. If the child sees that the parent cares for them and the child sees that the parent has credibility with what they're talking about, then the child opens up their mind and is willing to engage in a conversation with the parent.

Mijal: OK, I'm processing. Can you help me talk out one of the reasons why a parent wants advice on this? And then play out the advice you just gave and what that looks like?

Noam: Let's do the generational thing. I think that's a fun one. The kid is going through their own experiences and the parents have a different experience, and they each see Israel in different lights.

Let's go back to the come-with-me approach. You start with trying to understand their experience. You engage in that conversation. You express empathy for their experience, for what they've gone through.

I have found this to be the most insightful way to deal with the challenge. When older people say to younger people: I was your age too — not helpful. Much more helpful is when older people say to younger people: I've actually never lived through the age of social media that you live through and you're living through a different era.

Also ask them if they're interested to hear what your experience has been, what you've lived through. Then go into that and share the stories of your own experience. I have a history that you don't have, and I don't understand everything about what you're going through. People want to be understood. People are just waiting for other people to get them. Once people feel the other person gets them, once they show care and credibility, then there's the opportunity for dialogue and conversation.

Mijal: Let's say there's a parent who cares deeply for Israel, and they're supporting the war right now post-October 7. Their kid is at an elite university, and their kid believes that claims around antisemitism are blown out of proportion and that support of Israel is criminal. Would you advocate for the same advice?

Noam: See, this is where the authoritative approach is. Authoritative doesn't mean wishy-washy and it doesn't mean gentle.

Mijal: It sounded very gentle when you were saying it!

Noam: Well, maybe it was my tone. I could say it in a firmer way. It's not about asking permission. It's getting a sense from them if they want to hear from you or not.

Mijal: Yeah, we have different parenting styles, Noam [*laughs*].

Noam: I'm not saying I always parent like this [*laughs*]!

Mijal: OK, but can you respond to what I said with the example I gave? Would you advocate for this approach there?

Noam: For me, the goal wouldn't be to convince them about something. The goal for me would be ensuring that the relationship stands strong no matter what, because nothing is more important than that.

Mijal: So the core of your advice is: Focus more about your relationship as a parent and find ways to engage your child in a conversation. Your role is not to convince them of a particular position when it comes to Israel. It is to engage them and try to continue that engagement going forward.

Noam: And one more point: You can also be affirmative and passionate about what you stand for. That's a critical part of authoritative parenting: affirming to your child this is why I believe in and stand for my values.

Balancing Relationships and Principles

Mijal: I think it depends so much. There are different parents, different children, different situations, different challenges.

So I'll just say, this might sound obvious but I think this is often easy to forget, especially in the moment. When speaking with children, no matter how old they are, be honest about when you don't know something.

There's nothing wrong with saying: I don't know, that's a great question, this is really complicated. There's something really powerful about being honest about your own struggles and saying: I know X, Y, I might not know the rest, but I'm struggling because of the following reasons. And then you can invite them to learn with you.

I think it means a lot to children when they encounter their parents as real people who have struggles and it makes them trust you more. So that's just one thing.

I'll say two other things. The first is: I think you advocate focusing on the relationship and leaving some of the information stuff aside. But as parents we also have a responsibility to be informed. And second: There are no limits to how many resources are out there. Let's all get educated. Let's listen to Noam's other podcast, *Unpacking Israeli History*.

Noam: You said it for me. *Unpacking Israeli History!*[111]

Mijal: Exactly, I just opened the door for you.

Help Our Children Feel Loved

The last thing I'll say is that it's really important to focus on having conversations that center on first principles. All families have disagreements —

111 https://jewishunpacked.com/podcast-series/unpacking-israeli-history/.

religious, political. Sometimes relationships don't stand tall under the burden of those disagreements, and sometimes the relationships overcome the differences and are really strong and solid. A lot of it is about the ability of two people — in our case parents and children — to say: We might not agree on a particular policy or particular understanding of something that happened, but can we agree on first principles?

First principles might be love for the Jewish people, might be the right of all people to a safe haven. There's a bunch of first principles that can be put on the table.

I find it healthy for us to always remind ourselves before we go into challenging conversations with our loved ones: What are my first principles? And can we have a conversation that doesn't lose those?

Noam: Do you also have rules for times that are politics- and religion-free zones? Maybe at the Shabbat table, where we're actually going to agree to not focus on our differences? If we want to have the challenging conversation we could do it at a different time, in a different space.

Mijal: Yeah, that's really important — to be conscious and intentional as to when and with whom you're having the conversations and not to feel pressure to always have them.

I can think of examples in my own family. Sometimes we should have put rules and we didn't, and sometimes we had rules and they helped. And don't forget that often in a conversation one person can have the ability to engage in a detached intellectual debate, but for another person that same conversation can trigger a personal, vulnerable, intense place.

So there's real wisdom in curating discussions and thinking about how to be responsive, how to initiate, how to be a resource for our children and how to do so in the way, as Noam said, that lets them do so in the context of a relationship and in the context of becoming their own people.

Noam: I have one last piece of advice on this, Mijal. This is just a tactical piece. Sometimes young people feel that people are staring at them. It's the spotlight effect. Especially adolescents, when they're going through their identity development.

I learned something from my parents, who are clinical psychologists and social workers.

Mijal: Both of them? This explains a lot. My gosh.

Noam: It explains a lot, I know. One of the things I learned from them is that it can be very difficult to have a serious conversation with eye contact. Very hard.

But if you are casual, doing something else, shopping at Target, brushing your teeth in the same room, maybe driving, and you're just talking but not making it feel so heavy, the other person is much more open because they don't feel like they're being put on the spot or being challenged. You're not making it overly serious or heavy, which could shut some people down.

The goal in a relationship is to open people up. My dad always says — I love this line: Vulnerability is the currency of intimacy. The ability to be vulnerable with each other is really important in relationships. And how you do that really matters.

Mijal: Yeah, that's powerful. I'll add one more thing here. Ultimately, parenting is a work of faith. You invest, you plant, you love, you give, and you don't fully know what you'll see and when and how things turn out. I think the faith is that they will know they are loved and they will become wonderful people, right? They'll reflect that in the world.

I think a lot about the love that sustains me. My grandmother, my parents. What does it mean to walk around knowing that you're loved?

This matters for Israel conversations because I think we can get so caught up in what to say and the emotions and how difficult it is. And it's all true. I think that with all this, if we can always remember to help our children feel loved, that's maybe at the core of everything. And if we love Israel and we love them, it translates.

Noam: I love that. Mijal, that was a lot of parenting.

Mijal: Much easier to talk about it than to do it, right?

Noam: Yes. Thanks so much, Mijal. Great talking with you about this.

Mijal: Thanks to you.

Transforming Arguments into Learning Experiences

Abi Dauber Sterne

Abi Dauber Sterne is co-director of For the Sake of Argument *and co-author of* Stories for the Sake of Argument. *A long-time educator, she has served in leadership roles at Hillel International and The Jewish Agency for Israel. Abi is a rabbinical student at the Hartman Institute and Midrasha B'Oranim. She lives in Jerusalem with her spouse and four children. Her family dinner table is always a raucous mixture of laughter and disagreement.*

Arguments are generally no fun. But what if they could be? What if we could transform frustrating screaming matches into moments of learning, understanding, and closeness?

While many arguments feel intransigent, some kinds of arguments have the potential to unlock something important within all of us. What I hope to do in this short piece is lay out the different kinds of arguments that exist, help us set goals for each one, and then offer some tips on how to make certain kinds of arguments healthier. Finally, I will draw from rabbinic sources to present two metaphors that provide deep ideas for how to embody healthy arguments.

As you find yourself getting into an argument — be it about politics, a teenager's curfew, or religious practices — it is most important for you, as a parent, colleague, or friend, to try to clarify your intention. Most arguments seem to just happen and, not surprisingly, most arguments end in frustration. In order to help shape our arguments, to make them productive, setting an intention or desired goal is crucially important.

Through my work with For the Sake of Argument, my co-founder, Robbie Gringras, and I have developed methods, techniques, and framings aimed at shifting how people engage in contentious topics. We always begin with trying to understand — and even set — the goal of the argument. Generally speaking arguments can be categorized into three types, each with a different purpose or goal:

1. Debate: The goal of a debate is to convince the other or others that you are right. In formal settings, like a high school debate club or a court case, convincing the judge is the goal. However, in informal settings — like a political conversation around your dinner table or a late-night chat with your teenage son about abstinence — we often find ourselves trying to convince one another of our rightness. In these informal, often unplanned arguments, there is no judge to declare a winner, and sometimes they can turn into a fight. In fact, rarely do we leave the conversation saying, "You've convinced me. I'm wrong and you're right."

2. Negotiation: The goal of a negotiation is to come to an agreement. It's common to have to negotiate in work environments, political environments, or in parent–child interactions. Often, an agreement is crucial and in such interactions a compromise is almost always required. For example, you want your daughter to be home by 11:00 p.m. She wants to stay out until 1:00 a.m. Ultimately, you settle on midnight. Or maybe you're engaged in a real estate negotiation and in order to close the deal and come to an agreement both sides will have to give up on something important to them.

3. Healthy Argument: The goal of a healthy argument is to learn or grow. That is, if you can let go of trying to convince someone (debate), and if you don't need to come to some kind of agreement (negotiation), there is the possibility of having a disagreement with the goal of learning something new. It could be that you learn about the other person. It could be that you learn more about the topic at hand, whether or not you agree with the competing opinions. It could be that you learn something about yourself.

As you find yourself getting into an argument — planned or spontaneous, structured or unstructured — first assess the goal. Sometimes we need to make a decision or come to an agreement. But often we don't. If you find yourself beginning in debate or negotiation mode, ask yourself whether and why you need to win and whether that's even possible given the setting. Ask yourself whether you need to make a decision and come to an agreement. Many arguments, it turns out, don't need either. Many arguments can be most satisfying and fruitful when we're in a curiosity mindset with learning as the goal.

> *Think about a recent argument you've had or one you expect to have soon. How would you categorize it — as a debate, a negotiation, or a healthy argument? Why?*

Once you've decided to have a healthy argument, there are several rules of thumb or intentions that help enable this type of discussion. As in all good conversations, participants must be both attentive listeners and sensitive speakers. Accordingly, in the intentions below, there is some balance between listening and speaking.

1. Think of yourself as more of a gatherer than a hunter. Try to gather information rather than hunting for points to discount or prove wrong. In many settings we've become accustomed to listening for the sake of rebutting. To have a healthy argument, take the stance of someone who is truly listening and gleaning important information from as many people as possible (if many are involved in the conversation) and from as many perspectives as possible.

2. Go visit other opinions as if you are visiting someone's home. You are always free to leave and return to your own home. In other words, listening to someone else's opinion can be like being a guest in their home. Likewise, sharing an opinion can be like opening up your home and letting someone in. When you're truly listening to someone else's opinion you have a rare chance to get to know them, as if inhabiting their space. But by the same token, you do not need to move in forever. You do not need to take on those opinions as your own. Instead, once you feel you understand enough, or once you miss your own "home" — or your own opinions — you are free to politely thank the person you're speaking with and exit the conversation.

3. Be courageous. Offer your opinion, even an unpopular one, even though you don't know how it will be received. While sometimes in arguments we regret saying too much, many times we also regret not saying what we really meant. In order to learn from one another, we have to offer what's really on our minds. If you're nervous about offering your opinion, try couching it in a way that softens the tone, such as "I'm surprised to find myself thinking ..." or "I want to try this idea out but I may take it back in a few minutes."

4. You and whomever you are arguing with are allowed to change your minds or hold two competing truths. We often expect people to be consistent. We expect people to share a thought and to maintain it. In a healthy argument, we should actively allow for the opposite. While the goal isn't to change one's mind per se, it is natural to have new ideas if we are learning something new. It is desirable for each of us to be open to shifts and changes in our perspectives. In the course of a conversation, particularly a heated one, if you're concerned that changing your mind will make you seem wishy-washy, try saying something like, "I know earlier in the conversation I said *X*, but now I'm wondering if *Y*." By actively pointing out a shift in your own thinking — rather than glossing over it — you open up the possibility for further questioning and curiosity.

5. Assume you will end up feeling closer to your conversation partner/s. The mindset with which you enter into the argument is really important for how the argument will unfold. Through a healthy argument, you will get to know each other more intimately. Very often we assume that arguments can push us away from each other, and therefore we avoid them. Avoidance, however, has a cost. Avoiding sharing an opinion prevents us from truly getting to know one another. We remain friends at a surface level if we cannot share what is really on our minds. The understanding that sharing my ideas and beliefs can lead to greater intimacy, if done right, is core to a healthy argument.

With these goals and intentions in mind, you'll likely be off to a good start. But I recommend also trying to make sure that the timing and location is right. Sometimes a disagreement erupts and at least some of the people involved are not in the right headspace. I was once on a politically charged tour of Israel, and I sat down next to a colleague hoping to get into a deep discussion about what we had just experienced. She looked at me and gently told me that it wasn't a good time. She wasn't ready to share her thoughts. About an hour later, she came back and said she was ready to have a discussion if I was.

My colleague taught me an obvious but important lesson. Just because I was ready to talk didn't mean she was. So before getting into an argument — even a healthy one — it is a good idea to check in and ask your conversants whether they are ready and willing, and what they might need to enable a candid conversation. Sometimes a person isn't in the right frame of mind, or they might be feeling so volatile they're afraid of saying something they might regret. The setting is also worth noting and checking in about. People are often more likely to share their thoughts, particularly thoughts they fear may be unpopular, in a more private place with fewer people around.

In addition to the practical intentions or tips above, I believe it is also helpful to have images or metaphors of what a healthy argument can look like. They provide models for how we might embody our disagreements.

Our Jewish tradition is filled with disagreements, in particular disagreements about issues relating to Jewish law, *halachah*. Over centuries, rabbis and scholars have provided different explanations or metaphors for how to understand and hold these disagreements.

Beginning with a modern source, Rabbi Yechiel Michel Epstein (1829-1908), in the introduction to his great work of Jewish law called the Aruch HaShulchan, grapples with these disagreements. Given how much of Jewish practice had become standardized (in the Orthodox world in which Epstein lived), it would be easy to imagine that *halachah* is a corpus with great consensus. But as Rabbi Epstein reminds us, Jewish law is rife with discord. Because Jewish laws are seen by traditionalists as, in some ways, the word of God or some kind of ultimate truth, disagreements over these laws pose a challenge theologically and practically to the whole system.

He explains that these disagreements are "the glory of our holy and pure Torah. And all of Torah is called a 'song,' and the splendor of song is that everyone's voice is different. This is the essence of its beauty."

Rabbi Epstein reminds us that God calls Torah a song, "That this song may be a witness for Me among the people of Israel."[112] Rabbi Epstein borrows the word *song*, and applies the idea to the generations of interpretations and halachic arguments about the Torah itself. He expands the Torah-based metaphor to mean literally *song*, as when a group of people might be singing together. When one sings alone, the song is nice. But when a group sings together there are high and low tones, points and counterpoints. The music created when many different voices come together is much more beautiful than when one is singing alone.

So too, says Rabbi Epstein, are disagreements about Jewish law. If there were just one legal decisor, Jewish practice would be satisfactory. But as with many legal decisions, there are many voices about what we ought and ought not do. Jewish practice is a beautiful polyphonic choir resounding through the generations.

Looking a little deeper into Rabbi Epstein's metaphor, he reminds us that we must be singing the same baseline song. Or, put differently, the most productive arguments are ones in which we share at least some basic assumptions. An argument about Jewish law, for example, is only a productive argument if we both agree that the law is in and of itself important.

Within the context of at least some similar assumptions and values, we might ask ourselves how can we interact with those who disagree with us to create music rather than painful noise? How can we offer counterpoints that create harmony rather than cacophony?

The Tosefta, an ancient source from the second century, offers another metaphor for how we can hold differences of opinion. Our sages ask us to "make for ourselves a heart of many chambers."[113] They bring the example of a core disagreement between the great rabbinical academies of the House of Shammai and the House of Hillel[114] about what is pure and what is impure. This disagreement affects one of the most high-stakes of our laws determining who and what takes part in the world and who must be set aside (even if temporarily). These laws determine who or what is seen as living and who or what is to be seen as dead.

---

112 Deuteronomy 31:19.

113 Tosefta Sotah 7:7.

114 Called Beit Shammai and Beit Hillel in Hebrew, two schools of thought were founded by sages Shammai and Hillel during the period of the Mishnah; they lived during the last century BCE and the early first century CE.

In order to make the determinations of what is pure and what is impure, the rabbis of the Talmud described how they gathered in groups or assemblies[115] and offered competing opinions on these life-and-death issues. Rather than adjudicating, the Tosefta gives us clear — yet hard to understand — instructions for what to do with competing viewpoints: "Now make for your heart chambers within chambers and bring into it the words of Beit Shammai and the words of Beit Hillel, the words of those who declare impure and the words of those who declare pure."

A heart of many chambers, or rooms, is one that can hold differences of opinions. Often, when we engage in an argument, we experience a shutting down or closing out of others. Our impulse is to push away whatever is different or difficult to reconcile with our own ideas. The Tosefta entreats us not to shut down, but to open up deep into our core. It is asking us to open our hearts, to make room for multitudes. Interestingly, the Tosefta does not just tell us to open our hearts to make room, but rather to make *rooms*, in the plural. This heart doesn't blend everything together; it has compartments. How might we approach healthy arguments if we had many chambers in our heart?

Imagine being able to hear different opinions and letting them pierce your heart — not necessarily to the point of totally changing who you are and what you hold most dear. But imagine just being able to hold other people's ideas deeply inside you, nonetheless.

---

115 Those assembled were called *ba'alei asuffot.*

MANAGING

WORK AND FAMILY

Managing work and family requires that we determine what is truly important to us, what our most cherished ideals are, and then aim to align and realign our life along the lines of those chosen ideals. It is easier said than done, and it entails making time to reflect, to grieve, and to pray. "The key is not to prioritize what's on your schedule, but to schedule your priorities."[116]

The needs of work and family are not always at odds. When I was a teenager, my mother took a new job that allowed her to leverage her talents exceptionally well. The change elevated the well-being of our entire family and continues to inspire me to this day. This reminds me of an ancient Ethiopian saying: "Wisdom that stays inside, unexpressed, is like light that remains covered in a pot."[117] Our souls strive to express our gifts and talents in ways that illuminate both our family and the world beyond.

You may have heard this topic described as work–life balance, as if a magical formula exists that will allow us to pay just the right amount of attention to our professional and personal lives. Yet no such magic exists. There will always be demands on both sides. The aspiration to follow God's call to Abraham, and, by extension to all his descendants, to be a blessing,[118] can guide our way as we make tough choices in the management of work and family life.

In this chapter, Rabbi David Jaffe vulnerably shares insights from his experience managing work and family. He reflects on how meaningful it was for his family to establish a vision of negotiating work and family time, and staying accountable to that vision, while exercising flexibility to making changes over the course of the parenting journey. Ianna Raim explores why many people tend to be lopsided in balancing work and family, and what we can do about it. Bruce Feiler unpacks research on what sets happy families apart.

---

116 Widely attributed to Stephen R. Covey, the sentiment reflects principles found in Habit 3: Put First Things First, from his influential book, *The 7 Habits of Highly Effective People: Restoring the Character Ethic*, New York: Free Press, 1989.

117 I heard this in Hebrew from Penina Agenyahu, Director of the Jewish Agency's Global Partnership Network..

118 Genesis 12:2.

Reflections on Twenty Years of Trying to Balance Work and Family Life

Rabbi David Jaffe

Rabbi David Jaffe is the founder and principal of the Kirva Institute, where he teaches applied Jewish wisdom. His first book, Changing the World from the Inside Out: A Jewish Approach to Personal and Social Change, *explores how to walk a holy path that integrates deep spiritual wisdom with the daily work of peacemaking and social change. He brings these lessons to change makers and spiritual leaders throughout the country as an educator and consultant with such leading social justice organizations as Jews for Racial & Economic Justice, Keshet, and Bend the Arc, as well as communal and educational institutions such as the Hebrew College rabbinical school and Temple Israel of Boston. David serves as a faculty member at The Mussar Institute and the Institute for Jewish Spirituality retreats.*

I am writing this reflection in a moment of personal transition, as the parent of a nineteen-year-old who has just left home and a seventeen-year-old who is preparing to do the same within the next year. My emotions range from pride at how my boys are launching themselves into the wider world to heartbreak at the reality that we will no longer be in each other's lives on a day-to-day basis. I also feel pride in how I took advantage of the incredible opportunity these past nineteen years gave me to parent these two incredible human beings, along with a measure of regret. In reflecting back on two decades of parenting, four themes emerge as central in trying to achieve that elusive balance between one's work life and home / family life: Vision, Flexibility, Organization, and Shabbat.

This is a deeply personal essay, so I will begin with some context about myself and my family. I live in the Northeast of the United States, with my wife of twenty-one years and our two teenage boys. I am a rabbi, educator, and author, and over the course of my parenting journey my professional occupations have ranged from rabbinical student to high school educator to nonprofit entrepreneur. I dedicate a significant amount of time to volunteer activities, including community organizing and pastoral counseling. During this same period my wife alternated between full- and part-time work, starting up her own health consulting business and then becoming the full-time regional director of a national advocacy organization, all while dealing with a significant health challenge. Our boys attended Jewish day school, were homeschooled for several years, and went to public high school. We have no immediate family in the area, but are surrounded by a supportive cohort of other families — a community that has raised children together for twenty years. I share this context because the conditions of our lives have such a big impact on how we can approach work–life or work–family balance. Family contexts vary so much, from single-parent families to blended families to multi-generational families under one roof to nuclear families with two parents. As you read my reflections, I want you to be aware of my context, so you can adjust and apply what is useful to your context and leave the rest.

Vision

Why did God create the world? Judaism teaches that God wanted to bestow benefit on His creation. That was His vision, that was what led to the creation of the universe and all that is in it.

To create the work–family balance we want, it is incredibly helpful to define exactly what we want to achieve and to thereby create a vision. This may sound obvious, but I've counseled many families deep into their parenting years who are struggling with conflicts regarding their work and family life because they never articulated clearly how they envisioned the balance that was right for them. I can't emphasize enough how important it is to be up front with your partner about your vision for your work and family life. This is especially important for a woman partnering with a man and living in a modern, secular context, within which women are often expected to not only work outside the home but to also take responsibility for the majority of the parenting and home upkeep, while men are still expected to focus primarily on their careers.

While these expectations are changing in many Western cultures, unless expectations are made explicit at the outset about how roles in the family will be divided, this will most often become the default. This arrangement may be just fine for some families, but for those that want and expect a more egalitarian arrangement not setting expectations up front can lead to frustration and conflict down the line. These dynamics play out most intensely in male–female relationships, but some version will be present in any shared parenting. If you are single parenting, you will need to think about what support you need from family, friends, and other support people to approach your desired balance.

As part of our effort to express our vision for our family, my wife and I wrote a blessing that we recited at our wedding ceremony. We have this blessing framed and hanging on the wall next to our dining room table. At least once a year, on our anniversary, we read it together and reflect on how we are doing. Here is an excerpt from it that relates to work–family balance:

We will balance our work and community commitments with the holy work of nurturing our family life. We will support each other's professional aspirations with the knowledge that we both enjoy and are responsible for caring for our home life.

> *What might it look like for you and your family to consciously generate a vision? What advice do you have for yourself for steps toward creating such a vision?*

Having this vision clearly articulated and framed on our wall has played an essential role in holding ourselves accountable to our vision, particularly at times when one or both of us have been pulled toward pouring more time into work and running the risk of neglecting the home. To be honest, it was usually me and not my wife who needed to be held accountable, to bring back my focus on the family and not slip into the pattern of being a workaholic.

Desires and needs can change over time, and a family vision that needs updating can be renegotiated. I don't believe a perfect balance is ever achievable. We approach a balance, or work toward a balance, constantly adding a little to one side of the equation and taking away from the other by attending a parent–teacher meeting, sports game, or helping with homework, by skipping a board meeting or traveling to a conference. The opportunities for approaching balance are many; we need clarity about what we want and a detailed, enduring vision of what balance might look like to help make these daily choices in our parenting and work lives. Having this vision is all the more important because the stakes are so high. The choices we make about how we prioritize career, family, and home will have major implications for our advancements at work, on the one hand, and the attention we give our homes and children, on the other. Because of the high stakes and strong emotions involved in these decisions, creating a shared vision with your partner is essential.

Flexibility

The rabbis taught: "A person should always be soft like a reed and not hard like a cedar."[119]

The balancing of career and family life cannot be static. As children grow, they need different kinds of attention that impact how we achieve balance, how we prioritize and re-prioritize work and family commitments. The rabbinic statement I shared above is one I find deeply meaningful because it acknowledges the importance of flexibility. The rabbis go on to explain that the reed has many roots, and even though it bends with the wind it always ends up standing up in its place. The cedar, which doesn't bend with the wind, has short roots and can be blown over by especially strong winds.

I understand this metaphor shared by the rabbis to mean that we need to be firm in our priorities but also flexible and able to bend to different situations in life. When children are young, parents are called upon to give lots of physically demanding attention, from nursing to playing on the floor to night diaper changes to holding during tantrums. Parents of babies and toddlers are often chronically sleep deprived and physically exhausted.

During this period in our family, my wife was struggling with a debilitating chronic illness. I was grateful to have a stable income and regular daytime work hours with no night or weekend responsibilities, so that I could meet my home obligations. This was the period when I worked at a Jewish high school, first as a Talmud teacher and then as a dean and spiritual advisor for the school. Our children were in full-day preschool and then elementary school, and I could do drop-offs in the morning while my wife or support people picked up in the afternoons. I was home to manage bedtimes most nights. This was not the time in my life during which I developed entrepreneurial projects, traveled around the country for teaching seminars, or got involved in community activities. Parenting was very physically demanding and had to be the priority. Even when not dealing with the health issues we faced, parenting young children is a physically exhausting endeavor and parents need to pay attention to how they use and conserve their energy.

As our children grew older and we decided that homeschooling during the tween years was right for our family, my wife and I both needed to be flexible with our jobs. I changed from full time to part time in my regular job. To supplement my income, I focused on flexible options — picking up curriculum writing and evening teaching work. My wife also worked part time. This gave us the

---

119 Babylonian Talmud Ta'anit 20a.

availability we needed during the day for teaching our sons at home and driving them to activities. We also moved to a community where many of our friends already lived, so we could engage in a more communal form of parenting.

While it was a difficult decision to move from an area that we loved, the shared activities and childcare we were able to access in our new community became essential for this stage of our parenting. One year, for example, we shared homeschooling with two other families, trading off days so each family took responsibility for designing activities for our combined group of thirteen children, like Jewish learning and hikes in the woods. Other years, the kids played together in the afternoon and had dinner at different families during the week. We even had a parenting support group for a short period of time, where we would think through and discuss the social dynamics and developmental challenges we were seeing in our children. (I want to acknowledge the economic and class privilege we benefited from that gave us this type of flexibility with our work as well as the privilege of having such a robust community of friends.)

As our boys reached high school age, the balance of work and family changed yet again. Daytimes became fully available for work, but we needed to be available at night — not for bedtime rituals, as when they were younger, but for sports and homework or help with math and writing papers. At that point in my own career, I was doing a lot of freelance teaching most nights of the week. I realized that I only had several more years of parenting my boys at home and I wanted to show up for them, so I made the difficult decision to cancel all my evening classes and only teach during the day. I took on other projects that I could also do during the day, but gave up long-term night classes I had been teaching for years. This decision was all the more important because my wife had started working full time out of the home. Changing my schedule — being flexible — enabled us to rebalance our work–home–family responsibilities once more, so our balance was right for our family during this new stage.

Now that one of our sons is out of the house and the other is on his way, I can foresee that our balance between work and family and home life will recalibrate again. I share all these details of our personal choices to give one particular picture of how important it is to be flexible in balancing your work and home life. If your desire and vision is to be as available as possible to your children while also working and enhancing your careers, you will need to develop flexibility in order to best meet your own family's particular requirements over the years. You may also need to be flexible with how you access family and friends to join with you in the joyous and exhausting vocation of parenting.

Organization (Seder)

Mussar master Rabbi Shlomo Wolbe wrote that "Seder testifies to desire, and true desire must be expressed through seder."[120] The word *seder*, which many people know from the Passover Seder, means order or organization. It is the soul trait of being able to organize one's life in order to manifest one's vision. Rabbi Wolbe's teaching binds together desire, vision, and flexibility with the priorities needed to work toward balancing work and family life. We may know that we want time with our children, to talk about the day, or just be together without any chores or particular goals. A typical expression of that vision would be to organize a daily family dinner time. This seder may work for a period of time but, as many parents of teenagers know, once our children are more independent and choose to attend sporting or other activities in the late afternoon and early evening, family dinner time becomes very hard to maintain — at least it was for my family!

This is where being clear about your priorities and flexible with your seder comes in. When a particular schedule that was working for a certain period falls apart, the key is not to give up on the priorities, but to strategize about what new seder can be created to manifest these priorities. In my family, that looked like focusing more of our family time on Shabbat, which I will discuss more below. We decided that we would make Friday night dinner a sacred family time and rarely have guests. This decision enabled my wife and me to relax, knowing that at least for a few hours each week we would have focused time with our teen boys. In a way, this time made up for the inconsistent family dinners during the week and our haphazard access to quality time with our boys during their socially active teen years. What changes in expectations or weekly structure can you adopt to hold on to your work–family–home vision in the changing circumstances of your children's lives?

Shabbat

The Hebrew verb *lishbot*, which is the root of the word *Shabbat*, means to stop or to cease. Stopping and ceasing periodically from our work and communal activities is probably the most important thing we can do as parents to move toward balance in our family and work lives.

The newly freed Israelites are introduced to Shabbat shortly after the exodus from Egypt as a day to stay near home and not collect *manna*, their food in the

---

120 Shlomo Wolbe, *Alei Shur*, Volume 2.

desert. At that time, collecting *manna* was the closest thing the Israelites had to work or economic activity. Jews today celebrate Shabbat in many different ways, from the traditional twenty-five-hour cessation of all creative and weekday activities from one hour before sunset on Friday to Saturday night, to more flexible interpretations of the day of rest that may include a Friday night family dinner, a service at synagogue, or long walks in nature.

Highlights of Shabbat for everyone could include family or communal meals, singing, napping, playing board or card games, synagogue services, visiting friends, youth group activities, park visits, and other soul-nourishing activities.

Over the long term, Shabbat has probably been the most important factor in the life of our family to help us balance work and family. No matter how hard everyone was working during the week, no matter how many communal or youth activities we participated in, come Friday night the whole family has been together at the table. When our children were young, Friday night dinners were augmented with puppet shows about the Torah portion of the week and involved frequent breaks from the table to play with toys on the floor. As our boys got older and became involved in many of their own activities, these dinners became even more special as several hours of the week always spent together, uninterrupted by phone calls or screens. It is hard to overstate how important it was as a family to know we would have this time to reconnect every week.

Just as important as having our boys off their devices was the fact that my wife and I were also off our devices and committed to giving each other and our boys our full attention. We made special time every Shabbat when our children would take the lead and decide what they wanted to play, and we would follow along for however long they wanted to keep going. How different this was from weekdays, when we frequently had to cut short a game or activity because we needed to attend to this chore or that work call. We played card games like Uno or board games like Monopoly for hours.

As our sons got older I developed a ritual of playing whiffle ball with one of them every Shabbat afternoon after lunch. The specific activity is less important than the fact that you, the parent, decide to give your full attention to your child while participating in an activity of their choosing. Of course you can arrange such special times on a weekday, but Shabbat provides a built-in time when this type of attention is more available and encouraged. If you let it, Shabbat can provide a weekly reset to whatever imbalance that has developed between your work and family life. It is a time to breathe deep and stop the incessant activity of our often frantic modern lives. It is a time to turn inward toward your family — and toward yourself. While my focus in this essay is on family I must also point out that, for me, having at least a little alone time is an essential part of the weekly reset I experience on Shabbat.

If you already have a Shabbat practice, you probably understand what I am trying to convey in this section. If you don't have a practice and you are just starting your family life, please consider how you can make this powerful Jewish spiritual technology part of your life. If you don't have a practice and are already deep into the parenting journey, consider how you might integrate a Shabbat pause into your week — a time when you can give your undivided attention to your children. The important thing is to stop, refresh, and know that we are more than what we produce. Shabbat is a great gift, a gem of Jewish wisdom. I encourage you to use it as part of approaching balance in work and family life.

How might you revisit Shabbat rituals for yourself and for your family in a way that can help you with managing work and family?

Now that my boys are almost completely launched as adults, I can look back on the past two decades with some perspective as to how we approached balancing work and family. I honestly don't know if things were balanced, but I do know that because we articulated a vision for ourselves and held each other accountable, and always had Shabbat as a weekly opportunity to reset, my wife and I were constantly engaged in the question of balance. Perhaps that is the best we can do in the complex, unpredictable, ever-changing journey of parenting: Stay alert to the question. And Jewish life does provide us with many opportunities to keep asking it.

Rebalancing

Ianna Raim

Ianna Raim is a certified professional life and career revival coach who helps individuals and small business owners re-energize their careers to find more meaning and improve results at work and at home. Before developing her coaching career, Ianna spent more than 20 years in business, where she successfully founded several companies in a variety of industries including healthcare, import and export finance, and telecommunications. As a professional speaker, she has delivered motivational and strategy presentations to organizations and nonprofit groups as well as to her many private client organizations. A Harvard-trained MBA and Momentum educator, Ianna is also a board member at Weinbaum Yeshiva High School in Boca Raton and an active participant in Two's Company, a program that pairs Holocaust survivors with volunteers.

I've been an executive and leadership coach for over a decade, and in that time the words used to describe the ideal co-existence of work and life (everything that isn't work) have morphed several times: *Work–life balance, work–life integration, work–life blend, work–life fit, work–life rhythm,* and *work–life harmony* are just a few of the terms that have been used to describe that elusive achievement of simultaneous satisfaction with our lives at work and at home.

During the later years of the Industrial Revolution it was not uncommon for men, women, and even children to be expected to work sixteen-hour shifts in deplorable conditions with little pay. Today, there are laws that protect workers from such hardships. In fact, the pursuit of energized and happy employees has become an expensive and time-consuming focus for employers. Pre-pandemic, impressive recreation rooms, meditation spaces, gym memberships, and unlimited paid time off were some of the creative ways employers sought to impress their onsite staff.

When the pandemic forced us to retreat to our homes, the line between work and life became blurred. Instead of reclaiming time spent commuting and carpooling, many found themselves struggling even more to find balance as physical boundaries of work receded. More time was not necessarily the solution to the elusive work–life problem.

The pandemic prompted some movement. The Great Resignation saw millions of people choose to leave the conventions of corporate to pursue their self-employment or no-employment dreams and ostensibly find more meaning around life and work. Others practiced quiet quitting, getting by with minimal effort at work, which left more time for personal pursuits. Yet both movements fizzled. A 2023 Pew study found that 41 percent of Americans are working in a hybrid way.[121] And the buzz around having a healthy work–life balance persists.

Of course, no one would deny that technology has aggravated the problem. We are constantly connected and available. Still, it seems the real struggle is not an external one, easily blamed on unenlightened companies or inconsiderate bosses or even too much tech. To me, the issue seems to be an internal one — a fight within ourselves. Being busy has somehow become part of how we value ourselves.

A few years ago, I conducted an informal experiment in which I asked ten people within the span of a week: How are you? With the exception of three people, every answer I got was some variation of: *Ugh, I'm so busy.* Many of us wear our "busyness" — which surely is a lack of balance — as a badge of honor. It is as if our worthiness comes from continuous motion, as if we feel lost or, worse yet, guilty when we're not in motion. To avoid what feels like an awkward emptiness, we make ourselves busier to the point that busy becomes our normal.

We may fantasize about what it would be like to have days and days of endless downtime with no meetings, no errands, no phone calls, no appointments — but for many of us being busy has become part of our very identities. We have begun to believe that having quiet, free time means we're not important or needed or productive.

While research shows that different generations approach the balance question differently,[122] from my experience as a coach it seems that the struggle to prioritize what's important and actually feel good about our choices cuts across age, gender, and industry. The answer to being satisfied with how we manage work, family, and everything else in our lives starts with a keen self-awareness, a core honesty about our habits, beliefs, identity, and priorities.

---

121 Kim Parker, "About a third of U.S. workers who can work from home now do so all the time," Pew Research Center, March 30, 2023, https://www.pewresearch.org/short-reads/2023/03/30/about-a-third-of-us-workers-who-can-work-from-home-do-so-all-the-time/.

122 Nicholas J. Beutell, "Generational Differences in Work-Family Conflict and Synergy," International Journal of Environmental Research and Public Health, 2013, 10(6): p. 2544-2559.

In the Struggle for Time and Importance, Why Does Work Often Prevail?

Jewish mother is a ubiquitous label. Whether the term is hurled as an insult or meant as affectionate recognition, there is no doubt that the Jewish mother and, by extension, the Jewish family play a big role in our cultural identity. In the Jewish tradition family looms large, at least in concept. In practice, however, the focus on family can often take a back seat to other important Jewish tenets such as hard work, productivity, respect, giving back, and leading a purposeful life.

The simple reason is that most of these aspirations are far easier to attain through work than at home. As an executive coach, I have seen how people crave being productive, important, and impactful at their jobs. Striving for these achievements is motivating and admirable. Though we may have the opportunity to be all these at home, it is much easier to measure and feel our success in a work environment, where we have goals and metrics. We can readily see how what we do impacts co-workers, other departments, or customers. At work, either informally or formally at review time, we receive feedback. We are praised and complimented for a job well done. Often we are experts at what we do, and we are appreciated for that expertise and know-how. We feel important. We feel respected. The financial incentive for reaching goals at work is obvious. When we earn more, we can acquire more. The immediate rewards for working and over-working are tangible and instantly gratifying: a vacation, a new car, a new house. The rewards for working on our character and our family relationships are internal — and sometimes they take years to recognize.

At home, success is subjective at best. Relationships are emotionally messy. We are far from expert, because what our family needs from us is always changing. What it means to be a good father, husband, mother, wife, daughter, sister, son, sibling, or grandparent is evolving. Unlike at work, nothing really marks the end of a project or an engagement. The marathon of focusing on family is not only ambiguous, much of the time it's unnoticed. When was the last time your partner or kid thanked you for being a productive and impactful influence?

There are other reasons that we err on the side of overworking when the two realms of family and work collide. We tell ourselves: God only helps those who help themselves. We must do our part, our *hishtadlut*, effort. We are not permitted to sit around and expect God to provide everything for us miraculously. However, *hishtadlut*, if misinterpreted, can become a slippery slope. Where do my efforts end and divine will take over? What we may not realize is that, in the work arena, *hishtadlut* means doing what is expected or what is considered reasonable in order to get the results we want. Of course there are exceptions — working until midnight to make a deadline, traveling for weeks to close a deal — but when these become the norm we have to ask ourselves: Who is really in charge?

When Joseph is imprisoned in Egypt, he interprets the dreams of Pharaoh's butler and baker, who were also in prison. When the butler is released, Joseph asks him not once, but twice, to remember him and speak to Pharaoh on his behalf in exchange for the favor of interpreting his dream. In making his request twice, our rabbis say that Joseph was actually punished by having two years added to his time in prison. Why? The rabbis teach that, at Joseph's level of greatness, asking once would have been a fitting effort, but asking twice was considered excessive; it was as if Joseph was putting his faith not in God, but in a mere person.

The same can be said for us when we overwork. We may feel that we need to impress our boss; we may feel that working so hard is required to keep our job or to get promoted, or that if we don't work that hard we won't be able to afford the material things we like. The highest level of faithfulness and trust in God is to recognize that, while we are responsible for making an effort, we are not in control of the outcome. *Hishtadlut* at work has its limits.

On the spiritual, nonwork side of the equation, however, *hishtadlut* does not have the same limits. Prayer, learning Torah, improving our relationships, or working on our character traits — work that cannot be outsourced to a colleague or a consultant — is where we are encouraged to work overtime. Only we can work on ourselves.

What adjustments would you like to make to where and how you put in effort? Consider questions such as: Would you like to be married to you? Would you like to have a friend such as you? Would you like to be parented by you? Are you living in a way that your effort reflects your priorities?

Work As Religion

There is a further reason we tend to be lopsided in the work–life balance equation in favor of the work side. For many, work has actually become a religion within which we look for all things, including meaning and spirituality. In a 2019 essay titled "Workism Is Making Americans Miserable," author Derek Thompson wrote: "For the college-educated elite, work has morphed into a religious identity promising transcendence and community, but failing to deliver."[123]

The goal of work used to be to earn more free time. In 1930, economist John Maynard Keynes predicted that by the twenty-first century we would have a fifteen-hour work week (a five-day weekend!) and people would hardly know what to do with all their leisure time. People's identities would be defined not by their jobs, but by what they did in their free time. Today that prediction seems laughable. Now, starting from a young age, people are encouraged to find their passion at work, to find a job they truly enjoy, to look for work that can change the world. The concept of work has evolved from finding a job to investing in a career and following a calling. Work has become spiritual; it is the area within which people mistakenly search for their sole purpose. A 2019 Pew Research report showed that teens ranked having a job or career they enjoyed as higher in importance to them than getting married or helping others in need.[124]

Truthfully, this is not hard to understand. Society encourages us to define ourselves by what we do, not by who we are. When we meet someone for the first time, we ask: "So, what do you do?" We don't ask: "So, what values do you live by? How would you describe your character traits?" or even, "How do you most enjoy spending time with your family?" Work seems to be the hub of the wheel of our lives, from which everything else radiates. The irony is that, according to Gallup, only thirty-two percent of workers in the U.S. are engaged at their job.[125] Most people don't like their jobs. "Workism" has failed as a religion.

Religion should uplift, not enslave its followers. The Rambam explains that harsh labor, which describes the work the Jews were forced to do in Egypt, refers to labor that has no limit and no purpose.[126] According to the Midrash, Pharaoh commanded the Jews to build pyramids and tear them down once they were completed — that was endless work with no limit and no purpose.

The litmus test for the rightness of almost anything we do should be purpose and limit. Do we exercise to be healthy, to feel good and to look good, or do we work out excessively because our goal is to resemble Angelina Jolie? If the latter,

123 Derek Thompson, "Workism Is Making Americans Miserable," *The Atlantic*, February 24, 2019.

124 Juliana Menasce Horowitz and Nikki Graf, "Most U.S. Teens See Anxiety and Depression as a Major Problem Among Their Peers," Pew Research Center, February 20, 2019, https://www.pewresearch.org/social-trends/2019/02/20/most-u-s-teens-see-anxiety-and-depression-as-a-major-problem-among-their-peers/.

125 Gallup, State of the Global Workplace Report, 2023.

126 Maimonides, Mishneh Torah Hilchot Avadim 1:1.

then our endeavor has lost its way and its reasonable limits. Using food as another example, the purpose and limit guideline is challenged when we eat only for pleasure without any concern for our health, or we deny ourselves even small occasional indulgences and focus only on our weight. Similarly, when we work at our jobs beyond what is really required, to the detriment of everything else in our lives, we become our own pharaohs and enslave ourselves. We may rationalize that our work has great significance and purpose, but if it doesn't pass the litmus test of purpose and limit we have gone too far.

Torah Guidance on How to Approach the Work–Life Balance

When I was young, I had no idea that the 1965 hit by The Byrds, "Turn, Turn, Turn" — a song that we swayed to at summer camp and later became part of the soundtrack of *Forrest Gump*, one of my all-time favorite movies — took its lyrics from the book of Ecclesiastes. When I found out, I wasn't really surprised; so much of what we think of as modern pop psychology has its roots in the Bible — the Book of Jewish Values. This concept, that everything has its time and place, is no exception. Judaism recognizes the importance of designating certain times for certain things. In Leviticus, a list of biblical holidays is prefaced with this description: "These are the set times of God, the sacred occasions that you shall designate at their set times."[127]

There are three prayers in Judaism that are to be recited at certain times of every day and an additional one on Shabbat and festivals. Our sages teach, "Make your study of Torah a fixed practice."[128] There should be a fixed time for study, as well. Judaism understands that designating times, rather than letting time designate us, makes us more intentional and ultimately allows us to be happier about how we spend our time.

I've seen this concept play out in the coaching work I do. When overworked executives commit to actually scheduling time in their calendars for activities that are not work — such as time with family, going to the gym, time for self-reflection — it helps with managing work and family life.

It is important to acknowledge though that this requires discipline and follow-through. Here too Judaism helps us understand that our lives don't need to be balanced every single day. When we measure our balance on a daily basis, we are bound to be disappointed. A healthier way to gauge balance is by assessing

---

127 Leviticus 23:4.

128 Pirkei Avot 1:15.

it at different intervals over time. Judaism has set times for daily prayer and study, for the monthly celebration of the new moon, and for yearly festivals. The message we can take from the cyclical and metered nature of Judaism is that if striving for the "perfect" balance between work and life on a daily basis feels overwhelming, we can lean into a longer-range view. What if the goal becomes to achieve a certain amount of balance for a proportion of every month or every year? Or even every decade?

There are times when different aspects of our lives require more attention: when we are working toward a promotion at work, or when we are proving ourselves in a new role; when our kids are small, or when they are applying for college; when a relationship is suffering and needs extra attention, or when a health concern must become paramount. Expending more of our efforts on one aspect of our lives during a particular point in time and then on a different aspect at another point in time can also be viewed as balanced.

Balance Versus Balancing

Humans are the only creature that God created incomplete. Baby animals grow into adult animals with little intervention. Saplings become grown trees as a matter of course. But with humans, God said: "Let us make human in our image."[129] According to the Hasidic master the Baal Shem Tov,[130] God wasn't talking to the angels but to each and every one of us, his human creations. God was saying: Let Me help you become who you are destined to become. Let us work together to help you reach your full potential.

That process takes hard work; the journey of self-actualization is not for the faint of heart. It can be joyous and arduous at the same time. It's about acting, examining, and then recalibrating, constantly. In the Jewish tradition, the act of balancing, and improving that balance in the process, is far more admirable and realistic than reaching a state of balance. A balanced state might indicate that the journey is done. In Judaism, our journey of self-discovery is never done.

When we realize that things were designed to be out of balance precisely so we can be our own agents, working to find more balance, then we can begin to understand and even appreciate the struggle between working and spending time with the families we have been blessed with. Many things created by God

---

129 Genesis 1:26.

130 The Baal Shem Tov (1700–1760), Rabbi Israel ben Eliezer, was the founder of the Hasidic movement. He emphasized making Jewish practices of joy, prayer, and devotion in serving God accessible to all.

are in constant motion: The planets keep spinning, the rivers keep flowing, the winds never stop blowing. We, on the other hand, can stop. We can decide, intentionally, that we will pause and rest and self-reflect, and ask ourselves hard questions like: Am I looking to my work to define me? Is my family getting the best of me that I can give? Am I spending enough time on making myself a better person and improving my character? Is there a better way?

Set time to stop and reflect on these questions with a journal, a friend, or on a walk.

The ultimate goal is not to find the elusive "perfect" balance between work and life. That doesn't exist. Instead, we are instructed to work at our day jobs with dignity and honesty in order to elevate them, and to remember that work and making a living is only part of who we are; it is not our totality and it shouldn't be seen as such. It is something that supports everything else we do. Our job is what we do, but it is not what we were created to do.

Many times in my practice I have worked with executives who have to fire members of their team. Often there is a lot of doubt, indecision, and sometimes guilt around the act of letting someone go. This is understandable; most people don't relish causing someone else pain or discomfort. While compassion for the person being fired is apt, almost always that person is either replaced or their duties are absorbed by others. Work goes on. How different it is with family! Not only can we not get fired from our families, we certainly can't be replaced. And because there can be no replacement for us as parents, children, siblings, aunts, uncles, grandparents, cousins, and Jews, we simply have to work toward getting better at fulfilling these roles that exist beyond the four walls of the office. Improving our relationships, volunteering more, or working on ourselves takes time — often more time than we dedicate to the task — but the reward is worth the effort.

The Secrets of Happy Families

Bruce Feiler

Bruce Feiler is the author of seven New York Times *bestsellers, including* Life Is in the Transitions: Mastering Change at Any Age; The Secrets of Happy Families: Improve Your Mornings, Tell Your Family History, Fight Smarter, Go Out and Play, and Much More; *and* The Council of Dads: A Story of Family, Friendship & Learning How to Live. *His Ted Talks have been viewed more than four million times, and he teaches the Webby Award-winning TED Course* How to Master Life Transitions. *His latest book,* The Search: Finding Meaningful Work in a Post-Career World, *is a road map for finding meaning and purpose at work, based on insights drawn from hundreds of life stories of all vocations and backgrounds. A native of Savannah, Georgia, Bruce lives in Brooklyn with his wife and their identical twin daughters.*

I hit my breaking point as a parent a few years ago. It was the week of my extended family's annual gathering in August, and we were struggling with assorted crises. My parents were aging; my wife and I were straining under the chaos of young children; and my sister was bracing to prepare her preteens for bullying, sex, and cyberstalking.

Sure enough, one night all the tensions boiled over. At dinner, I noticed my nephew texting under the table. I knew I shouldn't say anything, but I couldn't help myself and asked him to stop.

Ka-boom! My sister snapped at me, telling me not to discipline her child. My dad pointed out that my girls were the ones balancing spoons on their noses. My mom said none of the grandchildren had manners. Within minutes, everyone had fled to separate corners.

Later, my dad called me to his bedside. "Our family's falling apart," he said. There was a palpable fear in his voice that I couldn't remember hearing before.

No it's not," I said instinctively. "It's stronger than ever."

But lying in bed later that night, I began to wonder: Was he right? What is the secret sauce that holds a family together? What are the ingredients that make some families effective, resilient, happy?

It turned out to be an astonishingly good time to ask that question. The last few years have seen stunning breakthroughs in knowledge about how to make families and other groups work more effectively. Myth-shattering research has reshaped our understanding of dinnertime, discipline, and difficult conversations. Trendsetting programs from Silicon Valley and the military have introduced techniques for making teams function better. The only problem: Most of that knowledge remains circulating only within those subcultures, hidden from the parents who need it most. I spent the last decade trying to uncover that information, meeting families, scholars, and experts in various fields ranging from peace negotiators to online game designers to Warren Buffett's bankers. I collected the life stories of hundreds of Americans in all fifty states.

In essence, I was trying to answer a simple question: What do happy families do right, and how can the rest of us learn to make our families happier? When I set out on this journey I had a conviction: I wouldn't force what I learned into some catchy list of things you absolutely must do to have a happy family. I continue to believe there is no such list. What my family needs is likely different from what your family needs, is likely different from what our neighbor's family needs. There is no single formula. Still, to my surprise, in my research I did keep hearing certain ideas over and over again as a number of overarching themes emerged. So at the risk of seeming hypocritical, here is my non-list list of things that happy families consistently do.

Consider the happiest families you know. What would you put on a list of what happy families do right?

Adapt all the Time

The idealized, mid-twentieth-century notion of the American family came with preset roles: The father did this, the mother did that, the children behaved in a certain way. There was a clear script, and millions after millions aspired to realize that script, even if few actually did. That script has been thrown out. Whether we're talking about the makeup of your family, the strategy you use to get your family out the door every morning, the way you feed your family, or the techniques you employ to discipline, entertain, or inspire your children, the smartest research shows you have to be flexible. You have to be agile. The most effective families know this.

Flexibility and agility can mean lots of things. It can mean, like the many families who took techniques from agile management practices, using more morning lists, chore charts, and other means of public accountability. It can mean, as became the case with my family, instituting weekly family meetings to evaluate how well your family is operating. It can mean simply looking at when you eat meals, how you give out allowance, or where you sit during family discussions, and changing things up from time to time. Above all, it means building into your family culture the idea that you are capable of evolution and change.

In their detailed studies of American families, Reed Larson of the University of Illinois and Maryse Richards of Loyola concluded that the most successful families employ a strategy of continuous renegotiation. "Collective family well-being depends not on fixed role assignments," they wrote, "but rather on flexible processes that allow the family to adjust and adapt."[131]

Management guru Thomas Peters coined a colorful term that captures this idea of continuous reinvention. The best way to keep up with the ever-changing nature of our times, he taught, is to follow what he called "perhaps the only sure-fire winning formula for success": S.A.V. Screw Around Vigorously.[132] Now there's a motto for our times. Want to have a happier family? Tinker with it all the time.

Talk a Lot

The second most-common attribute healthy families display is that they talk a lot. At mealtimes and on long car rides, from disputes between spouses to showdowns among siblings, from money to sex, my research consistently showed that the ability to communicate effectively is a key ingredient of successful families. As one group of high school girls shared with me regarding how they learned about the birds and the bees, "It's no longer 'The Talk.' It's a series of talks. It's a conversation." That credo could apply to nearly every aspect of family life.

But *talking* does not mean simply talking through problems, as important as that is. *Talking* also means telling a positive story about yourselves. Specifically, one powerful form of talk that successful families do together is create a family narrative. I first heard this idea from Marshall Duke, a psychologist at Emory University who has studied the importance of knowing your family history. Duke showed that the more children know about their parents and grandparents,

---

131 Reed Larson and Maryse H. Richards, *Divergent Realities: The Emotional Lives of Mothers, Fathers, and Adolescents*, New York: Basic Books, 1994.

132 Thomas J. Peters and Robert H. Waterman, *In Search of Excellence: Lessons from America's Best-Run Companies*, New York: Harper & Row, 1982.

especially their successes and failures, the more they themselves are able to overcome setbacks.[133]

The author Jonathan Haidt summed up the importance of storytelling in *The Happiness Hypothesis: Finding Modern Truth in Ancient Wisdom*. Feeling good about yourself involves stitching your experiences into a forward-moving, hopeful narrative: "If you can find a way to make sense of adversity and draw constructive lessons from it, you can benefit." When faced with a challenge, happy families, like happy people, just add a new chapter to their life story that shows them overcoming their hardship. This skill is particularly important for children, whose identities tend to get locked in during their adolescence.

Simply put, if you want a happier family, spend time crafting, refining, and retelling the story of your family's positive moments and your ability to bounce back from the difficult ones. If you tell it, they will come.

Go out and Play

Finally, don't just make adjustments and make stories. Make fun.

Playing games. Taking vacation. Having get-togethers. Inventing goofy traditions. Cooking. Swimming. Hiking. Singing Dad's favorite song that makes everyone's eyes roll. Tossing a football.

Going bowling. Getting lost. Making a giant domino trail on the dining room table. Whatever it is that makes you happy, doing it with other family members will make your family happier.

"Happiness consists in activity," the British writer John Mason Good said nearly two centuries ago. "It is a running stream, not a stagnant pool." Modern science has backed him up. As happiness expert Sonja Lyubomirsky observed, activities that give us durable happiness are ones that are earned. We don't just sit back and receive pleasure. We actually create the pleasure ourselves. "One of the chief reasons for the durability of happiness activities is that unlike the guilty pleasures, they are hard won," Lyubomirsky wrote in *The How of Happiness: A New Approach to Getting the Life You Want*. "You have made these practices happen, and you have the ability to make them happen again." When the source of positive emotion is yourself and the people around you, she continued, the happiness is "renewable."[134]

---

133 Bruce Feiler, "The Stories That Bind Us," *The New York Times*, March 15, 2013.

134 Sonja Lyubomirsky, *The How of Happiness: A New Approach to Getting the Life You Want*, New York: Penguin Books, 2007.

To be a good parent, be a parent who is good inside.
What do you already do that has you feeling good
inside? What further can you do?

This idea may not be particularly groundbreaking, yet it seems to be among the hardest to act on. If you want to have a happier family, gather your family members, find some time, and play.

What Tolstoy Knew

When Leo Tolstoy was five years old, his brother Nikolai told him he had recorded the secret for universal happiness on a little green stick that he had then hidden in a ravine on the family's estate in eastern Russia. Should the stick ever be found, Nikolai said, all humankind would become happy. There would be no diseases, no one would be angry with anyone; everyone would be surrounded with love.

The legend of the green stick became a consuming metaphor in Leo Tolstoy's life. Time and again, in his writings and in his quest for spiritual meaning, Tolstoy returned to the theme of a world free of misery and filled with happiness. In the notebooks he kept for his masterpieces *War and Peace* and *Anna Karenina*, he recorded a French proverb several times: "Happy people have no history." That proverb, with its implicit notion that happy people don't have a story and unhappy people do, became the inspiration for the opening line of *Anna Karenina*: "All happy families are alike; each unhappy family is unhappy in its own way."

Tolstoy may have been somewhat dismissive of happy families in his famous maxim, but he never gave up the search for happiness himself. In the last years of his life, he returned to the idea of a world purged of pain and overflowing with joy. He asked to be buried in the ravine of his family's estate, where he believed his brother had hidden the elusive formula. "There should be no ceremonies while burying my body," Tolstoy wrote. "A wooden coffin, and let anybody who will be willing to take it to the Forest of the Old Order, to the place of the little green stick."[135]

Tolstoy still rests there today, in an unmarked grave, covered in a mound of green grass.

---

135 Leo Tolstoy, *Last Diaries*, 1960.

Choose Happiness

The story of Tolstoy's lifelong quest for the little green stick perfectly embodies the final lesson I took from my experience. Happiness is not something we find — it is something we make.

The management guru Jim Collins made this point eloquently in *Good to Great: Why Some Companies Make the Leap...And Others Don't*. After relentlessly examining hundreds of organizations looking for common traits in those that are successful, Collins concluded, "Greatness is not a function of circumstance. Greatness, it turns out, is largely a matter of conscious choice." He explained that there is no grand defining action, no single step one can take toward greatness — there is just a commitment to making incremental changes and accumulating small wins.

For busy families, this idea of gradual victories is both comforting and energizing. You don't need a wholesale makeover, you just need to get started. I heard this idea repeatedly on my travels.

The surest way to have a poor-functioning family is to be content with the status quo. As Harvard professor Tal Ben-Shahar wrote in his book *Happier: Learn the Secrets to Daily Joy and Lasting Fulfillment*, "There is one easy step to unhappiness — doing nothing." The opposite of that dictum also holds: The easiest path to happiness is to do something. Tackle that challenge that's been nagging your family, tweak that routine that's not working any longer, have the difficult conversation, pull out the game from the back of the closet. Reach for the green stick.

You may not find it today, tomorrow, or even next month. You may not discover it until the kids get through an awkward phase, or you craft a new strategy for the mornings, or you make some time to get everyone together in the backyard. But you will reach that point, as long as you make the effort to start. In the end, this may be the most enduring lesson of all: What is the secret to a happy family?

Trying.

FACING

MENTAL HEALTH

CHALLENGES

Statistics don't lie. Millions of people suffer from mental illness — by some estimates, one in every five people struggles with mental health.[136] These numbers make it clear that the challenge of mental suffering impacts all of us. It is an inextricable part of humanity.

While mental illness can be a lonely journey for an individual and for their families and friends, its scope calls on us to face mental health challenges as a community and to approach it with compassion. The Hebrew word for compassion, *rachamim*, comes from the word for womb, *rechem*. It reminds us that compassion is about creating and holding space, as a womb creates and holds space for processes to develop with our loving patience. Like a womb patiently holds an embryo as it develops toward wholeness, our loving compassion can hold suffering to help it heal toward wholeness.

Three authors share expertise on the subject in this chapter. Dr. Edith Eger writes about healing our inner child. In supporting and nurturing the child within, we expand our capacity to support and nurture others, conveying confidence that someone who is suffering can access the tools they need and use them to cope. Carly Israel offers a vulnerable story about the cold and darkness of mental illness, using her difficult experience to express what it is she feels all parents should know. Chaya Lester explores how our flaws can also generate our greatness and how, for example, experiencing suffering can help us transcend fear to more compassionately be present in another person's suffering.

---

136 https://www.nimh.nih.gov/health/statistics/mental-illness.

Choose Freedom

Dr. Edith Eger

Trauma specialist, internationally renowned author, and Holocaust survivor Edith Eger, PhD, holds a faculty appointment at the University of California, San Diego, and has appeared on CNN and television programs such as The Oprah Winfrey Show. *Edith was a Hungarian teenager in 1944 when, as a Jew living in Nazi-occupied Eastern Europe, she and her family were sent to Auschwitz. Her parents perished in the gas chambers, but Edith's bravery kept her and her sister alive. After the war Edith moved to Czechoslovakia, met the man she would marry, and together they immigrated to the United States. In 1969 she received a doctorate in psychology before pursuing an internship at the William Beaumont Army Medical Center at Fort Bliss, Texas.*

When did your childhood end? This is one of the first questions I ask my patients. When did you stop being yourself and begin filling a role?

In my years of experience as a licensed clinical psychologist, the most common complaint I've treated has not been depression, anxiety, or post-traumatic stress disorder, but hunger. We hunger to know ourselves and to be known. We hunger for approval, for attention, for love and affection. To feed our hunger, we must learn to look inside ourselves. Find the little girl or boy who is crying, who is in pain, and show up for them. To truly be able to parent someone else, we first need to parent ourselves. We cannot give to others what we don't have. Self-love is self-care.

> *What is the little child inside of you hungry for? How can you satiate that hunger? When you wake up in the morning, go to the mirror and look at yourself with loving eyes. Assure yourself, "I love you." Speak lovingly to the little child inside, saying things like, "I am powerful." "I am worthy." "I am a good friend." "I am kind." "I am a good parent." Say it and also receive it.*

Feel Your Feelings

It isn't helpful to fight the past. If you have a feeling, sit down and say to yourself: *I am feeling something and that's OK*. There are no right or wrong feelings. Give yourself permission to feel your feelings — of pain, sorrow, grief, or any other "negative" feeling — without judging yourself. Grieve and let the feelings go through you.

I believe that we can't heal what we don't feel. We can't forgive without feeling rage. The opposite of depression is expression. The best thing to do with anger is to channel it in ways that don't hurt anyone until it dissolves. In my work, I advise individuals to revisit the places where they can relive their negative experiences. As a teenager, I survived the Holocaust. I went through the valley of the shadow of death. Decades after the war I realized that I needed to return to Auschwitz, to face the past. I needed to return to the place where my parents were murdered and to face what happened there. I wanted to revisit that site of terror and death and to assert, to proclaim, "I made it."

During the years between surviving the Holocaust and returning to Auschwitz, I got married and had children. I also went to college, became a teacher and then a clinical psychologist, earning my PhD at the age of fifty. With all my accomplishments, at times I felt like an imposter because I had not faced my past. Thirty-five years after escaping that hell, I still experienced panic attacks, at any hour of the day, on any day of the week. The attacks occurred not only because of external triggers, but because of the memories and fears that continued to live inside of me, haunting me. I needed to stop repressing and avoiding my feelings, and to stop blaming them on my husband or on other people.

We cannot always change our situations, but we can change the way we respond to them. In Auschwitz, Josef Mengele decided my fate. He condemned my mother to die yet chose life for my sister and me. It was not my choice to make. Yet before we were parted, my mother gave me this advice: "No one can take from you what you've put in your mind." Even in prison, in the hell of Auschwitz, I could choose how I responded. I could choose what to say and what to do. I could choose my thoughts. I could have chosen to throw myself onto the electrified barbed wire fence or I could choose, as I did, to struggle to live. I could choose to think of my childhood boyfriend, of my mother's baked goods, and of my sister, Magda, beside me. I could choose to eat a blade of grass. I could choose to close my eyes and retreat to my inner world. There is a difference between reacting and responding; I chose to respond.

The closer I was to darkness in Auschwitz, the closer I was to God. God showed me how to turn hatred into pity. I began to feel sorry for the Nazis, who had been brainwashed to hate me. At any moment they could send me to the showers, and I would not know whether gas or water was about to come out of the spouts. I had no control over my external circumstances, over living or dying. But the Nazis could not control my spirit. Mengele and the other Nazis would always need to reckon with what they had done. While their power came from dehumanization and extermination, my strength came from within.

The Key to Compassion

When my oldest daughter was a little girl, she came home crying because she had not been invited to a particular birthday party. I did not know how to be a mother to her, because I needed a mother myself. I had lost my mother at a young age and had not been able to learn from her example. Everything was upside down. I did not know how to be a compassionate listener for my daughter. I did not know how to show empathy. Instead of giving her room and opportunity to express and feel her feelings, I took her to the kitchen and gave her a slice of Hungarian chocolate cake and a chocolate milkshake.

It wasn't until I could feel my own rage and sadness and legitimize my feelings that I was able to forgive myself and others and become more compassionate. Self-acceptance did not come easily for me. My striving for perfectionism began in childhood; I wanted to gain my parents' approval. Afterward, feelings of guilt for surviving only strengthened my perfectionist tendencies. A need for perfectionism stems from the belief that you are broken, so you hide your brokenness with degrees, achievements, and false stories. When we can accept that no brokenness or pain limits our wholeness, we can shed the masks — such as perfectionism — that inhibit our living more authentic lives. We can offer ourselves and others positive regard, even during hard experiences. Once we are compassionate to ourselves, we can be compassionate to others. Empathy is the ability to enter under someone else's skin and keep their feelings company. We do that when we remember that the person in front of us is a diamond, a beautiful child of God.

In Auschwitz, I had a family of inmates. Those who struggled just for themselves did not make it. Caring for each other helped us survive. I learned that I could be myself, and others could stay true to themselves, but together we would be so much stronger.

When I came to America, I worked in a factory that had separate bathrooms for Black people. I was astonished and horrified. I joined the National Association for the Advancement of Colored People and I marched for civil rights with Martin Luther King Jr. We must all learn to let go of judgment and choose compassion.

When my children were upset because someone had excluded them or teased them during their childhood, I used to say, "I know how you feel." But later I realized this was not true. No one can truly know how someone else feels. We should not attempt to reason with someone to feel differently. In time I learned that empathy does not mean adopting someone else's inner life. Empathy is allowing someone to feel how they feel. Now, when my children and patients share their feelings, I say, "Tell me more."

Let Go of Guilt

It took me many years to forgive myself for surviving the Holocaust. Why had my sister and I survived, when our parents and grandparents and six million others had not? This guilt prevented me from truly celebrating any of my accomplishments or happy occasions. At the age of forty-two, as a mother of three, I graduated from college — and yet I did not attend my college graduation because I was too ashamed.

We feel guilt when we think something is our fault. It keeps us stuck in the past. It makes us feel like no matter what we do it will never be enough. We are not born with shame, but we may learn it at a young age. Yet ultimately, feelings of guilt and shame come from within, from a rejection of ourselves. Freeing ourselves from guilt means accepting who we are and whatever has happened to us. Freedom means giving up on our idea of perfection.

The best thing I did was go back to the lion's den, look the monster in the face, and reassign my shame and guilt where it belonged — to the perpetrators. I reclaimed my innocence. Guilt and shame are not assessments of who we are. They are patterns of thought that we can leave behind.

We can choose what to do with our lives. Guilt comes from a focus on the past. Worry comes from a focus on the future. Where we can *act* and make a difference is in the present moment.

The Choice Is Yours

In my work with my patients, I practice choice therapy. Freedom is about choice. At various points in our lives we will all suffer — it's impossible to avoid. We are all likely to be victimized in some way, at some point in our lives. Victimization comes from the outside, and unfortunately it's part of life. But there is a difference between victimization and victimhood. How we respond to the suffering we undergo is our choice. Victimhood comes from the inside. No one can make us victims but ourselves. If we hold on to the victimization we experience, we can create prisons for ourselves, constructed with the bars of rigid thinking, blaming, unforgiveness, and avoiding healthy boundaries. We can be our own jailors when we choose the victim's perspective.

They say time heals, but time alone is not what heals us. It's what we *do* with the time. Healing is possible when we choose to take responsibility for how we respond, when we choose to take risks, and when we choose to let go of past wounds.

Harnessing our power to choose will create positive change in our lives. It can free us from anger and from our past failures and fears. It can help us enjoy the feast of life.

We can choose how we speak *to* ourselves and *about* ourselves. We can rewrite our internal scripts. Reclaim our innocence. Become whole again.

When we heal ourselves, we are more likely to pass on to our children a legacy for a nurturing life. We did not choose what has and has not been passed on to us from our ancestors, but we can choose what we pass on to our children. What stories, values, rituals, teachings, and experiences from your family and ancestry do you want to pass on to the next generation to help them live a life of wholeness? What are the contours and content of your legacy?

What Do I Want Parents to Know?

Carly Israel

> *Carly Israel teaches high school in Cleveland, Ohio. The mother of three teenagers and author of the memoir* Seconds and Inches, *she has written about parenting, divorce, and recovery for the* Huffington Post *and other venues. Before returning to teaching, Carly was the host of three podcasts:* Northstar Big Book, *about sobriety;* In Your Corner Divorce; *and* Must.Love.Self. *Carly acknowledges that without her continued dedication to her sobriety none of her blessings would be possible.*

You must first understand where I have been to comprehend what I am about to say.

I Have Been to Hell

I am the granddaughter of Holocaust survivors. The blood of Holocaust survivors runs through my veins. My parents are sober. I am the mother of three teenage boys. I am a high school teacher. I have been an active sober member of Alcoholics Anonymous for over 25 years. I tried taking my own life when I was nineteen, and everything since is bonus time. I had been to the darkest, coldest caves and saw the ending. I begged God for it to be over.

Today, as a teacher, the parents I talk with are not the ones whose kids are doing well. They're the ones who are sent to me because I have been to hell, which I can confirm is not the hot, fiery version advertised in mainstream media. On the contrary, the hell I know is a cold, wet cave with no foothold for resting, where no one can hear your whispers or screams.

To be clear, mostly everyone involved does the best they can with what they have been given. Nothing about the subjects of mental health, including addiction and alcoholism, is simple. It is filled with secrets, embarrassment, guilt, and desperation. The families I get to share my story with do not leave feeling relieved. They walk away with a mission to save the lives of their loved ones and those who are impacted by these diseases.

Please take my guidance with a large grain of kosher salt. I speak to you with the heaviness of grief, with the freedom of being off social media for more than three years, and the introspection available without all that background noise. I speak to you as a perfect child of God who, on January 26, 1999, handed in her badge, lanyard, and keys and told God I was all done with His world.

Six years earlier, when I was thirteen, my parents — threatened by my Holocaust survivor grandmother, Lulu — finally got sober and active, but it was too late for the talks and the trust to be put in place. I was lost, and I trusted no one. They worked all the time, and when they were not working they dedicated themselves to repairing our family by staying sober, which takes a great deal of time and energy.

The following excerpts are from my memoir, *Seconds and Inches*.[137] The *her* in the passage below is my mother, daughter of Holocaust survivors, sober since 1991.

> I would not allow her or anyone to get too close to my heart again, because I didn't know if I would be able to survive another emotional tsunami. And as much as I loved her and as close as we became, I made sure to never let anyone close enough to hurt me, ever again. And as I went about the task of building ice walls around my heart, I poured and put anything in my body that promised to make the loud voices quiet down.

> Where we come from matters. I was full of the fire and the woods and the bombs and the secrets and all of the keep your outsides looking good so no one can bother you about your insides and the, "don't tells." And this is who I was when I stood on the edge of the beginning of my end.

I had a raging eating disorder, a high GPA, undiagnosed ADHD, no therapy, and a mouth on me.

> And when my parents got enough sobriety under their feet and tried to assert themselves and give me boundaries and curfews and consequences, I yelled at them, "A curfew? Now? Why?"

> My parents answered back, "Because we don't want you out at all hours —"

---

137 Carly Israel, *Seconds and Inches,* Jaded Ibis Press, 2020.

I interrupted them, "Oh, now you're going to try and parent me? I don't know if you're aware of this, but I have been taking care of myself since I was, like, nine!" Anything they came at me with I came back harder.

I was exhausting to argue with, inconsiderate and had a smartass answer for everything I did. When they told me I wasn't doing something that I needed to do, I argued back, "I get straight A's. I'm in D.A.R.E. and M.A.D.D. and Student Council and Yearbook and track. What more do you want from me?"

My disease caught fire in college, and my drug / alcohol use could barely disguise the mental torture I experienced just under the surface. For the first time, I began seeking out counselors who would prescribe me just about anything to get me out of their office. I would end up sitting in front of more therapists than I could recall — I was placed on sixteen different medications, each trying to triage the symptoms of the last.

I was exhausted. My grades were better than they ever had been. I made the dean's list every quarter, but I was all over the place. I dropped every course that wasn't theater, dance or English. On the outside, I had it all, but on the inside, I could barely hold all of the plates I was trying to balance on my arm. I fantasized about how I could end it all.

I drifted into a mindset where all I could do was imagine a time where I was no longer alive. I felt really untethered and at the same time trapped and I spent a great deal of time thinking about my own death. And how I wanted out, how I no longer wanted to feel all these feelings. I was tired and I was sick of feeling so out of control.

I thought about ending my life every single day. I wanted the pain to subside. While at one time drugs and alcohol made me tune out all of the noise and the insecurity, now they switched directions mid-song and amplified all of the hate within. If I got drunk or high, the fears and the voices grew louder. If I tried to not use, I couldn't breathe.

My parents ended the cycle of generations of alcoholism and

addiction on both sides of our family. And because of that brave choice, I would eventually become the first sober mother in all of my lineage.

To be clear, getting sober did not solve the problem. The work required to pull myself out of that cave was my only chance at survival.

The woman who helped me finally do the work was Julie.

"I'll help you if you're willing to do anything to be sober." Without looking her in the eyes (because I couldn't look anyone, including myself, in the eyes at that point), I told her, "I will do anything."

I struggled from the moment I dragged myself out of bed in the morning until the middle of the night when I couldn't sleep. My mood fluctuated nonstop, exacerbated by the side effects from the different medications my new psychiatrist put me on. I went from being a dean's list student to someone who could barely sit still in a chair. I spent many nights sitting next to Julie in a meeting, crying and smoking, and asking if this was ever going to get better. She said, "It will if you do the work."

The people in recovery told me I could believe in any God I wanted but that it needed to make sense to me. They asked me what I needed God to be. When I really thought about it, what I needed from God was courage because, without alcohol or drugs, everything in my life felt so big and challenging and I didn't know how to do it. But if God was courage and God was with me, then I could use that courage to do each Sisyphean task. And this began a relationship between me and God. A God that I had begged to take me out of this world. And God never punished me or made me feel anything other than loved and taken care of.

In that burning building, I found that the only way I could get out was to clear away what was blocking me from the exit door. That hallway that I had packed with stories of my childhood, the pain I carried with me, the loneliness I felt growing up in that house, the embarrassment, the names I was called, the humiliation, the regret from choices I knew were wrong — all of it had to come out. And Julie showed me how to do it.

What helps you to sit with your unpleasant feelings and memories? What helps you process them? Do you have a Julie figure who can be with you as you do such work? How might such a process support your and your family's health?

With her guidance and the courage God gave me, I got into action and excavated every last garbage bag and overstuffed box. Together, we examined the contents and found everything that was blocking me from God, and from breathing, and from living. During that first major cleaning, I discovered that almost every single story of pain and anguish I carried with me was no longer serving me. It was time to grow up, acknowledge the hurt, forgive, and move forward. I had to clean up my space and all the messes I left in my wake.

The excuses I used in the past to justify grabbing a bottle or whatever was offered no longer held any water. My parents were sober seven years and were living good lives. If I wanted to blame anyone for my misery, I only had to look in the mirror. There would be years and miles of healing ahead of me, but this was going to be on me.

From that point on, keeping the hallway clean between me and God would be my responsibility. And it would be my responsibility to get off the couch and clean up the mess.

As I continued to fight through the hallways and force myself to look in the mirror, I found myself face to face with my greatest enemy, who would eventually become my best friend.

I discovered through writing in my journal that I actually do enjoy connection with other humans, and I made a decision to be more open and trusting with my heart, and I realized that even if I do get hurt, that guiding voice of God will always be there for me.

I wrote, I am becoming my own best friend. I am becoming beautiful and lovable. I am becoming an extension of every man and woman who held the light in front of me to show me the way out of the cold darkness. This is living. I have already died. Now, today, this moment, this drop I savor, I shall live. I am learning to fly.

What I Learned

The drugs and alcohol and cutting and whatever else is out there are not the actual problem. Instead, they are sought as a solution for a pain that cannot be quieted on our own. It is where parenting, help, and super challenging, brutally honest talks are required. The structure and the bumpers are needed when our teens cannot knock down the pins without ending up in the gutter. That is where parenting is not only needed but wanted. The way you know your kid's needs and wants will be the exact opposite of what it should look like. At first, they will flail and fight and curse and spew hatred, with the clear intent of not only hurting you but also seeing if you will give up on them. And you won't. You will not because your love and God are stronger than their disease.

The most crucial piece of information I have for any parent who is deeply enmeshed in this disease is to go get help. My mom went to Families Anonymous. There is also Alanon. The members of these organizations know your pain unlike anyone else; if you find the right crew, they will save your life. To be clear, I did not say they would save your kid's life. That is the raw truth that I have to offer. Not all who require help will get it, and not all who need it will be saved.

If you have a loved one who is trapped in the disease of addiction, eating disorder, or mental health and has not found a solution, they believe what their head tells them. They listen to it all day. They see the pain they cause you, and they feel tormented by their own mind. They believe, I mean really believe — like if they were hooked up to a polygraph they would pass it. They believe that the world, especially you as their parents, would be better off without the drama and chaos they constantly cause.

As I got help, I was able to redirect my inner conversation more often.

If I measured my worth by other people's opinion of me, I would be hiding under a rock. But I'm not because their opinions aren't my business. One of the lessons I have learned along the way is that everybody has a story. Who am I to judge? Life is not a race. I only get this very short and precious life. What am I going to do with it? When I slow down enough, I remember my truth. I am a perfect child of God, and there's absolutely nothing I can do to change that. I have nothing to prove. I need no approval. I am enough. I am a soul. This is my body. This is my life. This is the truth of all of us. What are we going to do with our one precious life?

Long ago, there was an incredible woman named Ro Eugene who taught me that in order to do "hard," I needed to search for a lesson in the middle of the struggle. She shared that when one of her five children left their bath running and the ceiling in the kitchen began to rain, instead of yelling at them or feeling bad for herself, she thought, "thank God I have all these old towels to help me clean up." Her willingness to find the lesson and gifts has helped transform me into a woman who automatically looks for the gifts or lesson and all the growth opportunities that come my way. Because of her and so many others along the path, I can't walk this earth without seeing the gifts, lessons, and perspective.

What Parents Can Do

1. Get help for yourself. For example, join one of the groups mentioned above. Get help so you can manage whatever is ahead and set the bumpers and boundaries your kid needs.

2. If you have a feeling that something is wrong with your child, trust it. Too many children struggle without the attention and help they need.

3. Talk with your kid. Don't stop. Don't be afraid that you will give them ideas. Trust me, they have ideas.

4. Share your struggles with your kids so they can share theirs with you.

5. Trust your gut and get closer to God than you thought possible.

6. Allow the hard times to strengthen you so you can hold others up. I am a better human because I know what to say and not say to those going through hell. Our scars give us strength and the understanding we need to help others face their challenges. Today, I am beholden to my scars.

The Art of Being Flawesome:
A Jewish Path of Wholeness

Chaya Lester

Chaya Lester is a psychotherapist, author, inspirational speaker, and spiritual guide. Her goal is to help people heal and thrive. Chaya serves as co-director of Jerusalem's Shalev Center for Jewish Personal Growth, where she offers therapy, classes, workshops, and retreats. Her books include Lit: Poems to Ignite Your Jewish Holidays; Babel's Daughter: From the Bible Belt to the Holy Land, *based on her acclaimed one-women show about life in Israel; and* Ink from Ash: Healing & Empowerment during the Oct. 7th War.

Flawesome: The state in which your flaws also generate your greatness.

Living unafraid of imperfection is an elusive art form. We may think that flaws get in the way of our happiness, but embracing our flaws can actually lead to our greatest happiness. When we embrace our flaws, we access that unique state of being *flawesome*. Contrary to popular belief, you are not awesome in spite of your flaws — you are awesome because of them. For our flaws define our path forward and sculpt who we are destined to be in the world.

Flawesome is not merely a catchy wordplay. It encapsulates a Jewish principle that sits at the very root of existence. This principle shows that embracing our imperfection can radically alter the quality of our lives. To understand this principle, we turn to the biblical story of the creation of humanity itself.

The Original Flawesome

From stardust to dust mites, the biblical narrative depicts God masterfully crafting the cosmos in one busy "week." By day three the text begins to echo a stirring refrain: "God looked and saw that it was good." From beasts to beaches, from flying things to teeming things, each day's product is divinely inspected and declared *good*. This refrain culminates in the final act, the crowning sixth day of creation. Yet this day is punctuated with a deliberate shift in the chorus. It reads: "God looked and saw that it was VERY good." That *very* is in fact the very first superlative in the Torah.

The biblical commentators pounce on this most conspicuous insertion. The Midrash explains it with a perplexing riddle: "*Good* refers to the *yetzer tov*, the inclination toward the good; while *very good* refers to the *yetzer rah*, the inclination toward bad."[138]

The drive toward the bad is very good?!

Yes, the sixth day was very good because on it humanity was created. More specifically, on that day a very particular and peculiar aspect of humanity was created — humans' deeply embedded drive toward the bad. Paradoxically, *very good* refers to the inception of every base, greedy, grimy, lowly impulse within us. This deliberate bug in the system could spell the very downfall of the entire divine endeavor. And yet it doesn't.

As inconceivable as that may be, the divine will was such that God's crowning act of creation was implanting within it the possibility of its very undoing. The essential flaw in us is not some unfortunate mistake. It is not a divine blundering miscalculation. It is purposeful. It is superlative. It is the crowning *very goodness* of existence. According to Jewish wisdom, we humans are tailor-made as supremely flawesome.

Now imagine having that (divine) ability to look at all of your bad stuff and call it not just good — but very good!

Why Embrace Imperfections?

We embrace flaws simply because they exist; they can't just be ignored. No matter how hard we may try. We will be faced with flaws no matter how far or how high we look. They are purposefully woven into the very fabric of reality. The only way is to go through them — to work with the raw material of the flaws themselves.

Yes, the world is unavoidably full of untold acts of violence, corruption, and despair. Reality is rife with imperfection. And so are we. We all bicker and blame and batter ourselves, not to mention each other. Behind every success story are a thousand shame-faced failures.

So often we hear people say: How can there be a God if the world is so broken? It is the battle cry of atheists the world over. In a reality marred by war and suffering, it could very well be argued there is no God. A flawed world seems like evidence against God's existence.

But for Judaism that imperfection is an elegant expression of an inherent aspect of godliness itself.

---

138 Midrash Rabbah Bereshit 9:7-13.

Perfection & Perfecting: *Shlaymut* & *Hishtalmut*

This Jewish theory of flawesome is best given over by Israel's first chief rabbi, Abraham Isaac HaKohen Kook (c. early 1900). Rav Kook unfolds the kabbalistic teaching that, first of all, God is perfect. In Hebrew, *Shalaim*. Whole. Everything. And yet, if God contains everything, then that must necessarily include not everything. Rav Kook asserts that in order for Godly Perfection to be truly perfect, it must also include imperfection. Full wholeness necessarily and paradoxically contains lack.

The term he gives for this paradoxical state is *hishtalmut*. *Hishtalmut* is not a noun, it is more of a verb. In fact, it is a present participle. Present participles refer to things that are still actively happening; an ongoing process. To create the present participle, we add *ing* to the infinitive verb. (Or when it comes to God, the *ing* is added to the Infinite verb!) When the noun *perfection* is made into an ongoing active process, we get the word *perfecting*.

According to Jewish mysticism, Divine perfection necessarily encompasses a continuous process of perfecting. The core of this perfecting process is in fact us humans — the very ones created flawesomely "very good" on the sixth day of creation. We, with our myriad flaws, are the ongoing process of divine perfecting.

From the daily tiffs with our partners to the global rifts in governments and politics, it is all a deliberate part of the master plan. According to Jewish wisdom, even more wonderful than a perfect world is an imperfect world. For it engages us humans in the core *raison d'etre* of humanity — the act of perfecting. We are called to rectify a broken world. And that rectification process begins with encountering realities' many wrecks.

It is not a mistake that we make mistakes. In fact, we don't just make mistakes — our mistakes make us! They make us exactly who we are intended to be. We are flawed and that's awesome. We are perfectly imperfect. We are perfecting.

> *Toxic and difficult situations — and toxic and difficult people — can become opportunities for perfecting.*
> *The next time you experience feeling annoyed or vexed, take a deep breath and tell yourself, "They are flawesomely human, just like me." Then consider how this situation or person can offer you an opportunity for your own perfecting, for* hishtalmut.

The Sweet Spot of Perfecting

Does embracing flaws mean we just sit by and benevolently accept all the rank injustices of the world? Of course not.

Our job is to become master tightrope walkers, forever balancing between acceptance and improvement. Always wanting to be better and improved, and yet knowing that self-love means accepting ourselves just the way we are. It is the glorious — and often agonizing — dialectic of our lives.

Our work is to be continuously working on ourselves even as we are continuously reminding ourselves that we are perfect just the way we are.

A wise Jewish teaching says we must have two pockets — one with a note in it that reads: "I am but dust and ashes." Imperfect to the extreme. The note in the other pocket reads: "The whole world was created for me." Perfect just as I am.[139]

The question is knowing which pocket to dip in to when. What is the medicinal amount that you need at any given moment? Do you need to remind yourself to improve, or remind yourself to accept? The goal is to find the sweet spot of paradox between those two endeavors. Because we were made in the Godly image, perfectly perfecting.

A Personal Story

I want to end with a personal story about one of the most archetypally flawesome moments of my life.

It was the Shabbat before my eldest daughter's bat mitzvah. The first major life-cycle ritual of our family. My daughter led a beautiful Kabbalat Shabbat service in our home — overflowing with women, girls, *neshamas*, candles, dance, sparkly strings of fairy lights, and on and on. It was sacred-space-central. She led the songs perfectly, soulfully. It was simply exquisite.

I could say so many things about how glorious it was — and it was. It was Perfect.

But even more perfect was the perfecting. I want to share the most glorious part. And that was the backdrop — the dark backdrop — of all that brilliance. Because exactly one week before, we as a family weathered one of the hardest Shabbats we've ever had together. We had gathered in the living room after candle lighting with this sweet intention to sing together and have our daughter do a practice run of the Kabbalat Shabbat service. It was late and the kids were

---

139 Attributed to the eighteenth-century Hasidic master Rabbi Simcha Bunem. See Martin Buber's *Tales of the Hasidim: The Later Masters.*

overtired and underfed. The meltdowns started like hot dripping wax. One kid was literally stomping feet upset about all the attention the bat mitzvah girl was getting. Another kid stubbornly folded arms and refused to participate. Another was just piteously weeping outside the door. It was an archetypal mess.

Usually we parents are masters at managing the mess. We have meltdown protocols. We know just how to hush them, shush them, bribe them, and rush them through dinner and into bed. We are pros at triage, at pushing through the emotional outbursts, at sweeping it all forward and keeping it together. But this night we didn't hush or rush or sweep or swoop in for the save. We just let it drop. Even more, we joined in the meltdown. It was like the usually sturdy tabletop fell out and all the plates just shattered to the floor. We simply let all the negativity surface. Finally. Like our family had made an unconscious agreement to see the breaking through — for once. It was terrifying. And we did it.

All the tears came and all the ugly anger and rank resentments. All the toxic heartbreak and dynamics. It all surfaced in full fanfare. And we just saw it through. The meltdown must have lasted a good hour. Until slowly one child after another gathered in our bedroom. The tears of pain turned to tears of futility — the tears of just surrendering to it all. And then the hugs started. And then the processing, the sharing, and the wonder.

One of the kids reported a lightning strike of insight. They had finally understood a dynamic that had been happening since they were three years old. Three years old! They were never able to articulate it until that fateful night. A total breakthrough. Another kid uncovered a core hurt they had been nursing for months and probably forever. They finally shared it with us. We listened and held it with love and watched the healing unfold like a flower before our eyes.

The whole scene was truly hard core. That is, it revealed the hard stuff that sits at the core of our family dynamic. Usually we skate along placidly on the outer layers, but that night we let it crack open. And precisely because it all came up, we were able to hold all those deep broken places and transform them into the alchemy of connection and love.

It was the best psychological cliché of a breakdown that turns into a breakthrough.

It was the much-needed prelude to our incredible bat mitzvah weekend. It was the real mazal tov. An unexpected joy born of pain. A turning point. A next step. An arrival. Even more exquisite than all the pretty party lights and ceremony and song to come. This was the new song of the small tribe of our family. This flawed Shabbat gave us a very real taste of what was so "very good" about our family.

It was our family toiling away at that quintessential human act of perfecting. And it was every bit as perfect as the perfect bat mitzvah the next week. That night was the new song of the small tribe of our family. As our bat mitzvah girl said so wisely, "Sometimes you just need to fight a little bit more to really love each other."

We all experience so many challenges, so much heartbreak. Reminding ourselves that there is a rhyme and reason behind it all helps us push through the hardships and transform them into growth. This is the path of being flawesome — and it is a "very good" path indeed.

קַוֵּה אֶל־יְהֹוָה חֲזַק וְיַאֲמֵץ לִבֶּךָ וְקַוֵּה אֶל־יְהֹוָה

PUT YOUR HOPE IN GOD, BE STRONG AND OF GOOD COURAGE, AND PUT YOUR HOPE IN GOD. —PSALMS 27:14

וְתִמְלֹךְ אַרְצֵנוּ מִלֵּמֵד וְתִתֶּן־לָנוּ אַחֲרִית וְתִקְוָה

FILL OUR COUNTRY WITH LEARNERS AND GIVE US ULTIMATE SUCCESS TOWARD A FUTURE OF HOPE —TALMUD BERACHOT 16B

תִּקְוָה

וְיֵשׁ־תִּקְוָה לְאַחֲרִיתֵךְ נְאֻם־יְהֹוָה וְשָׁבוּ בָנִים לִגְבוּלָם

THERE IS HOPE FOR YOUR FUTURE, DECLARES GOD; MAY ALL THE CHILDREN [HOSTAGES] BE RETURNED TO THEIR COUNTRY —JEREMIAH 31:17

אַךְ לֵאלֹהִים דּוֹמִּי נַפְשִׁי כִּי־מִמֶּנּוּ תִּקְוָתִי

QUIET MY SOUL FOR GOD, FROM WHOM COMES MY HOPE —PSALMS 62:6

BEING AN AGENT OF
HOPE

Leaders, sages, and activists have all emphasized the centrality of hope for a life well lived.

Eli Wiesel, Holocaust survivor and Nobel Peace Prize recipient, was a living testament to the power of hope in the face of anguish:

We must hope in spite of despair, because of our despair; we must not give despair the victory. I do not believe the world is learning. And I cannot hide from that fact. And yet, I do not believe in despair. People speak of a leap of faith. I believe we require a leap of hope .... When the writer Tristan Bernard was arrested by the Gestapo, his wife noticed him smiling. She asked him why, and he replied, "Until now, I lived in fear; now I shall live in hope."

Wiesel goes on to say:

When two people come together to listen, to learn from each other, there is hope. This is where humanity begins, where peace begins, where dignity begins: in a small gesture of respect in listening .... Hope is a choice, and it is a gift we give to one another. It can be absurd. It does not rely on facts. It is simply a choice. Once you make that choice, to create hope, then you can look at evil without flinching, without falling. And this is the first step to fighting it, to protesting it.[140]

Elie Wiesel's sense of hope seems to be in keeping with many other Jewish teachers. First, we turn to Rabbi Jonathan Sacks, who explains hope by contrasting it with optimism:

These two concepts, often confused, are in fact utterly different. Optimism is the belief that things will get better. Hope is the belief that, together, we can make things better. Optimism is a passive virtue, hope an active one. It takes no courage — only a certain naivety — to be an optimist. It takes great courage to sustain hope.[141]

---

140 Ariel Burger, *Witness: Lessons from Elie Wiesel's Classroom*, New York: Houghton Mifflin Harcourt Publishing Company, 2018, p. 184 and 186.

141 "Time as a Narrative of Hope," *The Jonathan Sacks Haggada*, Jerusalem: Maggid, 2013. p. 102.

What can nurture the courage to sustain hope? In his book *Future Tense*, Rabbi Sacks explains the importance of focusing on the future and of practices that strengthen one's resolve to be an agent of hope:

> Human beings are the only life form capable of using the future tense. Only beings who can imagine the world other than it is are capable of freedom. And if we are free, the future is open, dependent on us. We can know the beginning of our story but not the end. That is why, as God is about to take the Israelites from slavery to freedom, God tells Moses that His name is "I will be what I will be[142]..."

> Judaism is a religion of details, but we miss the point if we do not sometimes step back and see the larger picture. To be a Jew is to be an agent of hope in a world serially threatened by despair. Every ritual, every mitzvah, every syllable of the Jewish story, every element of Jewish law, is a protest against escapism, resignation or the blind acceptance of fate. Judaism is a sustained struggle, the greatest ever known, against the world that is, in the name of the world that could be, should be, but is not yet.[143]

Commentary on ancient talmudic wisdom expands on what being an agent of hope entails. The Talmud teaches that after death a Heavenly Court will ask us a succinct list of questions, including: Did you look out for salvation?[144] This line is explained by Rabbi Abraham Isaac HaKohen Kook, Israel's pre-state first chief rabbi, who served in that capacity before the state was founded: "Regarding the hope which throbs in the heart of every Jew from generation to generation for salvation and redemption, our sages used the term look-out, *tzipita*, not the term hope, *kivita*. The role of a look-out person is to alert others to each event and to mobilize them to take action."[145]

---

142 Exodus 3:14.

143 Jonathan Sacks, *Future Tense*, London, England: Hodder & Stoughton, 2009, p. 251-252.

144 Babylonian Talmud Shabbat 31a.

145 *Maamarei Ra'ayah — Kodesh ve'Chol b'Techiyat Yisrael*, from the journal HaHed, 5691.

Rabbi Kook implies that hope is not about mere aspiration, mindset, or optimism, but rather about taking action to make a difference. Hope includes studying the problems around us and activating ourselves and others to address them. He closes by saying: "It is our responsibility to be on the lookout to leverage every [difficult] event on earth, so that through such events salvation can spring forth."

Time and time again from ancient history to current events the Jewish sages call on us to become masters of hope in the face of challenges. It is no wonder that the Israeli anthem is *Hativka* — "The Hope." Hope is a mainstay that has sustained the Jewish people and its spirit of living wondrously. May this spirit and the wisdom born from millennia of weathering challenges continue to enable humanity to navigate through a storm-tossed world.

The following three chapters explore three aspects of being an agent of hope: taking leadership, being a source of inspiration by infusing life with meaning, and contributing to a better future.

TAKING

LEADERSHIP

The Art and Practice of Living Wondrously

The year 70 BCE marked a turning point for Jewish leadership. With Jerusalem in flames and the Romans besieging the city, the Jews within its walls knew they were facing death. In the mayhem, one leader took a courageous risk that ultimately led to one of the most impressive transformations ever documented, one that saved the Jewish people — and, later, his top students articulated five principles that stand at the core of effective leadership to this day.

Rabbi Yochanan ben Zakkai, was this great leader. He recognized that the (Second) Temple's destruction was at hand and fashioned a plan. He had his disciples hide him in a coffin and smuggle him out of the city for alleged burial. Once out, he was brought to none other than Vespasian, the Roman commander of the enemy forces. Rabbi Yochanan confidently informed the commander that he, Vespasian, was about to become the next emperor of Rome. And, indeed, a messenger then approached, announcing that Vespasian had just been named emperor. Understandably impressed by the remarkable prediction, Vespasian asked the rabbi what he wanted — and Rabbi Yochanan replied: "Give me Yavne and its sages."

Vespasian agreed, seeing no harm in the humble petition. Little did he know that this agreement would ultimately lead to the Jews outliving the Roman Empire by thousands of years.

Rabbi Yochanan and a group of rabbinic colleagues retreated to Yavne, a small town on the Mediterranean coast. There they reconstituted Jewish leadership. They transitioned Jewish practice from being structured around the Temple and its priestly rites to being more enduringly mobile, leading to the Judaism we know today.

Rabbi Yochanan ben Zakkai's students took on the mantle of leadership from him. His challenge to his five star students was to "explore and envision" a path of leadership, "the right way to which any person should adhere" if they seek to serve God and reach their potential. Each gave a short response. The principles they communicated, which were recorded in the Mishnah,[146] align

---

146 Pirkei Avot 2:13.

with best practices today and offer guidance for soulful leadership:[147]

Rabbi Eliezer said: A good eye

Have a positive outlook. Frame situations with hope to highlight opportunities, draw out the best in others, and make the best of situations. Affirm strengths. Spotlight the success of others. Compassionately attend to fears and triggers — both yours and those of others.

Rabbi Yehoshua said: A good companion

Maintain good connections; value relationships. Foster trust to cultivate allies. Recognize the good and offer appreciation. Acknowledge, apologize, and address mistakes so you and others can learn from them and deepen relationships. Give and receive feedback effectively. Mentor others, elevating their knowledge and skills.[148] Obtain a spiritual mentor.[149]

Rabbi Yose said: A good neighbor

Manage conflict. When addressing discordant interests, strive to highlight underlying values. Pause in the face of any upset to buy yourself time, then listen and understand before responding. Integrate conflicting perspectives in a disagreement, balancing empathy and assertiveness to synergize different interests and create new opportunities for growth. Identify a shared vision to create a culture of belonging around it and use that to inspire with purpose.

Rabbi Shimon said: One who sees what is emerging

Pay attention to changing needs and emergent challenges and opportunities. Be prepared to overcome inertia, diagnosing and adapting to new realities — including shifting goals and strategies

---

147 Introduction to a curriculum: "Soulful Leadership" by Ronit Ziv-Kreger (2014).

148 Pirkei Avot 1:1.

149 Pirkei Avot 1:6.

when needed. Develop resilience. Foster curiosity. Attend to adaptive opportunities. Mobilize action around a shared vision.

Rabbi Elazar [ben Arach] said: A good heart

Nurture your core and your intuition with a regular practice such as prayer, meditation, journaling, or experiencing nature. Cultivate presence and strengthen your capacity to face and recover from intense experiences. Kindle joy. Celebrate successes, even small wins. Manage your boundaries; say no so you can say yes to what is most meaningful. Identify and leverage your personal strengths.

These five responses offer ancient context for — and, to some degree, align with — this chapter's contemporary articles, written by experts. Dr. Erica Brown, echoing the recommendation to be a "good companion" and a "good neighbor," explores listening as a leadership tool. Discussing different types of listening, she focuses especially on sacred listening — understanding, connecting, and hearing the divine spark in someone else's words — and how we can practice becoming more proficient with this important tool. Dr. Bill Robinson, in line with "a good eye" and "a good heart," tackles leading a family toward hope by becoming attuned to the world around us. Telling our children stories of overcoming familial adversity or personal failure can instill in them faith in their own abilities — not necessarily their current abilities, but rather what they can become through practice. Dr. Ronald Heifetz and Netaly Ophir Flint, reflecting "one who sees what is emerging" and "being a good neighbor," present central tenets of adaptive leadership for navigating the challenges of our era. They underscore that leadership belongs not only to those in positions of authority and offer guidance for how to mobilize others for good.

To Be Heard and to Be Seen: Leadership and Sacred Listening

Dr. Erica Brown

Erica Brown, PhD, is vice provost for values and leadership at Yeshiva University and founding director of its Rabbi Lord Jonathan Sacks Herenstein Center for Values and Leadership. She previously served as director of the Mayberg Center for Jewish Education and Leadership. The recipient of the 2009 Covenant Award and renowned author of thirteen books, her latest book is The Torah of Leadership: Essays on the Weekly Parsha.

Melissa Daimler's 2016 article in Harvard Business Review is titled, "Listening Is an Overlooked Leadership Tool." Listening as a skill is often neglected in favor of developing technical leadership skills like fundraising, reading budgets, or mastering software, and the skills of presence like public speaking or social media optimization. The focus remains only on getting the message of the organization or cause out. But listening is vitally important. This overlooked leadership tool may actually be the most important asset in any leader's skillset. When you listen with full presence, curiosity, and compassion, without judgment, you help bring out someone's light, the part of them that shines and often resides within and waits to feel safe before finding outward expression.

I'd like to call this particular kind of focus *sacred listening*, which is listening with the goal of understanding, connecting, and hearing the divine spark in someone else's words. It is not transactional in the leadership sense of listening to glean how to enhance one's position or status or organizational importance. It is listening purely to see and to honor someone else's humanity — the place where one soul touches another through the gift of silent attention.

> *When have you felt listened to in this way?*
> *When have you seen someone attend to*
> *another with such sacred listening?*

Leaders who practice sacred listening can work wonders in a boardroom or behind the closed doors of an office, yet we lead in so many other spaces that also require this type of spiritual intention: in family rooms and kitchens, in sanctuaries and soup kitchens, in classrooms and the hallways of power. Just think of all the people in your family and immediate circle who might benefit from being truly heard and seen by you, who would shine because of the light you place on them through your attentiveness. Each child. Each parent. Each spouse. Each friend.

Judaism places great importance on the value of listening. Our central statement of monotheism, and one of the most well-known verses of Jewish prayer, is all about listening: "Hear, O Israel: The Lord our God, the Lord is one."[150] It asks that we listen to our truths and integrate them into our lives. God listens too; throughout the book of Psalms we reference God's capacity to listen as an aspect of healing and solace: "I love the Lord, for He heard my voice; He heard my cry for mercy. Because He turned His ear to me, I will call on Him as long as I live."[151] These verses speak to a lifelong relationship built out of the power of hearing a voice and a cry. It reminds us that when someone does turn an ear to us, we see that person as someone we can turn to again and again.

We anthropomorphize God as having ears as a way of viewing God as the ultimate Listener: "In my distress I called to the Lord; I cried to my God for help … my cry came before Him, into His ears."[152] We don't only cry before God with the expectation of sacred listening; we also make requests and state our needs: "In the morning, Lord, you hear my voice; in the morning I lay my requests before you and wait expectantly."[153] We realize that even though our requests may not be fulfilled — the answer may be *no* — there is value in the articulation of our needs and solace in the knowledge that they have landed somewhere. Someone has heard us. Someone sees us for who we are, in our joy, in our pain, and in our neediness.

---

150 Deuteronomy 6:4.

151 Psalm 116:1-2.

152 Psalm 18:6.

153 Psalm 5:4.

Leaders cannot always fix problems. But leaders, in imitation of God, can always listen attentively. Listening does not solve problems. It cannot repair wounds. It does not resolve complaints. But there is much that sacred listening *can* do. Listening can make followers feel whole and respected. Listening can help dignify the issues and difficulties of volunteers and professionals. Listening can build trust. Listening can strengthen relationships. Listening can take the sting out of problems and soften the hurt of wounds. While it cannot resolve complaints, sacred listening can minimize their significance.

The very act of intentional listening creates deep trust. When someone listens well, we are open to making ourselves more vulnerable and opening up more. In her article "The Art of Listening," essayist Megan Minutillo describes her parents' gift of learning about people quickly and deeply; they have the capacity to take in others fully. Those who speak to them want to reveal more of themselves:

> They have an uncanny ability to connect with people, and it doesn't matter if you've known them for fifty years or five minutes — everyone who meets them tells them their life story. And they do so because they listen. They listen without judgment, or pretense, or ulterior motive. They listen — not to indoctrinate, come up with a witty retort, or insert their own story.
>
> They listen so that whoever is sharing their words, hearts, and stories, feels seen, heard, and loved.[154]

The incremental trust-building that happens with genuine, sacred listening is especially necessary when someone is hurt, has experienced trauma, or feels misunderstood, which so often happens in leadership situations. We find a tender example of just this kind of attention in the book of Ruth: Ruth, a poor outsider who had converted to Judaism and moved to the Land of Israel, feels marginalized and excluded. Boaz, a spiritual role model and wealthy landowner, shows Ruth grace. Ruth, used to being invisible, feels unworthy of such gentleness:

> "Why are you so kind as to single me out, when I am a foreigner?" Boaz said in reply, "I have been told of all that you did for your mother-in-law after the death of your husband, how you left your father and mother and the land of your birth and came to a people you had not known before. May the Lord reward your deeds. May you have a full recompense from the Lord, the God of Israel, under whose wings you have sought refuge!" She answered,

---

154 Megan Minutillo, "The Art of Listening," medium.com, October 13, 2020.

"You are most kind, my lord, to comfort me and to speak gently to your maidservant — though I am not so much as one of your maidservants."[155]

Boaz had heard of Ruth's sacrifices. He named them, and honored her by repeating them. He listened carefully to her story and, as a result, gave her a renewed sense of dignity. We all need a Boaz in our lives.

Leaders often listen with judgment. They have ulterior motives: They listen because they want to raise money, or recruit, or sell an idea, or generate awareness. Or they listen so they can find an opening to tell their own story. But that kind of listening is not listening at all. Think of the best listener you know. Describe that person. Chances are that person is also highly curious, and asks a lot of good questions. If you want to get good at listening, you might think of your leadership job as being on a series of interviews and you're the interviewer. That's a privileged role. Get good enough at it and people might list you as the best listener they know.

So how does a leader become a sacred listener?

Listening Is a Discipline

We humans have been talkers since our earliest days. We might take classes in speaking, but never in listening. Our daily conversations are often examples of just how underdeveloped our listening skills are. Ever call someone to share your pain and suddenly find yourself at the Suffering Olympics?

"I just came back from the dentist. I had a cavity."

"That's nothing. I had a root canal last week."

You hang up the phone feeling invalidated, perhaps angry at yourself for even sharing your problem.

Or maybe you wanted to share good news, but as soon as you mentioned it you were interrupted by someone who was so excited that she didn't let you finish.

"So our daughter just got engaged ..."

"Mazal tov! When's the wedding?"

You had more to say about your own happiness, but got quickly cut off.

Listening requires discipline and intention. The psychoanalyst Erich Fromm,

---

155 Ruth 2:10-13.

who wrote a book called *The Art of Listening*, called it an *art form*.[156] Deborah Tannen, a professor of linguistics, explains why listening is as difficult as it is. It's really two activities: "... pay attention not only to the *message* (the meaning of the words), but also the *metamessage* (what it says about the relationship that you say these words in this way at this time). We often think we are responding to the *message*, but, in fact, we are responding to the *metamessage*: tone of voice, unspoken implications."[157]

Yet out of our enthusiasm to connect, we often don't allow others to finish a sentence. We regard a pause as an opportunity to jump in, to add, or to expand. We feel obliged to fill in the natural lulls in conversation and believe that not doing so creates awkward moments rather than a time to process and understand what's been said.

In her article "New York Conversational Style," Tannen researches and discusses, in part, the speech patterns of Jews as a subset of New Yorkers. The way we speak to each other is often socially conditioned and constructed; we adhere to cultural norms even if everyone within a demographic or ethnic group does not conform to these conventions. Tannen describes a typical Jewish conversational pattern as "high involvement concentric overlapping."[158] One person speaks, and the listener speaks over that person in response; each interrupts the other repeatedly but they are often unaware they are interrupting. Internally, they are just speaking.

In many leadership seminars I conduct, I give participants time to answer a personal question about their leadership style in writing. I then ask them to pair up with someone in the room they do not know or do not know well. Each participant has one uninterrupted minute to share what they've written. If they don't use their full minute, they are welcome to sit in silence or to go deeper into their answer than what they put on paper. I ask the listener in the pair to give the speaker the luxury of deep and engaged listening and invite them *not* to think about what they want to say in response. Just be there, fully and totally.

When the minute is up, I don't want participants to switch roles. I ask the listener to say one simple sentence: Tell me more. The speaker then gets an

156 Erich Fromm, *The Art of Listening*, New York: Continuum, 1994.

157 Marianna Pogosyan, PhD, "How We Talk and Listen Affects Our Relationships: Linguist Deborah Tannen shares insights into human communication," *Psychology Today*, July 27, 2018, www.psychologytoday.com/us/blog/between-cultures/201807/how-we-talk-and-listen-affects-our-relationships.

158 Deborah Tannen, "New York Conversational Style," International Journal of the Sociology of Language, 30, 1981: p. 133–149.

additional uninterrupted minute with which to respond. Only then, after two full minutes of one person talking, can they change roles.

Inevitably, when processing this exercise afterward, many listeners share how challenging it was to give even one minute of their full attention to someone else. Some say what a relief it was to be there in the shared space without worrying about what they were going to respond. The invitation not to think about a response helped them be fully present. One woman in a senior lay leadership position approached me sheepishly after a leadership seminar, berating herself: "I've always prided myself on being a good listener. I even *tell* people I'm a good listener — until just now. I realized how difficult it was for me to spend one minute listening to someone else." She did not realize just how much company she has.

> *Consider sharing this exercise with someone and using a timer to try it out, both as a listener and as a speaker.*

At an executive board meeting in an elegant art museum, I used the same technique to have board members discuss a difficult and controversial decision so each person, especially the introverts in the room, were able to voice an opinion and be heard. The whole exercise took just under five minutes. At the end of the evening, a veteran board member pointed to her conversational partner: "I'm embarrassed to say this, but the two of us have been sitting at meetings together for a while now but I learned more about her in those few minutes than I have in three years."

The easiest way to develop the discipline of sacred listening is literally one minute at a time. Try it. Time it. And if you want to deepen the bond, just say those three magic words — *tell me more* — and then sit back and relax into the gift of listening. As Tannen writes, "A perfectly tuned conversation is a vision of sanity — a ratification of one's way of being human and one's way in the world."[159]

Leadership Listening

Listening well is a tool for being a good human being. It's also critical for

---

159 Deborah Tannen, *That's Not What I Meant! How Conversational Style Makes or Breaks Relationships,* New York: William Morrow, 2011, p. 19.

emotionally intelligent leadership. We can think of listening within three general categories:

- *Informational listening* (listening to learn)
- *Critical listening* (listening to evaluate and analyze)
- *Therapeutic or empathetic listening* (listening to understand feeling and emotion)

As a leader, you have ample opportunities to engage in these three types of listening. Informational listening is important when considering new strategic options and learning about new technology or information-based skills. Leaders are thrown suggestions all the time. Critical listening enables leaders to evaluate new ideas and decide which to pursue and how to create more buy-in. But the kind of leadership listening that I've called *sacred* is the third category, therapeutic listening — the kind of listening that can be healing.

Leaders are constantly putting out fires, managing complaints, and solving problems. Often, as cheerleaders-in-chief, leaders try to protect or defend their causes and organizations by pushing back or resisting what they're hearing. When they do that, they simply make more work for themselves. Defensiveness does not, cannot, build trust. It only makes people feel unheard and undervalued. Many times critics have an agenda or an axe to grind. Leaders who are critical rather than empathic will make the situation worse. When someone has a complaint, try that uninterrupted minute, followed by *tell me more*, to de-escalate a situation and to honor the person's dignity, even if you cannot fix the problem.

We can divide sacred or therapeutic listening into two further categories: active listening and accountable listening. Active listening demonstrates that the person doing the listening is fully present at that moment. Accountable listening stretches into the future. Let's define and explain the terms.

Active listening indicates to the one speaking that you are attentive, hear what is being said, and can parrot what was said back to them. This involves not only speech but attentive body language, eye contact, and audial indicators that you are paying attention.

"We are way over budget and that's my fault."
"Sounds like you think the budget problems are all your fault."

or – if you want to vary the language:

"Sounds like you're blaming yourself for this problem."

Mirroring, a very effective technique, has the listener repeating one word of the speaker as a question.

"That meeting was really rough."

"Rough?"

"Yeah. All that arguing. It was pretty brutal."

"Brutal?"

"Honestly, I felt really bad about what I said."

These techniques may seem artificial at first, but with practice they become more normative and natural. They demonstrate to the speaker that a leader is checking in for meaning and understanding.

Accountable listening is listening with a sense of personal or professional responsibility to the future. For example, someone might say they are unwell. An accountable listener will not only listen clearly at the moment of this admission, but also inquire at a future date about the speaker's health. Leaders often hear volunteers, board members, professional staff, clients, donors, stakeholders, or customers share a piece of information about a need or want and follow up later with ideas, answers, or results. Following up makes a speaker feel particularly valued and important.

"I can't believe you remembered my birthday and sent a card."

"I am so touched that you called to find out how I'm doing. I feel much better."

"Thank you for your email. Even though it didn't resolve the problem I have, I appreciate that you looked into it and got back to me."

Categorizing different acts of listening and thinking about leadership within different frames of listening can help leaders pay more attention to their leadership style and work on their leadership deficiencies, experimenting with different techniques and evaluating the impact each has. Good leadership has an experimental quality that enables us to grow and develop; as the saying goes: What we pay attention to grows.

Pirkei Avot, an ancient anthology of rabbinic quotes, discusses qualities inherent to wisdom that are foundational to better leadership:

The wise person does not speak before one who is greater than he in wisdom; he does not interrupt his fellow's speech. He is not in a rush to reply. He asks what is relevant and replies to the point. He speaks of first things first and of last things last. Of what he has not heard he says, "I have not heard," and he acknowledges what is true.[160]

There is no interruption or rush to reply in the search for true wisdom. There is only sacred listening, the kind that leads to authentic and meaningful leadership.

---

160 Pirkei Avot 5:7.

Leading a Family Toward Hope

Dr. Bill Robinson

> *Dr. Bill Robinson is executive director at Na'aleh: The Hub for Leadership Learning. He was dean of the William Davidson Graduate School of Jewish Education at the Jewish Theological Seminary from 2014 to 2019.*

Is There Still Hope?

I have for many long years put my faith in the redemptive saying: The arc of the moral universe is long, but it bends toward justice. Yet, I am not so sure anymore. All around us, we see the emerging ecological collapse, a worldwide political turn to fascism, the destitution and struggles created by economic inequality, the uncertain threat (and, yes, the promise) of artificial intelligence, and everywhere spiritual malaise. Then, even more immediate to my (and perhaps your) life is the increase in anxiety among children and young adults. An honest accounting of our historical progress leads me to perceive, instead of a slow, inexorable advancement, a piling up of too much debris.

Though as a perpetual optimist and a parent, I cannot accept such a singularly despairing vision. Rather, I choose to see both the good and the bad of progress, even when the good is harder to notice. As the author and activist Rebecca Solnit asks: What might not have happened if we didn't put forth the effort to improve our world? "Young women often don't know that sexual harassment and date rape are new categories; most forget how much more toxic rivers like the Hudson once were; who talks about the global elimination of smallpox between 1967 and 1977?"[161] The world is filled with both devastation and renewal, and thus also despair and hope.

We live in a world in which each moment is filled with potential for further wreckage or repair. We have a choice to mindlessly contribute to the wreckage or intentionally work toward repair. This is how I understand leadership: as a choice to act with others in common purpose. Anyone can lead if they so choose, and

---

161 Rebecca Solnit, *Hope in the Dark: Untold Histories, Wild Possibilities,* Chicago: Haymarket Books, 2004, p. 71-72.

anyone can learn to lead better. But not everyone will become an effective and inspiring leader. In order to lead people along the path of hope and redemption, each of us must become attuned to the opportunities for repair that lie before us and learn to tell stories that inspire others to join us in this sacred endeavor.

First though, we need to accept that learning to lead better — like most else in life that doesn't come easy — involves lots of practice. In the book of Proverbs it is written: "Seven times the righteous person falls and rises, while the wicked are tripped by one misfortune."[162] A straightforward reading of this text may be that one who is righteous, unlike one who is wicked, will rise from misfortune. Another reading, which I prefer, is that through falling and rising, over and over again, a person becomes (more) righteous. We learn how to lead a life of repair through failing to do so. In the lingo of entrepreneurs, we learn to *fail forward*. This occurs when our failures lead us to shed old habits and strive to build better ones, when we replace myopic ways of seeing the world with those that reveal the daily possibilities of living virtuously. It is the way in which we and our children become more compassionate, curious, and courageous, as well as filled with hard-earned humility and well-deserved pride.

Attuning Ourselves and Our Children

When we fail in the process of becoming more righteous, our hearts soften and our minds open. And we pause before rising again. In the pause, we reflect on how we might rise differently, and how in rising we might align our actions toward fulfilling a vision of the world redeemed. We take a moment to become fully present, and in so doing we can pre-sense the emergent possibilities before us.

This involves attuning to the world around us. Consider the example of going to a classical music concert, particularly if it's your first time. As the orchestra begins to play, you hear a clamor of sounds coming all at once from the woodwinds, the strings, the brass, and the percussion. Then, as you continue to listen, you begin to hear the distinct sounds of different sections. You become conscious of melody, harmony, and repeating themes of the pieces. You can even begin to sense what comes next. We can learn to do this in our everyday lives.

To do so, however, we must first get out of our own heads. I know I can easily walk through my days absorbed by the thoughts inside my head, if I don't intentionally focus on the world around me. In the Torah, when Jacob left his family on his journey to his mother's brother, he stopped for the night to rest and

---

162 Proverbs 24:16.

he dreamed of angels ascending and descending a ladder. Upon awakening, he declared: "Surely God was in this place, and I, I did not know."[163] This is not the typical translation, but it is more faithful to the text, which includes both the word for *I* (*anochi*) and the words for *I did not know* (*lo yadati*). Why the repetition? It is to teach us that in order to make room for the Divine Other, we need to let go of our own ego. If we are too filled with ourselves, there is no room for God.[164] Similarly, in order to be fully present, to be able to pre-sense the possibilities for repair in the world, we need to get out of our own head.

When we attune to the world around us, we become more aware of both the beautiful rhythms of the world and its discordant notes. In this way, when we rise we sense the possibilities for repair — where life is not yet thriving and where together with others we can make a difference.

For instance, global hunger and homelessness pervade our neighborhoods, even if we haven't yet noticed. There is work to be done! It is unlikely that we can solve global hunger or homelessness in the immediacy of rising — but we can volunteer for organizations that feed people and help families to find housing. We can donate to advocacy organizations working toward systemic change, and we can give *tzedakah* (righteous charity) to the homeless person on the street. We can support efforts at long-term change and help those immediately around us to rise up when they have fallen. A multitude of opportunities are before us, though we often go through the world unaware of them until we set aside our own concerns and attune to those of others.

Moreover, we get better at leadership the more we practice. The twelfth-century Jewish philosopher Maimonides asserted that the primary purpose of giving *tzedakah* is to develop the virtue of generosity within us. Thus, he states, it is better to give small amounts multiple times than one large, single contribution.[165] Ideally, make giving and leadership into a daily practice.

Attuning can also change us. When we notice the beauty in the world and become aware of discordance and despair, a sense of responsibility rises up within us. We feel the urge to respond virtuously. We just need to see through the detritus of the modern world that has dulled our senses. It may be as simple as noticing a swan "rising in the silvery air — an armful of white blossoms, a perfect commotion of silk and linen," as the poet Mary Oliver offers. She asks us: "And have

---

163 Genesis 28:16.

164 From Lawrence Kushner, *The River of Light: Spirituality, Judaism, and the Evolution of Consciousness*, Chappaqua, NY: Rossel Books, 1981.

165 From Maimonides' commentary on Pirkei Avot.

you too finally figured out what beauty is for? And have you changed your life?[166]

We can strengthen our and our children's capacity for attunement through daily practices such as listening to pieces of classical or jazz music. Similarly, Judaism contains an aspirational practice of saying one hundred blessings a day.[167] We can begin each morning with the *Modeh Ani* (Grateful Am I) prayer[168] and end each day with recounting something we are particularly thankful for. But one hundred each day?! It requires that we learn to pay close attention to what's around us so we have many opportunities to bless the beautiful, the good, and the new. This could simply involve evening walks with our children, where we might see an unusual sight such as a swan or a small act of kindness. Maybe make a game of it: How many opportunities can you find to say a blessing? The author and poet Marcia Falk offers a creative, spiritual version of the *Shehecheyanu*,[169] a blessing for almost any occasion: Let us bless the flow of life that revives us, sustains us, and brings us to this time.[170]

> *Consider keeping a journal — not a diary for recording events but rather a journal for attuning to what you care about and find meaningful in your day. Notice what blessings you see, what you can celebrate about the day, and what you'd like to evaluate. Attune to what you do, how you do it, and why. Attune to the people around you, what they do, how they do it, and what you can learn from them. What steps can you take to strengthen the people and things that matter most to you?*

166 Mary Oliver, *"The Swan,"* in *Swan: Poems and Prose Poems*, Boston: Beacon Press, 2010.

167 Menachot 43b.

168 The traditional English version of this blessing is: "I thank You, living and enduring Majesty, for You have graciously returned my soul within me. Great is Your faithfulness."

169 The traditional, English version of this blessing is: "Blessed are You, Adonai our God, Majesty of the world, who has kept us alive, sustained us, and brought us to this season."

170 Marcia Falk, *Night of Beginnings: A Passover Haggadah*, Lincoln: University of Nebraska Press, 2022.

The Power of Storytelling

This work is hard and hope easily falters without a sense of collective achievement and future possibility. We need to believe that our daily actions have historical resonance and sustainable impact. This is where the power of storytelling comes in. It connects our (otherwise) seemingly meaningless daily efforts to a larger pattern of significance. It inspires us to continue the work, to rise up again after each fall.

Consider the Jewish stories you may have heard growing up: the Passover story of the Israelites' escape from slavery and their journey through the wilderness to the Promised Land, or Rachel's more personal and ultimately tragic struggle to secure love, children, and prosperity for her family. And then there are popular American stories we may have read or watched in the theater, such as *Harry Potter, Game of Thrones*, or *Star Wars*. In all these stories, people seek to overcome the daunting challenges before them. In the process, they discover who they are, where they came from, and what they are truly capable of. Sometimes, though, this needs to be revealed in conversation. For example, we might ask our children: What do you think Harry or Ron or Hermione learned when they at first failed? How do you think their struggles help them to learn what they were truly capable of? Can you think of a time when you felt like them?

We can also share our own family stories that connect our children to their particular history: stories of immigrant struggle or overcoming personal tragedy, stories of a neighbor's act of kindness that changed a life. We may be hesitant to tell our children stories of familial adversity or personal failure. But these stories will instill in them hope amid a broken world and faith in their own abilities — not necessarily as they are now, but what they can become through practice. The best stories for doing so are what the psychologist Marshall Duke calls "oscillating stories" that share the achievements and the setbacks of your family.[171]

The power of stories to sustain us and carry us through, especially when we may feel overwhelmed and doubt our own abilities, is central to Jewish tradition.

> When the great Rabbi Israel Baal Shem Tov saw misfortune threatening the Jews, it was his custom to go into a certain part of the forest to meditate. There he would light a fire, say a special prayer, and the miracle would be accomplished and the misfortune averted. Later when his disciple, the celebrated Magid of Mezritch, had occasion, for the same reason, to intercede with Heaven,

---

171 Reference to Marshall Duke's work on storytelling can be found in Bruce Feiler's "The Stories that Bind Us," *The New York Times*, March 15, 2013.

he would go to the same place in the forest and say: "Master of the Universe, listen! I do not know how to light the fire, but I am still able to say the prayer." And again the miracle would be accomplished. Still later, Rabbi Moshe-Leib of Sasov, in order to save his people once more, would go into the forest and say: "I do not know how to light the fire, I do not know the prayer, but I know the place and this must be sufficient." It was sufficient and the miracle was accomplished. Then it fell to Rabbi Israel of Rizhyn to overcome misfortune. Sitting in his armchair, his head in his hands, He spoke to God: "I am unable to light the fire and I do not know the prayer; I cannot even find the place in the forest. All I can do is to tell the story, and this must be sufficient." And it was sufficient.[172]

This traditional Hasidic tale is at once a story of loss and a story of hope in continuing the journey. We may not have the power that our ancestors did, but we can tell our stories and that will have to suffice.

What is a story you find deeply meaningful?
Imagine how you could craft it and find
opportunities to share it with others?

We will need many stories to bend the arc of history. In Judaism, we have a practice that involves offering small interpretations of traditional texts, often through relating personal stories, called informally *drashing* (from the word *lidrosh*, to seek). My first encounter with *drash* storytelling as part of Torah learning came from the poet and scholar Alicia Ostriker. I recall a story she shared about a group of women who were studying Torah together. They were reading the Akedah, the sacrifice of Isaac, in which "early next morning Abraham saddled his donkey and took with him two of his servants and his son Isaac."[173] The Torah doesn't mention Abraham having a conversation with his wife, Sarah, before he leaves on this journey. And notably, soon afterward Sarah dies without seemingly seeing Abraham again. So what happened in between the lines of Torah? What did Sarah say or feel? Her words are left unrecorded.

Under Ostriker's facilitation, the women explored when they have felt like

---

172   Elie Weisel, *The Gates of the Forest: A Novel*, New York: Holt, Rinehart, and Winston, 1966.

173   Genesis 22:3.

Sarah, and how their own experiences may illuminate the meaning of the text. The emotionally fraught example the women gave was the experience of placing their child on a school bus for the first time, when suddenly their child was beyond their control and care. Yet it was also a moment of trust and growth, as well as a connection among generations of parents. Decades later, I still recall this creative *drash* and my own difficult experience of doing the same with my oldest child. In weaving traditional text and personal narrative together, the singular moments of our lives are woven into a larger narrative of our people's continuing covenantal journey.

We Each Have a Unique Responsibility

Each moment of our lives offers opportunities to lead in ways that move us closer to healing our souls, our communities, and the world. Each day we have a choice between hope and hopelessness.

I learned from my teacher Rabbi Irving (Yitz) Greenberg that we are all created in the divine image (*b'tzelem Elokim*), and thus each of us is born equal, unique, and infinitely valuable. Each of us is also born with the divine capacities needed to fulfill our covenantal responsibility to repair the world.[174] Rav Sholom Noach Berezovsky, the Slonimer Rebbe, took this traditional Jewish teaching further.[175] He taught that because we are each unique, each of us has a unique mission to fulfill in the world. No one else could fulfill this mission, so if we don't it will be left undone. The good news is that we are also endowed with the potential capacity to fulfill it.

Discovering our personal mission and helping our children to do so can be a lifetime project. While we can learn how to lead our lives from the stories of others, the story of our own life will be unique. In the end, what matters most is that we have led our lives righteously in our own way.

Another Hasidic tale relates this simple and hard truth of life and leadership:

As he lay dying, Rabbi Zusya began to cry uncontrollably. His students tried to comfort him. They asked, "Rabbi, why do you weep? You are almost as wise as Moses, you are almost as hospitable as Abraham, and surely heaven will judge you favorably." Zusya answered them: "It is true. When I get to heaven, I won't

---

174 For more on Rabbi Greenberg's thought see his book *The Triumph of Life: A Narrative Theology of Judaism*, Philadelphia: The Jewish Publication Society, 2024.

175 Rav Sholom Noach Berezovsky, *Nesivos Shalom*, 2013.

worry so much if God asks me, 'Zusya, why were you not more like Abraham?' or 'Zusya, why were you not more like Moses?' I know I would be able to answer these questions. After all, I was not given the righteousness of Abraham or the faith of Moses but I tried to be both hospitable and thoughtful. But what will I say when God asks me, 'Zusya, why were you not more like Zusya?'"[176]

The ultimate practice of leadership is knowing and living your unique responsibility in the world while walking arm in arm with others toward a larger, common purpose. In this way, helping each other rise when we fall, attuning to one another's unique concerns and contributions, and telling stories of our shared journey — together leading toward hope — will the arc of the moral universe eventually bend toward justice.

---

176 Martin Buber, *Tales of the Hasidim*, New York: Schocken Books, 1991.

Embracing Adaptive Leadership for Navigating the Challenges of Our Time

Dr. Ronald Heifetz and Netaly Ophir Flint

Dr. Ronald Heifetz, Founder of the Center for Public Leadership and King Hussein bin Talal Senior Lecturer in Public Leadership at the John F. Kennedy School of Government, Harvard University, has advised heads of governments, businesses, international organizations, and nonprofits for four decades. He is one of the world's foremost experts on the practice and teaching of leadership.

Netaly Ophir Flint is a partner at Konu, an international leadership development and organizational change firm, where she works with individuals, executives, and organizations to help them adapt and thrive as they tackle complex challenges in a rapidly changing world. Formerly, Netaly served as CEO of the Reut Group, an influential strategy and leadership think tank based in Tel Aviv.

The Urgency of Leadership Today

We are living through a moment of profound complexity. In a post-October 7 world, our Jewish communities face unprecedented challenges — crucial disagreements on how best to secure the future of Israel, a resurgence of antisemitism on our streets and university campuses, deepening divisions between Israeli and Diaspora Jewry, as well as global issues like the climate crisis and eroding democracies. The fabric of Jewish unity is being tested by the conflicting visions of Israeli society, lack of a shared commitment to find a path toward peace, waves of hatred, political unrest, and societal breakdowns, as we've witnessed firsthand in the streets of Tel Aviv where Netaly lives and works and in the protests across American campuses like Harvard where Ron works.

As these challenges grow, there is a palpable yearning within our communities for leadership that can rise to the occasion — leadership that can unite rather than divide; lead with strategic imagination, discipline, and empathy; and mobilize people to confront tough trade-offs and realities. Yet paradoxically, as the problems around us intensify, it often feels as if the political echelons that once provided stability and guidance appear overwhelmed and ill-equipped to navigate the complexities of our time. Against this backdrop, we hear many of our clients and students asking: How can we address these problems we're witnessing every day in our work, homes, and communities? And what can we do to step up?

To cultivate this kind of leadership, we must first recognize that the old models of authority, rooted in top-down expertise and control, are no longer sufficient. What we need now — more than ever — is a form of leadership that mobilizes widespread learning across the divisions and factions in Israel and within the Jewish world, fosters productive debate and collaboration so that we discover better options, gets our people ready to embrace complexity and risk, and encourages resilience in the face of our demanding and changing world. We believe the Adaptive Leadership framework provides key principles that can help guide us through these turbulent times.

Leadership and Authority Are Not the Same Thing

One of the most common mistakes we see people make is to conflate leadership with authority. If you step back and think about it, we all know intuitively that leadership and authority are not the same thing — all of us have seen people gain senior positions of authority who do not practice leadership, and we all know people who have practiced leadership without gaining a senior position of authority. We saw this during the COVID-19 pandemic when all sorts of everyday people around the world stepped up without being elected, appointed, or anointed to meet the challenge of providing leadership for their families, classrooms, businesses, and government agencies to keep the death rate low, while others misled their people toward tragically high death rates. We also saw many heads of governments lead adaptively and many mislead their people.

Effective leadership isn't about holding a formal position of power but about mobilizing people to address tough challenges that require their own responsibility and problem-solving attention — challenges that cannot be offloaded to authorities to simply "fix the problem." These adaptive challenges demand that we learn new ways, sifting through what's precious and essential to conserve, what must be given up, and what innovations will enable us to take the best of our tradition into the future.

We don't need leadership when the problems we face are amenable to authoritative expertise. We need simply to hire and elect the right people. But when challenges are adaptive, they demand a different kind of response. That's when we need leadership. Authorities often fail to practice leadership because they get stuck in treating all problems as if they were technical, amenable to authoritative solutions from on high, rather than getting the relevant people to engage with the problem. Leadership is about mobilizing people to face adaptive challenges that require new learning, changes in values, or shifts in our behavior. It's about helping people figure out how to adapt together to changing conditions, especially when no one person has the right answers or a clear solution. In other words, leadership is an activity, a practice, and thus anyone can choose to exercise leadership — including YOU — even if you don't hold a formal position of authority.

There are key differences between leading from a high position of authority and leading either from below or outside the social system. Authority brings certain kinds of power and resources, but it also brings certain kinds of limitations, like having to meet a large number of expectations to stay in power. Practically speaking, one has to analyze how these resources and limitations shape the way one goes about exercising leadership, depending on one's location in the social system, one's authority or lack of it. In our books, articles, online courses, and consulting work, we analyze these resources and constraints and how to operate with and without them.

The key insight here is that leadership is not the domain of the few. As the late Rabbi Jonathan Sacks wrote, we are called to be a nation of leaders.[177]

If you feel a call to exercise leadership on a challenge your family or community is facing, here are some of the basic components of adaptive leadership to keep in mind:

Stay Diagnostic and Keep the Work at the Center

The most common failures in leadership are diagnostic failures. There's often so much pressure to solve a problem that we tend to jump into action without clearly understanding the nature of the challenge at hand. A common mistake is to treat adaptive challenges — which require new learning, innovation, and changes in perspective — as if they were technical problems that can be solved by applying existing knowledge or authoritative expertise.

---

177 See, for example, https://rabbisacks.org/covenant-conversation/yitro/a-nation-of-leaders/.

For example, responding to a sudden rise in antisemitic incidents isn't just about increasing security or changing laws (technical solutions); it also requires addressing the underlying societal factors fueling hatred from various and very different sources. These are adaptive challenges in nature, not only for the people across the political spectrum harboring antisemitic views, but also for those of us who must come to terms with the moral and strategic conflicts in our own Jewish community and Israeli society as we wrestle with the sharp differences among us in how to "be a light unto the nations" – to realize the values of democracy, justice, and peace.

We have an extraordinary tradition upon which to draw. The Jewish community began to develop a culture of adaptability with examples of adaptive leadership since our earliest days. Adaptive challenges are as old as we are. They leap off the pages of the Tanakh, Talmud, and the writings of subsequent generations. The Five Books of Moses are filled with powerful illustrations that not only distinguish leadership from authority, but also explore the demands of taking a slave-minded people and turning them into a self-governing community, with faith in an ineffable God. Our response to the destruction of the Second Temple in 70 CE again illustrated our adaptability in developing answers in our rabbinic academies to the key questions: What's essential, what's expendable, and what innovations will enable our people to survive and thrive in the diaspora.[178]

In contemporary Jewish life, we often face similar situations where what appears to be a technical problem is actually an adaptive challenge. For instance, the challenge of engaging young Jews in community life might seem like a technical problem solvable by offering more programs or modernizing facilities. However, the real adaptive challenge often lies in helping young people find meaningful connections to their heritage in a rapidly changing world, which requires rethinking certain fundamental aspects of how we approach Jewish identity and community.

By staying diagnostic and recognizing the true nature of the challenges we face, a parent or teacher or rabbi can choose to guide their communities through transformative experiences that address root issues rather than just symptoms. This might involve:

- Bringing the "juice" in Judaism, the spiritual experience, into our families and synagogues.

---

178 For additional examples and to dive deeper into how adaptive leadership is demonstrated in the Bible, see Lord Rabbi Jonathan Sacks' teachings and Professor Ronald Heifetz's "Foreword" in Lessons in Leadership: A Weekly Reading of the Jewish Bible, Jerusalem: Maggid-Koren Press, 2015.

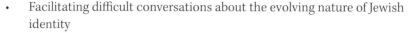
- Facilitating difficult conversations about the evolving nature of Jewish identity
- Encouraging community members to take ownership of their Jewish journey
- Reimagining Jewish traditions to resonate with contemporary values while maintaining their essential meaning

The key is to resist the pressure for quick fixes and instead engage in the deeper, often more conflictual but exciting work of adaptive change. This approach allows leaders to keep the real work — the adaptive challenge — at the center of their efforts.

> *Consider a technical challenge you have faced recently where knowledge and skills — either yours or someone else's — were able to create a needed solution. Now consider an adaptive challenge you currently face that requires learning and input from different perspectives. Keep this adaptive challenge in mind throughout this article.*

Respect the Pains of Change and Manage Losses

The work of leadership requires us to help our communities navigate the changes necessary to address their adaptive challenges. Change, even positive change, almost always comes with loss. It's that loss, not the change itself, that we truly fear and resist. An adaptive challenge requires us to distinguish between what is precious and essential and what can be discarded. These distinctions are very hard intellectual and emotional work, and they truly require leadership. They require tough decisions regarding what must be abandoned to move forward, and how each loss will affect the people around us in our organizations, our communities, and our families.

The threat of loss requires sensitivity, empathy, and even reverence. Loss of material wealth can be a staggering blow to a family or a community. Loss of competence can be even more intimidating: To move beyond the bounds of our intellect to an area we're unfamiliar with, even with the promise of learning something new, can be a struggle. Loss of identity — personal or collective — can crumble what seemed like reliable foundations.

In Jewish life, we can see this challenge in the ongoing transformation of Jewish education. For decades, many Jewish communities relied heavily on traditional Hebrew school models for transmitting knowledge and culture to the next generation. However, as society has changed and younger generations have different needs and expectations, Jewish leaders have had to confront the need for adaptive change in education.

Consider the shift toward experiential Jewish education. This approach emphasizes hands-on learning, community service, and immersive experiences over traditional classroom instruction. While potentially more engaging and effective, this shift comes with significant losses:

- Loss of familiar structure: Parents and educators must let go of the traditional classroom model they're accustomed to.

- Loss of perceived competence: Teachers skilled in traditional instruction may feel less competent in facilitating experiential learning.

- Loss of certain traditions: Some time-honored practices, like rote Hebrew reading drills, may need to be discarded or significantly altered.

- Loss of identity: The community may struggle with a shifting identity as what it means to be educated Jewishly evolves.

Jewish leaders must help their communities navigate these losses. This requires:

- Acknowledging and honoring what's being left behind

- Helping community members see the potential benefits of the new approach

- Providing support and training to those who feel de-skilled by the change

- Continually connecting the new practices to enduring Jewish values and identity so the losses are understood to be much smaller than all that is being conserved.

The same principles are true when we try to address challenges in our family systems. Consider, for example, a family that recognizes the need to change their lifestyle to a healthier one after the father suffers a heart attack. This shift might involve moving to a plant-based diet, giving up smoking, cutting down on snacks, and dedicating more time to exercise. While beneficial, these changes present an adaptive challenge that requires managing several potential losses, including loss of familiar comfort foods that feel like home, loss of leisure time in exchange for exercise, loss of the kick and comfort of cigarettes, loss of social conformity as the lifestyle may diverge from peers and extended family, and loss of routine.

To address these losses using adaptive leadership principles, the parents could:

- Have open family discussions about the reasons for the changes and acknowledge the difficulties everyone might face
- Involve children in meal planning and preparation, turning it into a fun family activity
- Gradually introduce changes, starting with Meatless Mondays, to ease the transition
- Regularly check in with family members about their feelings and adjust approaches as needed
- Maintain flexibility, allowing for occasional treats or exceptions to prevent feelings of deprivation

By managing these losses thoughtfully, the family can turn this adaptive challenge into an opportunity for growth, learning new skills, and developing a shared sense of purpose. This approach allows the family to make significant changes while respecting each member's feelings and challenges.

When we practice adaptive leadership, we learn not to run from or fight change. Instead, we learn to honor and hold reverence for the challenges of change. Change is the work, not a distraction from it, and making progress means continuously navigating the change in order to make progress on the challenge.

Give the Work Back to Those with the Challenge

Another common leadership mistake is thinking that we can solve such problems alone or in a vacuum. Often, many of us gain a sense of competency, control, and authority by taking the problems off others' shoulders and giving them solutions. However, that approach rarely works when dealing with adaptive challenges. Instead, exercising adaptive leadership involves bringing together those with the problem, engaging them with the challenge, and asking them to be part of the solution. Those with the problems are welcomed into the room, encouraged to have a seat, and guided to take part in — and responsibility for — making progress on the challenge. In that sense, the people with the problem are an important part of the challenge, and exercising leadership means putting the work back on their shoulders as opposed to solving the issues for them.

Let's take the example of grappling with rising antisemitism on college campuses. A traditional approach might involve Jewish organizations or university administrations implementing top-down policies or programs. However, exercising an adaptive leadership approach recognizes that the most effective and sustainable solutions often come from within the affected community itself.

In this case, exercising leadership may involve bringing together diverse stakeholders: Jewish students, non-Jewish allies, faculty, administration, and local Jewish community leaders to brainstorm new actions or policies, coupled with an initiative led by students to create spaces for dialogue where all parties can share their experiences, concerns, and ideas.

Instead of trying to solve the problem alone or impose solutions from above, you're creating a framework where the campus community itself becomes equipped to address antisemitism. This approach helps the campus community develop its own capacity to combat antisemitism and promote inclusivity by developing better strategies to diagnostically assess the various sources of antisemitism on campus and then engage and challenge these different antisemitic sources differently. For example, Jewish students might need to learn together the history of antisemitism, the history of the Arab-Israeli conflict, and the legitimate debates within Israel in favor of and critical of Israeli policy before they can engage productively with non-Jewish students who are critical of Israeli policy but have also been propagandized to draw on antisemitic tropes and to make false analogies between colonialism and racism, on one hand, and Zionism, on the other hand.

Another example — one that Netaly as a parent to teenagers is currently dealing with — is coping with children's excessive screen time, which affects family interactions and children's sleep patterns. We've seen that, in order to deal with this challenge, the initial instinct of many parents is to impose strict rules — only to find out that their children did not adhere to those boundaries and instead found sophisticated ways to gain more time with their electronic devices. In this case, after lots of family tension and frustration, Netaly and her husband took a different approach. Instead of deciding on the solution, they convened a family meeting to discuss the issue, ensuring everyone had a chance to express their views. Together, the family defined what healthy technology use looks like for them, and each family member, including the teenagers, proposed ideas to reduce screen time and increase family engagement. They agreed to test their new approach for a month, with everyone committed to giving it an honest try. While the problem didn't go away, they were able to make progress and, most importantly, the children took ownership for the issue, increasing the long-term likelihood for success.

In both these examples, we see how adaptive leadership involves distributing responsibility, empowering others, and ensuring that solutions are developed and owned by the community facing the challenge. This approach not only addresses the immediate problem but also builds the community's capacity to face future challenges.

> *Think about bringing together different stakeholders and distributing responsibilities to manage an adaptive challenge you are facing. What might that look like?*

Choose to Step up and Engage

As we attempt to navigate the growing complexity of our times, each and every one of us has the ability to exercise leadership — from whichever position we hold, as parent, community activist, student, teacher, or rabbi. Exercising leadership in this moment will not ask: How can I get others to follow me? but rather: How can I engage those affected by this challenge in shaping the future? By embracing the principles of adaptive leadership, we can navigate the complexities of our time with wisdom, empathy, and resilience. It begins with a personal choice to step up and make a difference. This is our watch. And it is possible.

INFUSING OUR LIVES WITH
MEANING

You may have experienced a *flow* state at some point — that sense of fluidity between your body and mind, when you are totally absorbed in something. Time feels like it has slowed down. Your senses are heightened. You are at one with the task you are engaged with, immersed in what can feel like effortless momentum. This state was studied and popularized by positive psychologist Dr. Mihaly Csikszentmihalyi, who writes: "The best moments in our lives are not the passive, receptive, relaxing times.... The best moments usually occur when a person's body or mind is stretched to its limits in a voluntary effort to accomplish something difficult and worthwhile."[179] His research shows that flow is universal; that it has been reported to occur across all ages, cultures, classes, and genders; and that it can be experienced during many types of activities.

More than 450 years ago, Rabbi Judah Loew, a leading rabbi in Prague, described the goodness that comes from God as a *flow*. Rabbi Loew likened the goodness we receive to a river that nurtures its surroundings. He taught that we are meant to keep the flow moving and we must avoid hindering its way. Appreciating the wonder of the gifts we receive and sharing them with others will keep the flow in motion, but hoarding, he taught, stops the flow.[180]

The generosity, curiosity, passion, joy, and love that keep us connected to the flow of meaning are explored by the three authors of this chapter. Rabbi Dr. Ariel Burger examines the importance of questioning in Jewish tradition and asserts that the way we make meaning as Jews, and as human beings, is by asking questions. The path he charts guides us to experience life as a continuous unfolding of meaning. Sivan Rahav-Meir shares her most important teachings about meaning and motivation: If we fill our lives and mind with sources of life wisdom, these will be available to us during times of pain and sorrow. Dr. Tal Ben-Shahar, an expert in positive psychology, explores a set of practical strategies for making ourselves happier.

179 Mihaly Csikszentmihalyi, *Flow: The Psychology of Optimal Experience*, Harper & Row, 1990.

180 Rabbi Judah Loew of Prague (the Maharal), *Netivot Olam, Netive Ha'Tzedkah*, Chapter 2.

Discovering Meaning in the Face of Sorrow

Rabbi Dr. Ariel Burger

Rabbi Dr. Ariel Burger is the founding director and senior scholar of The Witness Institute, whose mission is to empower emerging leaders, inspired by the life and legacy of Elie Wiesel. He is the author of the award-winning book Witness: Lessons from Elie Wiesel's Classroom. *In 2019 he was chosen as one of the Algemeiner Top 100 people positively influencing Jewish life today. When Ariel is not learning or teaching, he is creating music, art, and poetry.*

Questions

Torah asserts that life has intrinsic meaning. As Elie Wiesel, the renowned Holocaust survivor, author, and Nobel Prize-winning human rights activist, put it, "No life is a means to an end; every life is an end in itself." Yet it is still possible for human beings to sometimes experience life as meaningless. In the face of suffering, or chaos, when we consider war or hunger or the myriad other sorrows of our world, we might well ask: What is it all for?

Some religious approaches ask us to censor such questions, to renounce them; they argue that our role is not to question, but to accept, to trust. While faith is an essential Jewish value, I personally do not accept such an approach, such censorship. Neither, I believe, does Judaism. After all, if we look at the Bible, we find its principal characters have one thing in common: They ask questions.

The first to ask a question is actually God, who asks Adam, "Where are you?"

A story is told of a great Hasidic master, the founder of the Lubavitch movement, who was being held in prison for a period. He was asked by the warden, "What kind of a God did not know where Adam was?"

To which he replied, "God knew; *Adam* did not."

The first question in Jewish tradition is therefore an existential one, asked of man by the divine: Where are you? Meaning: To what do you devote your time? What are your thoughts, your ambitions, your memories, your dreams? How do you spend your time, and for whom?

How might you reflect on these big questions? While Eskimos have many words for snow, Hebrew and Aramaic have many words for question.[181] *How might questioning be part of your infusing life with meaning?*

As we meet other characters in the Bible, we find that they also ask questions. While defending the wicked city of Sodom, which has been slated by God for destruction, Abraham asks, "Will the God of justice not do justice?"

Later, while they are on their way to the mountaintop upon which Abraham has been commanded to sacrifice his son, Isaac asks his father, "Where is the lamb for the sacrifice?"

Later, Isaac, now elderly and blind, asks his son Jacob, who is disguised as his brother Esau, "Who are you?"

Later still, Jacob asks his own son Joseph, "What is the dream you have dreamed?"

These are merely a few examples. The Bible is filled with questions, and it teaches us to celebrate questions. The way we make meaning as Jews, and as human beings, is by asking questions. Some questions can lead us to concrete answers: Whom we should marry, which career path we should choose, which community we want to settle down in, which preschool is best for our child — these are questions to which we can generally find answers through clear thinking, gathering data and information, and asking advice of family and friends.

Some philosophical or scientific questions cannot be answered so easily: what the best way is to live a life, how do we define good, what the relationship is between the Earth and the sun, how cellular reproduction happens — these questions are too powerful to be answered within a single lifetime. They have required generations of thinkers and writers to ponder, to discuss, and to add to one another's conclusions. This is why we must learn, and benefit, from the work of earlier generations.

Other questions can never lead to answers at all, because the questions are too big, too profound. They can lead only to *responses;* to ways of behaving that are informed by the question. There can be no answer, for example, to the question of how God could allow a Holocaust to happen; could permit the destruction of over a third of the world's Jews, including one million children — but there can

---

181 Hebrew and Aramaic words for *question* include: *she'ela, chakira, ba'aya, drasha, chidah, kushia, sheilta, kasha, tama, he'etir, iba'ayeh, parcha, tavah.*

be *responses*. One response can be making a commitment to preventing other tragedies, other suffering. That was Elie Wiesel's response.

Not Knowing

We live in a time and a culture in which the big questions are not often celebrated; those who have *answers* are lifted up as the heroes, the stars. A politician who makes clear, declarative statements is more likely to be elected than one who says "I don't know," or even, "on the other hand…" There is so much pressure to know, to have the answers. Many people today suffer from a feeling of ennui, meaninglessness, existential fatigue, and it is in large part because they feel they must pretend to know things all the time.

When I was very young, my grandfather taught me that it is admirable to say, "I don't know." He showed me examples in which the great biblical and talmudic commentator Rashi, who was known for his strict economy with words, made the choice to comment on a verse, only to write, "I do not know what this means." Why did Rashi speak up only to declare that he had no answer? To teach us, explained my grandfather, that it is not a shortcoming to say "I don't know" — on the contrary, it is a great strength.

The quest for meaning in life begins with this phrase: *I don't know*. When we allow ourselves to ask many questions, we find something fascinating happens within us. We develop our natural curiosity. And with curiosity comes wonder. We experience moments of childlike *joy* at the world around us; its people, animals, plants, stones. We *wonder* at the events of our lives; all the millions of tiny factors it took to bring us to *this* point, to *these* relationships. We feel *gratitude* for the people in our lives, the stories we are living, even the struggles we experience. We see that these are all gifts, if only because *they could easily not have existed at all*. Perhaps this is why the first prayer a Jew says upon awakening is Modeh Ani: "I thank You, God, Living King, for You have given me my soul back with mercy; great is Your faithfulness."

There are two important points to mention with regard to this essential prayer. First, the Hebrew word for *thank*, *modeh*, can also mean to admit, to confess. So this prayer can be read as, "I *admit* that You have given me my soul back" — it is not something I am taking for granted. Second, the final phrase of the blessing, "great is Your faithfulness," implies that we rely on God to give us life each day. But the word *emunah*, faithfulness, can also be translated as faith, and the phrase can therefore read, "great is Your faith in me." You have given me another day of life because You believe in me — in my ability to do something good today, to grow, to learn, to help someone else, to create something beautiful.

In short, we Jews begin our day with an assertion of meaning. We do not take our lives, our time here on this Earth, for granted. We cultivate gratitude and radical wonder at the mere fact of our lives. And we remind ourselves that we are here for a purpose, and that the Creator has given us this day because of *His* faith in *us*. *Modeh Ani* is a formula for meaning-making throughout our days and throughout our lives.

Discovering Meaning

Once we choose to search for meaning, to begin with gratitude, wonder, and an acknowledgment of our not-knowing, we can begin to experience life as a continuous unfolding of meaning. Jewish tradition celebrates questions, especially in the context of Torah study, often done with a friend or group. Those of us who have been privileged to spend time in places of deep focus on Torah study have learned certain methods of reading texts. For example, we know that when we read a verse in the Torah we are meant to look for issues; we are not meant to be passive readers, accepting everything we read on the page. We are meant to seek out contradictions, strange phrasings; we are taught to notice patterns. Why does this verse use an extra phrase or seem to repeat itself? What motivates these biblical characters to act as they do at this juncture in their lives? What are we to learn from their flaws and mistakes? The Jewish way of studying is to embark on a passionate quest for meaning within text, and this quest applies equally to the study of our own lives. It teaches us to read our lives, too, as sacred text. This is one meaning of the phrase that can be heard during the High Holy Days: "May we be written in the Book of Life." The Book of Life is the translation of our actions, the events of our lives, into a part of eternity. Judaism teaches us to read life like it, too, is a sacred text; to look for patterns, to seek meaning, to ask questions.

The traditional Jewish perspective is that the book of our lives has an author, and that author is the Creator. We do not create meaning; we *discover* the meaning that is already there, hiding below the surface of life. From a traditional theological perspective, the act of seeking meaning is the act of listening for God's voice in every experience. What does a particular moment teach me about myself and others? What does it mean to experience what I am experiencing, to feel what I am feeling? Where is the opportunity for growth here?

Seen through this lens, waiting in a long line at the gas station might be transformed from an inconvenience to a chance to work on patience or an opportunity for a small act of kindness. Experiencing a financial challenge may be taken as an opportunity — to cultivate and nurture trust, or to develop humility and the willingness to ask for help, or to increase empathy for those who suffer from even greater poverty. Finding yourself in conflict with a close friend could become an opportunity to grow skills as a peacemaker.

If we are looking to grow, every event, every moment, can be filled with meaning.

Consider setting a regular time to discover and explore learning and growth opportunity in your experience.

A Call

There is profound reassurance in the notion that we can live lives of meaning-seeking and that, when we seek, we can find new understanding and new chances to improve ourselves. There is comfort in knowing that we are not alone in our quest; that God, the Source of meaning, is communicating to us through the events of our lives, encouraging us to keep asking, to keep searching — and cheering us on. But this perspective also comes with real responsibility. Because we are seekers of meaning, we know that there are patterns in everything, and opportunities to grow, for us as individuals and for all of humanity. When we see the brokenness of the world — hunger, social conflict and violence, persistent injustices, and gratuitous suffering caused by human beings — we can no longer remain quiet. We cannot claim that such events are random, meaningless, or accidental. Once we assert the meaningfulness of every aspect and every detail of life, once we begin to listen deeply to life, every personal or collective challenge becomes a call to us to respond. And we are living through a time in which these calls to respond are constant and loud.

There is a particular kind of strain that comes from living in a time like this. We are experiencing great social and political tension, a widening divide between entrenched positions, the rise of hatreds we thought had finally been marginalized. And this all leads to uncertainty, anxiety, and discomfort. It is tempting to try and alleviate this discomfort by turning our backs, pretending that the world has no meaning and that it therefore makes no demands of us. But we must fight against that urge. For those of us who yearn for meaning, there is tremendous opportunity in moments like these: opportunity to challenge the accepted notions of how society must be designed; to interrogate the systems of thought and cultures that developed and the policies that emerged from them that have consistently led to destruction and human suffering. The urgency, anxiety, and discomfort we feel should push us to change our own behavior and to challenge these patterns.

To be a seeker of meaning is to be uncomfortable, to reject complacency, and to live a life of profound concern for others. It is to remain awake when you are tempted to hit the snooze button on the alarms you are hearing. It is to imagine new possibilities, new and better ways of living. And it is to find others who are also seeking, who are also questioning, who are choosing a life of meaning. The good news is that you are not alone. There are many of us who live this kind of life, and there always have been, from the most ancient times of the Bible until the present day. This might be our greatest hope: that those of us who insist on searching for meaning can come together to ask questions, to seek answers and responses, and to imagine a new world — one of kindness, sensitivity, and respect for all life.

Most Important Lessons I Have Learned About Meaning and Motivation

Sivan Rahav-Meir[182]

> *Sivan Rahav-Meir was voted by* Globes *as the most popular female media personality in Israel and by* The Jerusalem Post *as one of the 50 most influential Jews in the world. She works for ILTV Israel News, writes a column for* Yediot Aharonot *newspaper, and hosts a weekly radio show on Galei Zahal (Army Radio). Her lectures on the weekly Torah portion are attended by hundreds and the live broadcast attracts thousands more listeners throughout the world.*

*M*eaning. It's probably the most important word in life. Since October 7, we see this is especially true. There is much discussion now about the war on terror and antisemitism, about security, about diplomacy, about the importance of explaining Israel's position to the world. But the root of everything that is happening now is found in one word: *meaning.*

Do we know why we are struggling? What is the reason for this war between good and evil, between light and darkness? Why is it that evil chooses us as its enemy, each generation anew? The Jewish people must know who we are, know that we have a mission, that we are not here randomly, and that we have an essential voice to transmit to the world.

At the most personal, intimate level as well, not only at the national level, what is your meaning? What is the engine that drives you? Do you want more money? More publicity and likes? More success and social status? None of these will last for very long.

When you have no sense of meaning, when you lack motivation and purpose, it is very difficult to get up each morning and function during challenging times.

But when you have a sense of meaning, when you have motivation and purpose, you're only too ready to wake up and begin doing — *especially* in difficult times.

---

182 Translated by Leah Hartman.

On a personal level, since October 7, I have taken a deep dive into this subject. I published a booklet called *To Be a Jew: Faith and Hope in Challenging Times*, of Rabbi Jonathan Sacks' writings, in Hebrew and in English. Hundreds of thousands of copies are being distributed for free across the globe, and you are welcome to find it online. I wrote a children's book called *L'gdol* (*To Grow*). It is a collection of stories about the hope and growth that rise out of crisis. I speak about this subject often, and about the Lubavitcher Rebbe's understanding of crises, after having interviewed numerous Chabad emissaries on the topic.

But mainly, I have met thousands of heroes in person. Men and women and children who inspire motivation all over the Jewish world through their actions and words.

I will attempt here to summarize several ways of answering the biggest question: How do you experience meaning?

And to those who have visited Israel, perhaps an additional question needs to be asked: Did you feel meaning when you visited the Land of Israel? How can you hold on to this upon returning home? How can you preserve the *wow* for the long run, throughout your life, not only as a one-off?

I offer here four guidelines I have learned:

God Determined This World Has Meaning

At times it seems as if evil is winning. As if chaos has taken over. We must tell ourselves again and again, and educate ourselves and our children, this is not so. God is good, and God is guiding this world toward good. Even if there are difficulties on the way. And even more than this: God needs us. We are God's partners. Not passive partners, but active ones. We aren't spectators, watching the game from the sidelines. We are players on the most elite team.

The Lubavitcher Rebbe's first discourse following his acceptance of the mantle of leadership of Chabad is called *Bati L'gani* (*I Have Come to My Garden*). God comes to this world, for *this* is His garden.

Notice the choice of words: It is not a wild jungle — it is a garden. It was created with intention, with order and thought. Every tree, bush, and flower has meaning to it. Someone planned and wanted each one to be exactly in its place, and it all fits together as a marvelous creation. And in this garden, we are the gardeners. We must act, care for it, make it grow, bring it to its final destination.

Each year, on the anniversary of becoming the Rebbe, he would share an additional discourse under the title *Bati L'gani*, in which he would further explain the task of our unique generation: to continue working in God's garden.

Even if in the latest news edition evil is winning, this will not be so forever. On the contrary.

"The Door to Happiness Opens Outward"

This saying by Kierkegaard states that in order to emerge from a crisis, we sometimes have to emerge from ourselves. To look outward. The Hebrew word *simchah*, joy, is used over and over in the Bible alongside the act of giving to another, to the weak, to someone who doesn't have. You are happy when you eat in Jerusalem together with the orphan and the widow. This is true, pure joy. Joy that is connected to others — not egoistic joy.

Here is a remarkable story told to me by Meirav Berger, the mother of hostage Agam Berger. While her daughter is in Gaza, she tells us what gives her strength:

"After the kidnapping I didn't leave the house. I was very down, I really didn't function. A few months after the kidnapping, it came time to celebrate the bar mitzvah of Ilay, Agam's younger brother. I was connected to Rabbi Mendy from the Chabad house of our city, Holon. The first time I left my home was to go there, to the Holon Chabad house. I was broken, shattered, barely functioning. We came to plan the bar mitzvah, but it was a Thursday, the day on which they do a ton of *chesed* [acts of loving-kindness], packing meals and distributing to those in need. When we arrived, they were at the peak of all this, at the height of the war. And suddenly we found ourselves ... packing rations for the needy and helping with the distribution. This was a moment that got me out of my despair. The giving gave me strength to go out into the world."

It is not a cliché: One who gives, receives. The ability to help another gives us strength and helps us. You're invited to try.

To Study Torah

Are you familiar with the coffee analogy? Imagine a person arriving at work and making himself a cup of coffee. On his way to his office he physically bumps into a colleague, and the entire cup of coffee spills. Now ask yourself: Why was it coffee that spilled? The simple answer: because he'd filled the cup with coffee. If he'd filled it with orange juice, orange juice would have spilled. If he'd filled it with milk, milk would have spilled.

In other words: What we take in is what comes out in times of crisis. If we fill ourselves with resilience, with strength, with optimism, with faith and, in particular, with Torah, this is what will spill forth.

We'll still have difficult moments, but we'll always have an anchor, a source of comfort and hope.

And here is yet another level: This is not just a personal matter. The Torah is the operating mechanism of the Jewish people. When you learn Torah, you connect with all Jewish souls, and recall who we most truly are.

Rabbi Sacks discovered his Jewish identity as a young student, and he summarized his conclusions as follows: "Non-Jews respect Jews who respect Judaism, and they are embarrassed by Jews who are embarrassed by Judaism."[183]

How do we honor our tradition? By studying it. Here is a fundamental passage of Rabbi Sacks' on the study of Torah. Sometimes it seems to us that because we already have the State of Israel, or because the times in which we live are more modern and advanced, there is no need for intensive Torah study. On the contrary:

> Jews were dispersed throughout the world, they were not part of the same political jurisdiction, but they continued to see themselves as a single nation, a distinctive and persistent group, often more closely linked to other Jews throughout the world than to the peoples among whom they lived.

> They did not share the same culture. While Rashi and the Tosafists were living in Christian France, Maimonides inhabited an Islamic culture, first in Spain then in Egypt. Nor were their fates the same at any given time. While North European Jewry was suffering massacres during the First Crusade, Spanish Jewry was enjoying its golden age. While the Jews of Spain were experiencing the trauma of expulsion, the Jews of Poland were thriving in a rare moment of tolerance.

> They did not use the same language of everyday speech. Ashkenazi Jews spoke Yiddish, Spanish and Portuguese Jews spoke Ladino, and there were as many as twenty-five other vernaculars, among them Judeo-Arabic, Judeo-Slavic, Judeo-Yazdi, Judeo-Shirazi, Judeo-Esfahani, and Judeo-Marathi, as well as Yevanic, a form of Judeo-Greek .... Nothing united them at all — nothing, that is, that would normally constitute nationhood.

> What united them? Rav Saadia Gaon in the tenth century gave the answer: "Our nation is only a nation in virtue of its religious laws." Wherever Jews were, they kept the same commandments, studied the same sacred texts, observed the same Sabbaths and fast days, and said essentially the same prayers in the same holy language.

---

183 Jonathan Sacks, *A Letter in the Scroll: Understanding Our Jewish Identity and Exploring the Legacy of the World's Oldest Religion*, New York: Schocken Books, 2000, p. 212.

They even faced the same spot while doing so: Jerusalem where the Temple once stood and where the Divine presence was still held to have its earthly habitation. These invisible strands of connection sustained them in a bond of collective belonging that had no parallel among any other national grouping. Some feared this, others respected it, but no one doubted that Jews were different. Haman said so in the book of Esther: "There is one people, scattered and divided among the peoples, whose laws are different from all others."[184]

That is the paradox. In their own land, the place where every other nation is to some degree united, Jews were split beyond repair. In dispersion, where every other nation has assimilated and disappeared, they remained distinctive and, in essentials at least, united.[185]

This is our challenge in this unique generation. To unite the Jewish people around the Torah, which will come forth from the Land of Israel.

Combining the Three Previous Guidelines — Teach the Torah to Others

In my opinion, if we will all apply the fourth guideline, the entire world will be in a much better state. Now that we've learned that this world has a purpose, now that we've learned about giving to others, now that we've learned the power of the Torah, we can bring it all together. To give to another not only physical help but spiritual help. The highest degree of charity is to allow a person to return to their roots and their identity. One who wanders in the world without knowing who they are, suffers. Such a person is not connected to truth, is not able to connect the past to the present to the future, or to find their role in all of this confusion.

This is a time for increased Jewish pride, a greater sense of Jewish identity. On campuses, in synagogues — which are now seeing new people attending — with solidarity missions arriving to Israel, and essentially everywhere. If our enemies want us to be less Jewish, we will be more Jewish.

And so, if you have knowledge (and if you are reading this book and if you are connected to Momentum, then you have knowledge) — share it with others. Don't

---

184 Esther 3:8.

185 Rabbi Jonathan Sacks, *Future Tense, Jews, Judaism, and Israel in the Twenty-first Century*, New York: Knopf Doubleday Publishing Group, 2012, p. 34.

be timid. Millions of our brothers and sisters in the Jewish world are waiting for you. You need only to knock on your neighbor's door and invite him to a Shabbat meal, or to initiate bringing Jewish wisdom and what you are learning into your conversations and interactions, including into the workplace.

> *Consider how you might take on one or more of these ideas. For example, have a "news fast" for a few days periodically. People spend an average of one hour a day getting news[186] and that news all too often focuses on doom and gloom. Consider infusing yourself and your environment with well-being and meaning by fasting from watching or scrolling through news media and engaging instead in any combination of the three guidelines.*

I remember meeting with a delegation of female Chabad emissaries from campuses throughout the United States. One of the women, whose Chabad house is located on a particularly hostile campus in the United States, told me, "Not long ago, they published an ad on campus about 'Ending Israeli Apartheid Week.' My husband said to me: 'Good, I need to prepare more mezuzahs and tefillin for next week, and it's likely that on Shabbat students who've never come will join our meal.' We simply see, through the numbers of people showing up, how the darkness increases the light."

But there is no need to be an official Chabad emissary. Every Jew is an emissary.

These are not ordinary times, and this article is not ordinary either. Therefore I will also close with a personal request: Write me your thoughts on what was said here. Tell me what you think, to my personal email: sivanrahavmeir@gmail.com.

These words were written in Jerusalem, in the midst of a war. How I wish you will read them in a situation that is much better and much safer.

Maybe in the past I would have written in a more subtle and formal way, not explicitly demanding of people to do something. But I believe we are living in a time of urgency. The Jewish people must wake up and come back to themselves. Every big crisis can also be a big opportunity. It depends on us, here and now.

---

186 Rutger Bregman, *Humankind: A Hopeful History*, New York: Hachette Book Group, 2019, p. 14.

How to Be Happier

Dr. Tal Ben-Shahar

*Tal Ben-Shahar, PhD, consults and lectures internationally on topics
including leadership, ethics, happiness, and mindfulness. The co-founder
of the Happiness Studies Academy, in 2011 he co-founded Potentialife to
bring positive psychology to people's daily lives. Tal is the author of the
international bestsellers* Happier: Learn the Secrets to Daily Joy and
Lasting Fulfillment *and* Being Happy: You Don't Have to Be Perfect to
Lead a Richer, Happier Life, *which have been translated into 25 languages.
He is the narrator of the 2012 documentary* Israel Inside: How a Small
Nation Makes a Big Difference. *Tal taught at Harvard, where his classes on
positive psychology and the psychology of leadership were among the most
popular in the university's history.*

As a student and teacher in the field of happiness studies, people often assume I'm always happy. Surely, someone who has dedicated himself to studying the science of happiness has it all figured out, right? The reality is a happy life doesn't mean being happy all the time. In fact, to understand happiness it's equally, if not more, important to accept and embrace painful emotions.

Therein lies the paradox of happiness.[187] We know it's a good thing, but at the same time research shows that people who pursue it are more prone to depression. In other words, their quest for happiness makes them less happy. So if not happiness, what then should we strive for?

I've found answers in my 25 years as a positive psychologist, examining and conducting research using questionnaires or brain scans like EEGs and FMRIs in labs, from New York to Beijing.

---

187 Iris B. Mauss, Maya Tamir, Craig L. Anderson, and Nicole S. Savino, "Can Seeking Happiness Make People Unhappy? Paradoxical Effects of Valuing Happiness," Emotion, 2011, 11(4), p. 807–815.

Focus on What Works

Happiness, it turns out, is best pursued indirectly. Just think of the sun. Observing it with the naked eye is unpleasant — painful, even. Yet when Isaac Newton experimented with letting sunlight pass through a clear glass prism, he discovered the rainbow of colors that make up the whole. We are more successful finding happiness when we break it down into its elements.

What makes positive psychology different from traditional psychology is that instead of trying to fix what's wrong, we focus on what works.[188] Here, I'll explore three major metaphorical colors of the rainbow, the elements of happiness.

Permission to Be Human

> Those who don't know how to weep with their whole heart, don't know how to laugh either.
>
> — *Golda Meir, Prime Minister of Israel, 1969–1974*

Sadness, anger, disappointment, guilt, fear, frustration, envy — these emotions can be painful. There are only two kinds of people who do not experience them: psychopaths and dead people. If you're experiencing painful emotions, we can deduce you aren't a psychopath and you're alive. And that's a good place to start.

Feeling bad isn't a bad thing, but in our society it's not exactly something we are taught to feel proud of or to embrace. Scroll through your social media and you might get the sense that everyone is doing great — much better than you are. We don't post about the fight we had with our partner last night, our children's tantrums, or our jealousy over an acquaintance's picture-perfect vacation. Instead, we portray ideal versions of our lives and ourselves, and we get distorted expectations because of it.

Some of the best advice I ever got was from our pediatrician. Six hours after my son David was born in Boston, our pediatrician, Dr. Shapira, came to check on him and my wife. Just before he left the room, he paused. "Over the next few months, you're going to experience every single kind of emotion to the extreme — extreme joy, extreme frustration, extreme love, and extreme anxiety. It's fine, it's natural, and we all go through it."

---

188 Martin P. Seligman and Mihaly Csikszentmihalyi, "Positive Psychology: An Introduction," American Psychologist, 2000, 55(1), p. 5–14.

After about a month, for the first time since my wife and I connected at the Bnei Akiva youth movement at the age of 14, someone else was getting more attention than me. I noticed I was starting to feel some envy toward David. Normally, I might have judged myself. What kind of person is jealous of their newborn son? But because I had Dr. Shapira's words in my mind — "it's fine, it's natural, and we all go through it" — essentially giving me permission to be human, I accepted the emotion and it passed, making room to feel love for my son.

When we repress and suppress painful emotions, they intensify. When we acknowledge them and allow them to flow through us, they don't overstay their welcome. What we resist persists. When we embrace unpleasant emotions, they flow through us and leave. So how can we better embrace the full scope of our emotions? Consider any of the following: keeping a journal, venting to a friend, speaking to a therapist, or having a good cry. With acceptance, we have control to choose the best course of action.

> *What can support you in experiencing your feelings,*
> *even when a friend isn't available? Has journaling,*
> *music, or exercise been helpful for you? You can*
> *try this: close your eyes and imagine your emotion*
> *as a wave or a cloud. Watch it as it approaches,*
> *passes over you, and then slowly dissipates.*

So if we want to experience happiness, we must allow ourselves to also experience unhappiness. Indeed, the research backs this up. To understand why this contrast is so essential, think of the last great biography you read, watched, or listened to. I often say the best self-help books are biographies. They include the ups and downs, the weaknesses and strengths. And it's no coincidence that the Torah is filled with biographies and stories about people who make mistakes, experience painful emotions to their extremes, and move ultimately forward with acceptance. Those stories teach us perspective. When we see the high points of someone's life juxtaposed with their lowest lows, we gain insight about how acceptance of our emotions, trust, and a plan of action combine for a meaningful life.

Change Your Relationship with Stress

The richest banquet, the most exotic travel, the most interesting, attractive lover, the finest home — all of these experiences can seem somehow unrewarding and empty if we don't really attend to them fully — if our minds are elsewhere, preoccupied with disturbing thoughts.

— Tara Bennett Goleman,
Emotional Alchemy: How the Mind Can Heal the Heart

You've likely heard by now that stress isn't good for you. "Stress a Silent Killer," "Your Heart's Worst Enemy," news headlines warn.[189] The World Health Organization says we're dealing with a stress pandemic and governments around the globe are taking steps to address it.

"The amount of information we take in each day has rapidly increased over the years.[190] Research shows that in 2011, Americans absorbed five times more information each day than they did 25 years earlier. This equates to roughly 174 newspapers of additional information."

But what if I told you that stress is not the enemy? Through decades of research, my colleagues and I have found that stress can actually be good for us. Take your exercise routine, for instance. You go to the gym and lift weights to stress your muscles so they'll grow bigger and stronger. This is antifragility, a concept introduced by Nassim Taleb, in practice. Resilience is the phenomenon of putting pressure on a system and seeing it bounce back once that pressure is lifted. Antifragility goes a step further: The system actually grows stronger from stress. The same idea applies to psychology. The science of happiness teaches us there are conditions we can put in place to increase the likelihood of growing from hardship.

So if stress isn't the problem, why is it making us so sick? Again, think of the gym analogy. If you lift weights every day and never give your body time to recover, chances are you'll get injured. If we don't prioritize recovery, we suffer. The goal, then, is not eliminating stress from our lives completely. It is energizing our lives with periods of recovery when we meditate, spend time with a friend, take a walk around the block, work out at the gym, or share a meal with family.

These bouts of recovery can look different. A colleague of mine once worked with a Wall Street firm. The organization was seeing high levels of burnout, sick employees, turnover, and a lot of stress. My colleague suggested that every two hours the company's workers take 30 seconds to close their eyes and take three

---

189   Riyan Ramanath, "Stress a Silent Killer, Say Doctors," *The Times of India,* September 29, 2023.

190   Daniel J. Levitin, "Why It's So Hard to Pay Attention, Explained By Science," *Fast Company,* September 23, 2015.

deep breaths. They set reminders, determined to fix their stress pandemic. And what do you know — those 30 seconds, or micro-breaks, as psychologists call them, might seem insignificant, but with consistency they make a big difference.

So do mid-level breaks, like a good night's sleep. Research out of Stanford, UC Berkeley, the University of San Diego, and UC Riverside has shown the benefits of sleep for both mental and physical health.[191] Or think of God — He took a day off. We too can get more done in six days than in seven. With rest, we're more creative, more productive, and happier. Lastly, there's macro-level recovery. This is the kind of rest you get from taking a vacation, and U.S. workers aren't getting enough of it. A staggering number of people say that even while on vacation they spend about an hour a day working.[192]

Mindfulness is another way to foster antifragility. Professors Jon Kabat-Zinn and Richard Davidson conducted a study in which people who had never meditated before were put on an eight-week program.[193] By the end of the study, with meditation they found anxiety levels had plummeted, and participants were more social, friendly, generous, and kind to other people. Even more incredible, when the researchers collected blood samples from the group, they found the meditators actually strengthened their immune systems. These benefits were equal regardless of whether the students meditated for as much as 50 minutes a day or as little as twice a week.

All this psychological research reinforces something that Judaism has been teaching for thousands of years. Our tradition is constructed around recovery. *Brachot*, prayers, help us on a micro-level. They provide a chance to pause in the day-to-day rush; beyond a 30-second micro-break, they connect us with meaning. Likewise, Shabbat gives us mid-level recovery every single week, rain or shine. Then there are longer, macro-level opportunities for recovery, like holidays. We take time off, slow down, and adhere to nature. Each of these traditions also encourages mindfulness — the importance of being in the present moment.

But it's not only breaks that are important, it's also how we approach a task.

191 Diane C. Lim, Arezu Najafi, Lamia Afifi, Claudio LA Bassetti, Daniel J. Buysse, Fang Han, Birgit Högl, Yohannes Adama Melaku, Charles M. Morin, Allan I. Pack, Dalva Poyares, Virend K. Somers, Peter R. Eastwood, Phyllis C. Zee, Chandra L. Jackson, "The Need to Promote Sleep Health in Public Health Agendas Across the Globe," The Lancet Public Health, 2023, 8(10), e820-e826, https://doi.org/10.1016/s2468-2667(23)00182-2.

192 Luciana Paulise, "54% of Individuals Continue to Work on Vacation: What Is the Cost?" *Forbes*, June 19, 2024.

193 Richard J. Davidson, Jon Kabat-Zinn, Jessica Schumacher, Melissa Rosenkranz, Daniel Muller, Saki F. Santorelli, Ferris Urbanowski, Anne Harrington, Katherine Bonus, John F. Sheridan, "Alterations in Brain and Immune Function Produced by Mindfulness Meditation," Psychosomatic Medicine, 2003, 65(4), p. 564–570.

The Jewish idea of doing actions with intention, *kavanah*, emphasizes the value of being present. *Kavanah* is the act of directing our attention to an action so it is done with purpose and meaning rather than in a rote, mechanical manner. If we cannot be present, if our mind is elsewhere, we will not enjoy the blessing of the moment and will miss the joy it can offer.

Appreciate the Good

> Gratitude is not only the greatest of virtues, but the parent of all others.
>
> — *Marcus Tullius Cicero*

Embracing painful emotions and giving ourselves the recovery time to process and meditate on them is critical — but how do we then cultivate pleasurable emotions? The answer is gratitude.

Research shows that keeping a gratitude journal makes us happier and healthier. Even spending one minute a day — or one minute a week — to write down what you are thankful for can have remarkable benefits. Or you can go even further, and write a gratitude letter.[194] The founder of the field of positive psychology, Marty Seligman, once asked his class to write a letter of gratitude and then share it with the person they wrote it to. He said that in his 40 years of teaching, he had never encountered a more positive experience. So I tried it with my own students.

John was a big guy, playing on the Harvard varsity football team. I could see him all the way at the back of the lecture hall where he'd take his seat every day. But a week after I had assigned the gratitude letter, instead of filing out of the room when class was over he made an appointment to visit me during my office hours. The next day, the football star sat in my office, visibly uncomfortable. He told me he had written his letter to his father and read it to him over the weekend. "After I read my father the letter, my father hugged me for the first time since I was eight years old."

That's why my favorite English word is *appreciate*. It has two interconnected meanings. Its first definition is to say *thank you* for something, but its second

---

194 David Stefan, Erin Lefdahl-Davis, Alexandra J. Alayan, Matthew Decker, Josie Wittwer, Tracy Kulwicki, J. Parsell, "The Impact of Gratitude Letters and Visits on Relationships, Happiness, Well-Being, and Meaning of Graduate Students," Journal of Positive School Psychology, 2021, 5(2), p. 110–126, https://doi.org/10.47602/jpsp.v5i2.256.

meaning is *increasing value*. When you appreciate the good, the good appreciates. Too often we forget the miraculousness of day-to-day life. In his research on terminally ill patients, Irvin Yalom, professor emeritus at Stanford, commonly heard things like "for the first time in a very long time, I truly appreciate my life." The challenge for us as humans is not to wait for something external and tragic to happen to appreciate what's inside us and around us. It's not hard to do, but we need reminders. Rituals such as our family Shabbat dinner go around can provide them.

Gratitude is a powerful thing. As a family, every Shabbat dinner we go around the table and say one thing we are grateful for and a kind act we did or observed in others. If nothing comes to mind, we make one up. It's important for all of us to hear for one simple reason: We often take for granted the goodness around us.

"The basis of the Torah is gratitude," said Rabbi Berel Wein. "Gratitude to our parents, teachers, elders and even to governmental authorities. The attitude of Judaism towards life generally is that everything is really a privilege, even life itself. It is easier to deal with the challenges that life impresses upon us if one views it from the vantage point of privilege rather than of entitlement and rights."[195]

Put Ideas into Practice with Rituals

We've explored the benefits of gratitude, recovery, and wholeness. Yet the real challenge is putting them into action. In his book *The Effective Executive: The Definitive Guide to Getting the Right Things Done*, consultant and educator Peter Drucker discusses the importance of introducing behavioral change as rituals.

Consider which prism is especially important for you at this stage in your life — giving yourself permission to be human, providing yourself with recovery time from stress, or focusing your attention on the good. Next, find a manageable action you can regularly take — something small — to put this priority into practice. Go for the low-hanging fruit.

Introduce these ideas as rituals day in and day out, and your neural pathways will change. When your neural pathways change, your behavior will change. When your behavior changes, the behavior of those around you will change too. If you increase your levels of well-being, you are not only impacting the quality of your own life, but you are impacting the quality of all those who you encounter. Happiness is contagious.

---

195 Rabbi Berel Wein's Weekly Blog, "Privileges and Rights," https://www.rabbiwein.com/blog/post-1992.html.

CONTRIBUTING TO A

BETTER FUTURE

The first reference to the Jewish people outside of the Torah is on the Merneptah Stele, an Egyptian inscription dating back to the thirteenth century BCE. It reads: "Israel is laid waste. Her seed is no more." Clearly, the future is not written in stone or, in this case, granite. In the words of Rabbi Sacks, "The Jews are a people who outlive their obituaries." Persistent belief in a better future and our role in creating it is, as Rabbi Sacks taught, "a fundamental feature of Jewish spirituality. We believe that we cannot predict the future when it comes to human beings. We *make* the future by our choices."[196]

But when we make choices, it is too easy to think myopically. How can we orient our thinking toward making the future we seek? The famous polio vaccine pioneer, Dr. Jonas Salk, said: "The most important question we must ask ourselves is, 'Are we being good ancestors?'"[197]

In 2013, Mexican-American Jewish thought leader Ari Wallach coined the term *longpath mindset* to describe the importance of actively countering our instinct for the short term and instead embracing the possibility and potential of the future. We know that our actions have consequences. The longpath mindset invites us to consider not only implications for us and our children, but also for our children's children and for their children.

Hope presupposes a belief that our shared future can be better than the past we inherited or the present we inhabit. The son of a Polish Holocaust survivor who was a member of the Jewish underground during World War II, Wallach now runs Longpath Labs, dedicated to inspiring people to become great ancestors.

He wrote in 2022:

> At its heart, the belief in a longpath ... mindset is a Jewish one. After all, we're the people who have dragged our story along to every outpost — the people who have waited on and insisted upon a future return. And just as our Passover story promises a transformation that does not happen overnight,

---

196 Lord Rabbi Jonathan Sacks, "A Word of Torah: On Not Predicting the Future," *The Detroit Jewish News,* December 16, 2021 (originally written in 2015)..

197 Roman Krznaric, *The Good Ancestor: A Radical Prescription for Long-Term Thinking,* New York: The Experiment, 2020.

the longpath view says that, yes, you can be an agent of change, not just a slave to the current climate, but it's going to take some work.[198]

How, exactly, should we understand that "work"? In this chapter, Dr. Zohar Raviv compares us to mountaineers who may at any moment again encounter a Sinai calling that reorients our quest. He invokes the wisdom of the prophets to remind us that the power of prophecy is its potential to spark forward-looking human action. Nigel Savage explores a central Jewish focus for a life of relationship, commitment, freedom, and hope that can promote a more sustainable world for all. He contrasts this focus with the western pursuit of happiness. Dr. Marilyn Paul and David Peter Stroh discuss how even the smallest acts can trigger an avalanche of positive change to entrenched systems, especially when they are taken in tandem with personal growth.

Words often attributed to Anne Frank famously remind us that, "Our lives are fashioned by our choices. First we make our choices. Then our choices make us." Contributing to a better future is a way of living *hope* as a verb, to improving ourselves and our world for generations to come.[199]

---

198 Ari Wallach, "When Judaism Considers the Long Term, It Looks to the Past," *The Times of Israel,* September 14, 2022.

199 This introduction was mostly written by Jessica Berkowitz, Momentum's senior education specialist.

Hope Is a Mountain: The Divine Pledge As a Human Charge

Dr. Zohar Raviv

Zohar Raviv, PhD, is the international vice president of educational strategy for Birthright Israel. He also serves as scholar in residence for Momentum Unlimited and The iCenter for Israel Education.

Wander and Wonder

As these words are being written, the unfolding 2024 year arguably continues to be one of the most heart-wrenching times for the Jewish people and for Israel. As each morning ushers in another form of mourning, it is indeed a period deeply engulfed by angst, trepidation, frustration, even despair. While traveling the world these past months, working with multiple Jewish leaders, educators, policy makers, and communities, I could not but deeply empathize with such feelings, let alone realize the high stakes for hope and human agency when addressing the daunting challenges in our complex contemporary world.

It is within this mind frame that I return, once again, to the wisdom of our ancestors — particularly, in this case, the prophets of Israel. And lest the reader's intuition lead them to think that I am in search of a prophecy of comfort à la Isaiah chapter 40, rest assured that such is not my intent here. Rather, I return to the prophets for a valuable lesson that they have taught us throughout the centuries: that leadership (leading oneself included) and despair do not go hand in hand, and that hope is an intrinsic element within the often-baffling event we all call *life*. As we embark on unpacking this statement, what better prophet serves us by way of beginning than The Master of all Prophets: Moses.

The Mount Sinai Model

I have always been fascinated by the Mount Sinai story — not merely for its unique and towering standing in the dramatic unfolding of our saga as a people, nor simply for its seminal role in shaping the ethical foundations of our civilization. My fascination lies with the message it sends each and every one of us, for whereas in some theological constitutions we find divinity descending to Earth (e.g., Christianity) or a prophet ascending to Heaven (e.g., Islam), the Mount Sinai model features a simultaneous interface wherein Moses ascends while God descends. On top of that mountain, at this seminal divine–human rendezvous point, something quite profound takes place.

Exodus 19:19 describes the intimate moment of God and Moses' rendezvous: "And when the voice of the horn waxed louder and louder, *Moses spoke, and God answered him by a voice.*" The profoundly intimate interaction between God and Moses, seemingly featuring a "conversation" between the divine and the prophet, did not escape our sages, who now asked: Why do we read that God "replied him *with a voice*" instead of just stating that "God replied" (which renders the term *voice* redundant or superfluous)? The answer that we find in Mechilta D'Rabbi Yishma'el (second century CE) is truly astounding: God answered with Moses' own voice.[200]

Finding Our Voice — Ascending Our Sinai

This remarkable interpretation presents a compelling question, one whose ramifications are arresting: If God replied with Moses' own voice, who exactly did Moses hear? Was Moses having a conventionally perceived "dialogue" with divinity, or was he in turn engaged in an enlightened monologue, the result of a soul intimately aware of its place, as well as responsibility, having been created "in God's image"? The question here does not lie within the realm of religious practice or piety alone, but is woven into the very fabric of our human condition as beings whose foundational existence is the search for meaning, conviction, and worth.

Mount Sinai, we realize, is not presented simply as a physical and majestic location to marvel at or as a historical event to be pinpointed in space and time. Mount Sinai calls upon us to also view it intimately and eternally, beyond the myopic scopes of space and time, from within, as the mental landscape that invites us to become the mountaineers of our own lives: to move beyond the contracting shackles of ignorance, mediocrity, or self-indulgence and to ascend the formidable mountain in order to find divinity replying to our quest in our own voice!

Mount Sinai is a moment of enlightenment that awaits us at each corner, each event, and each second of our lives on this earth; it is neither a singularly human arena, nor that of the divine alone. Rather, it is the diffusion of one within the

---

200 Mechilta D'Rabbi Yishma'el, DeVaChodesh 4.

other, the intimate and quite enigmatic realm of true fulfilled spirituality — the rendezvous point wherein each human understands their potential as one who was created in God's image.

> *Take a solo hike in nature, perhaps uphill, and mindfully reflect on what mental mountains are most important to you to be climbing to actualize your calling. What guidance does your inner voice offer you regarding this climb? What obstacles and challenges obstruct your way to an expansive view? How can you approach them as an adventure?*

The Mountaineer's Charge: Return

It is arguably within this mind frame that we can also approach all the other prophets of Israel, for indeed — and contrary to popular belief — they by and large were neither fortune tellers nor soothsayers nor crystal ball handlers. Had we needed to provide the prophetic mindset some sort of visualization, the prophet's face would probably assume the semi-grotesque appearance we find in Picasso's paintings: one eye set on God and His charge, the other set on humanity and its conduct, and a mouth that articulates the disparity between the two.

> *Consider having a visual reminder to approach challenges as a mountaineer in conversation with the divine — perhaps a print of a Picasso painting that invites you to keep one eye on God's charge for you and the other eye on current reality.*

The prophet thus becomes an axis of moral intervention, aiming to realign humanity's thoughts and deeds with the divine ethical charge. In that light, the hallmark of prophecy lies not within a *predetermined* future (such and such will *surely* happen), but rather with a possible future (such and such can happen) — a future whose realization relies not on the prophets' vision but on human choices and actions.

It is therefore that we find the byword of prophecy to be *shuvah* (return / repent), namely the willingness of women and men to heed the social and ethical charge set before them, realign their lives with such charge, and ascend toward the level of morality that realizes their potential as humans — an act that is *always* reciprocated by divinity's pledge to descend and meet them halfway.[201]

The Prophetic Paradox

The Jewish idea of a covenantal human–divine partnership runs in fact so deep that it flies in the face of any intuitive concept we might have about prophecy. Realizing that any future is not predetermined but rather depends on human behaviors and choices poses a paradoxical conundrum to the very notion of prophecy: for upon reflection, it becomes obvious that an effective prophet — that is, a prophet whose vision and warnings of possible outcomes have managed to stir the hearts of their audience and affect positive change among humans — ends up being the prophet whose prophecy ultimately did not come to pass! This deep paradox raises many questions in the Bible concerning our very ability to distinguish between true and false prophets — but we are transgressing here. Suffice it to say that a true prophet, according to the Bible, seeks no profit. Returning to our discussion, the true prophet enters the arena not only to highlight the disparity between the divine charge and human conduct, but to reaffirm the power entrusted with humans to *change* their realities.

Jonah: The Best Prophet, the Worst Prophet

A wonderful example of the intricate mechanisms of prophecy and its interface with human choice and responsibility is found in the biblical story of Jonah. Much like other prophets, Jonah is at first reluctant to assume this heavy burden, even attempting to flee as far as possible from the sin city of Ninveh, where he was commanded to deliver God's displeasure with its people and prophesize their impending doom.[202] After turns and tribulations Jonah ends up in Ninveh and delivers the word of God: "Yet forty days, and Ninveh shall be overthrown."[203]

Nothing out of the ordinary thus far. However, we learn that the people of Ninveh took Jonah's prophetic warnings very seriously indeed. Not only did they repent and cover themselves in ashes, but so did their cattle and livestock at the

---

201 See prophetic passages such as Ezekiel 18:21, Jeremiah 3:12-22, Hosea 6:1, Joel 2:12-13, Jonah 3:10. We will revisit Jonah later in this essay.

202 Jonah 1:2: "… and proclaim against it; for their wickedness has come up before Me."

203 Jonah 3:4.

king's command. And based on the prophetic model we have already outlined above, the result of their choices and conduct should not surprise us: "And God saw their works, and that they turned from their evil way; and God repented of the evil which He said He would do unto them; and He did it not."[204]

Had the story ended here, we could have easily crowned Jonah as one of the most successful prophets in the biblical narrative. Whether through charisma, outstanding oratory, or persuasion skills, Jonah has managed to fulfill the prophetic charge brilliantly. Alas, the story does not end here. The fourth and final chapter of this little book shows that while the people of Ninveh aligned perfectly with the prophetic model and indeed altered their possible fate, the one who did not fully understand its true purpose and mechanism was, ironically, the prophet himself. Jonah, we learn, was "[exceedingly] displeased and angry," feeling that God made a mockery out of him by not realizing the punishment Jonah had prescribed unto the people of Ninveh: "for I knew that You are a gracious God, and compassionate"[205] and won't have the stomach to realize that wrath.[206]

Here Jonah proves himself to be a failed prophet, having completely missed the point of prophecy within the context of human agency and moral accountability. Feeling betrayed by God's withdrawal from the envisioned punishment of Ninveh, Jonah focuses on being proven "right" rather than being an agent of true ethical and social change. He saw his prophecy as an end rather than a means to a higher end, namely a social shift toward humanity and a change for the better on behalf of humanity's future trajectory. That change, as we saw, was realized by the people of Ninveh themselves, for no one else could have made that decision in their name.[207]

Hope: Memory and Courage

The great promise that we find throughout our prophetic writings is the intersection of choice, responsibility, and hope. Indeed, even when surrounded

---

204 Jonah 3:10.

205 Jonah 4:2.

206 Albeit beyond the frame of this particular discussion, it is worth noting that other interpreters of this story ascribe Jonah's disapproval of God's mercy toward the Assyrian city of Ninveh in the context of his foreknowledge of the role Assyria would play in the destruction of Israel's Northern Kingdom.

207 God's treatment of Jonah and the lesson God teaches him about prophecy, humility, and humanity are a worthy read in and of themselves (see chapter 4 of the book of Jonah).

by displays of human depravity, degeneracy, and withdrawal from moral clarity, our charge is to remember that hope can never be highjacked from us. Rather, it continuously relies on our ability to assume ownership over our own humanity, as individuals, as a family, as community members, as a people, and as citizens of this world. Fortified by lessons of old and realizing that we forever are the captains of our own journeys, hope is articulated by the will to lead oneself and others on a path often forsaken: the unwavering belief (albeit at times excruciatingly difficult) in our ability to turn the world in which we live into a world in which we believe.

While our shared past is a fact, our shared future remains forever a choice. And as we continue through life, hoping to leave our own imprint for the sake of future generations, we must take heed and remember our past and its lessons. For at the end of the day, a generation that does not remember its past forfeits its own moral right to be remembered by its future! Such choices not only define us as humans but also inform our place, commitment, and contribution to the ever-evolving story of our people.

Let us choose and let us climb, for we have the souls of mountaineers.

On Life, Liberty, and the Pursuit of Happiness: How Jewish Tradition Engenders Happiness by Creating a Better World for Others

Nigel Savage

Nigel Savage founded and led Hazon — today Adamah — which under his leadership became the largest environmental organization in the American Jewish community. Today he is based in Jerusalem, where he co-founded and leads the Jewish Climate Trust.

Here's my question: When the United States Declaration of Independence begins by affirming the right to life, liberty, and the pursuit of happiness, what's the Jewish take on that?

Part of that phrase has strong Jewish roots. The founders of the United States were deeply influenced by the Hebrew Bible. A remarkable proportion of them could actually read the Torah in Hebrew. That commitment to life and liberty traces back to the biblical story of the People of Israel fleeing from Pharaoh.

But what about the pursuit of happiness?

Those four simple words are a snapshot of something that, even 250 years ago, was already becoming central to the American psyche. In the years since they first were written, the pursuit of happiness has become an indelible — an inalienable — American right. It is reflected across presumptions of American life that are so core we barely notice or question them, and they have spread from the U.S. to a substantial part of the West. You can do anything you want nowadays, be whoever you want to be, do what you want to do, eat what you want to eat, wear what you want to wear. *You do you* — a quintessential contemporary phrase — could not have arisen in more traditional societies. It implies the radically naked individual, independent of context, family, belief, tradition. *You do you* is shorthand for today's understanding of life, liberty, and the pursuit of happiness.

Before I critique it, I want to note, first, that I like happiness and freedom as much as you do. As human beings we are tuned to want what is pleasurable and to avoid what is painful. None of us is against happiness.

And more than that: If my alternative to contemporary American life is, for instance, to have to live under Chinese communist rule, or as a woman under the Taliban or in Iran, or as someone who is gay in Nigeria or Saudi Arabia, then of course I choose life in the West without hesitation. The pursuit of happiness requires life and liberty, and as liberal westerners we too easily take the great gift of these things for granted. Our societies may be fallible and flawed in many ways — but the alternatives are far worse.

Still, it is striking that Jewish tradition has no equivalent phrase to "the pursuit of happiness." What it does have sounds radically different — *ol malchut Shamayim,* which means something like the burden of the kingdom of Heaven.

If Jewish tradition thinks we should be pursuing something, this is pretty much what it is. This idea has been inscribed in the rhythms of Jewish life for twenty centuries. The traditional daily recitation of the Sh'ma[208] is understood by the rabbis as an expression of *ol malchut Shamayim.* At the start and end of each day we redirect what might be our own pursuit of happiness, and instead commit to this curious and counterintuitive idea of somehow subsuming our freedom.

So I want to try to explain what *ol malchut Shamayim* has meant in practice in Jewish life, how radically different in ethos and orientation it is from our contemporary world — and yet, most startlingly, how it may offer a healthier and more attainable route to a happy life, for ourselves and for others, than anything encompassed by the western pursuit of happiness.

Before I proceed, I want to make a point about my own observance and my own Jewish journey. I'm not orthodox. I'm not consistently halachically observant. In a formal theological sense I think of myself as a Jewish spiritual humanist. I say this because, on the face of it, *ol malchut Shamayim* certainly implies a traditional theology. It takes for granted a belief in God in general and in the Jewish God — the God of the Torah — most especially.

But despite its theological basis, I want to detach the notion of *ol malchut Shamayim* from formal questions about God or the nature of belief in God. Jewish life is a practice. We do, of course, have our own theologies. But we care far more about what a person does than what they think. And so I want simply to ask: What does *ol malchut Shamayim* mean in practice, and how does it connect to our contemporary happiness?

At its core, it is a commitment to Jewish observance, traditionally understood. What should I eat? How should I spend my time? When should I rest? To whom do I owe obligations? If someone knocks at my door wanting help, what should

---

208 The twice daily recitation that begins with the famous words: "Listen, Israel, *Adonai* our God, *Adonai* is One," and in its entirety includes three short biblical paragraphs.

I do? If given the chance to gossip about somebody, should I do so? How should I react if I am feeling angry? Is there anything I need to do if a friend's parent has died? Or whose child is sick? Should I go to this funeral or not? Should I give charity? To whom, and why, and how much, and in what way?

Ol malchut Shamayim is why Jews have traditionally lived within walking distance of each other. It's why we have kept Shabbat and kept kosher. It is why we have been enormously committed to our kids' education, to the betterment of the broader communities in which we live, and to a messianic determination to try to make the world a better place.

The point I want to make is that Jews have done these things, for twenty centuries, because we believed ourselves *obligated* to do so; that this obligation has been a self-imposed limitation on our wider freedoms, and that the consequences of this have immeasurably enriched our own lives and created strong communities that nurture others. This is not abstract. Let me give a few examples.

Over the years any number of people I didn't know — friends of friends — have invited themselves to meals in my home, especially to Shabbat or holiday meals. I have not experienced this as an encroachment on my freedom. To the contrary, it has immensely enriched my life. (And these rhythms are reciprocal. I was recently in Paris over Shabbat. At the last minute I texted a fairly vague friend and asked if we could go to her for a Shabbat meal. She invited us to her parents where, as it happens, we had Friday night with an Egyptian Muslim who grew up in Saudi Arabia and lives now in Berlin. A fabulous evening.)

The commitments of community extend in multiple directions. Giving money to a homeless person in the street. Offering a student loan guarantee to a cousin's son. Having friends, and friends of friends, stay in my home. Taking food to a *shivah* house. Helping to make a *minyan,* a prayer quorum of ten. Listening to someone in need. Offering career advice. Acting as a *shadchan,* introducing two people who are single who I think would like each other.

These are all things I have done many times. As has my sister. As have many — most — of my friends. As did my parents before me. What these actions do, in aggregate, is create skeins of community — invisible lines that connect us to others in an endless crisscrossing pattern, weaving a world of relationship, commitment, freedom, and hope.

Reflect on actions you and the people around you do
that contribute to such skeins of community.

And that's how this all loops back to these wider questions. How can I live more healthily? How best can I nurture my kids? How, given finite time and money, can I contribute to making the world a better place, when the world sometimes seems so broken and so overwhelming?

I've been involved for the last twenty-five years in addressing issues of sustainability within and beyond the Jewish community. For the world's sake, and the sake of those who come after us, we have to reimagine how we live. We need to burn less carbon and emit less methane. We need carbon taxes, we need to eat less meat, we need to drive less, fly less, consume less.

It is a little overwhelming.

But underneath our overconsuming of the world, I'm increasingly persuaded, is *fear*. Social support networks are weakening across the West. Health services are straining. The social fabric itself is fraying.

In this fear we grab tight to things that make us feel safe. We want more money, more things. We want a car in which we are insulated — or think we are — from the chaos that surrounds us. We want a home and then a larger home and then another home. If we have these, we think, *then* we will feel more safe.

What do you associate with safety in your life?
Make a list of people, relationships, practices, and
experiences in your life that make you feel connected
and secure. Compare it to a list of material things you
believe provide safety. Reflect on which list feels more
sustaining over time.

The lessons of Jewish life are that overly relying on material things provides false securities, just as populism is a false security; and just as infinite freedom and the pursuit of happiness are false freedoms.

That's how *ol malchut Shamayim* connects the dots. In our commitment to others we find ourselves held and respected and loved. In our commitment to the lived practices of Jewish life we find ourselves supported in the community. In our determination to give to others, we receive so much. In our understanding of obligation, we discover a different kind of freedom.

Ol malchut Shamayim in the twenty-first century is a frame that, certainly for me personally, weaves together a commitment to traditional Jewish practice with a commitment to striving to create a healthier and more sustainable world for all. For twenty centuries Jewish people have asked: Is this food kosher? Meaning, literally, is this food fit to eat? That's a question that for many of us encompasses not just how an animal was killed, but how it lived. Or to give another example: Jewish tradition has always believed in *hidur mitzvah*, literally beautifying a mitzvah. That's where our tradition of beautiful Kiddush cups or challah covers or holiday *hanukkiot*, candelabra, comes from. I celebrate *hidur mitzvah* in that sense. But *hidur mitzvah* nowadays can encompass not just our homes but our schools, our parks, our colleges, our public spaces. *Ol malchut Shamayim* involves a certain humility, a commitment to a larger whole. It is thus a frame for living both more richly and more ethically.

> *With whom might you reflect on and discuss*
> *this notion of* ol malchut Shamayim
> *and what it can mean for you?*

And so I end with this: the distinction between *happiness* and *joy.*

Happiness is very much an American word, inscribed as it is in the Declaration of Independence.

A Jewish word that sounds similar, but is quite distinct, is *simchah.* The late Rabbi Jonathan Sacks once memorably translated *simchah* as the joy we share with others.[209] That is indeed what a *simchah* is in Jewish life — a wedding, a bat mitzvah, a joyous occasion whose joy would not be possible were we not with others.

So may we be blessed to live a rich and joyous life; to learn, by living it, our own understanding of *ol malchut Shamayim.* And in doing so may we richly receive the blessings of life, liberty, and happiness.

---

209 Jonathan Sacks, "Covenant & Conversation: Collective Joy," Re'eh, The Rabbi Sacks Legacy, 5779, https://rabbisacks.org/covenant-conversation/reeh/collective-joy/.

We Can Transform the World, Bite by Bite

Dr. Marilyn Paul and David Peter Stroh

Marilyn Paul, PhD, is co-founder and principal at Bridgeway Partners, building bridges for social and environmental change and offering organizational and management consulting. Her consulting focuses on facilitation, organizational diagnosis, systems thinking, and leadership development. She is the author of It's Hard to Make a Difference When You Can't Find Your Keys: The Seven-Step Path to Becoming Truly Organized *and* An Oasis in Time: How a Day of Rest Can Save Your Life.

David Peter Stroh is recognized internationally for enabling leaders to apply systems thinking to achieve breakthroughs around chronic, complex problems and develop strategies that improve system-wide performance over time. He is the author of the best-selling book Systems Thinking for Social Change: A Practical Guide for Solving Complex Problems, Avoiding Unintended Consequences, and Achieving Lasting Results. *David is a co-founder of Innovation Associates, a consulting firm whose pioneering work in the area of organizational learning formed the basis for fellow co-founder Peter Senge's management classic* The Fifth Discipline: The Art & Practice of The Learning Organization. *He is a founding partner of Bridgeway Partners.*

S everal years ago, we were surprised to learn that people worldwide throw out more than 1.3 billion tons of food a year. One-third of all perfectly edible food goes to waste. How could we not have known this? Throwing out food? What a terrible waste when so many people are going hungry. And although it's not what we usually think of as a way to contribute to a better future, it turns out that food waste is a serious problem. It's very costly for our beleaguered planet. When we throw leftovers into the trash, it releases massive amounts of methane, a gas that's worse for the planet than carbon. It's also expensive! On average, people in the U.S. throw out more than 200 pounds of food per person annually. American households discard well more than $2,000 worth of edible food each year. Where did all the food waste come from? Our first answer was: "Not from us!" But then, as we observed ourselves in action, we realized that our family *was* contributing to the problem. And we could contribute to a better future every day through reducing our food waste.

While it's true that much food waste is created by farmers letting food rot in their fields, grocery stores tossing unmarketable food at day's end, or restauranteurs pitching tons of leftovers, twenty-five percent of American food waste comes from average citizens — you and me — throwing out food in our homes, on the road, and at work. Think of it: All that labor, all that water, all that soil, and all those toxic fertilizers going to grow food that ends up in landfills because of our personal habits. What's going on here?

For us, as for millions of busy people, getting food on the table took place in a hectic rush, sometimes tinged with a hint of desperation. We eat on the run, often preparing easy meal kits or just ordering meals for delivery. We need convenience because we squeeze our meals in between activities we think are more important. We lose track of food, throw out leftovers, or just don't plan well and buy too much in the first place. We didn't plan for this, it's just that dinnertime would arrive with no food ready to eat.

We *can* prevent this level of waste. It turns out that addressing food waste is actually one of the best ways we have to fight climate change and thus create a better future. We don't have to wait for the whole broken food system to be fixed to make a difference.

But often we talk ourselves out of even the smallest changes. It happens when we are tired, overwhelmed, lonely, or hurting in some way. In that mental space of fatigue and moderate despair, it's hard to think about contributing to a better future. We feel daunted.

Yet it is important to remember that our small changes can build up to systems change. How? By talking about what we are doing, encouraging others, and modeling new possibilities. Research tells us that people change when their friends and neighbors change, and this can add up to systems change. We want to create a better future together.

Stepping Out of Old Patterns Makes a Difference

A better future starts now — right in this exact moment when we can choose something different. We can pause, even briefly, and notice our habitual mind telling us about how daunted and tired we are. When we bring awareness to our old ways of thinking and our habit of being disheartened about change, we have a chance of stepping out of our old patterns. When patterns are broken new worlds emerge. So now our new choices change our personal world and the larger world as well. Not only do we reduce food waste, but our behavior affects others. And that can lead to systemic changes.

Small Changes Can Alter Systems

To contribute to a better future for all of us, we need to change the systems we are in. But systems don't change in the way we think they should. In fact, often the harder we push for what we want, from the type of thinking that created the problem in the first place, the worse things can get. When we encounter a system that seems stuck we often ask: Who is to blame for this mess? How can we change those people? What actions can we take to change them? We look for the bad guy and point the finger at them. While this might help us feel better in the short run, blaming others just disempowers us. But what if we switch to think new thoughts like: What can I do from where I am to make changes? How can I talk to people in encouraging and supportive ways that lead to working together on making even small changes?

Ask Different Questions About Change

To create real change, we can learn from change agents to ask a different set of questions. These include:
- What are the contributing factors to the current situation, and how are they connected?
- What are the root causes of this tough situation?
- If we know the solution, why haven't we been able to implement it?
- What are the payoffs to the current situation — not just its costs?

Surprisingly, perhaps the most powerful question to begin with is: How might we be contributing, however unintentionally, to the very problem we are trying to solve? Adopting this viewpoint of personal responsibility is not intended to shift blame to ourselves, but rather to empower us to initiate change where we have the greatest control. Systems thinking teaches us that the greatest control any one of us has over a larger system is through *our own intentions, our own thinking, and our own behavior.* As we change our intentions and thinking, we make new choices that lead us to take new actions.

With regard to a change you would like to see, one that is of small or medium magnitude, consider: How might I be contributing, however unintentionally, to the very issue I'm seeking to solve?

Change Begins with Us

How do we make these better choices? Contributing to a better world asks us to learn, grow, and take our responsibilities to other people and nature seriously. In other words, our larger systems change only when *we* do. We are reminded of the story attributed to the renowned Jewish teacher Rabbi Yisrael Salanter:

> When I was a young man, I wanted to change the world. I found it was difficult to change the world, so I tried to change my nation. When I found I couldn't change the nation, I began to focus on my town. I couldn't change the town, and as an older man, I tried to change my family. Now, as an old man, I realize the only thing I can change is myself, and suddenly I realize that if long ago I had changed myself, I could have made an impact on my family. My family and I could have made an impact on our town. Their impact could have changed the nation, and I could indeed have changed the world.[210]

Our Food Waste Example

Let's look at how this applied to us as we were reducing our food waste. Like many people, we knew that we are in the middle of a climate crisis and at risk of losing our planetary home. Yet like others, we were trying to block out the bad news and justify our inaction. Most people are really hoping that something will happen to rescue us from the very depressing reality of increased extreme weather events, loss of species, warming oceans, and the loss of our glaciers and icebergs.

But we learned there is another option. That option is to join in the massive movement of people contributing to a better future by changing systems at multiple levels. These systems include:

---

210 Rabbi Yisrael Salanter, *Social Justice Texts*, Meyerhoff Center for Jewish Studies.

- The economic system that threatens our natural world
- The political system that seeks to protect the economic system on the one hand and recognizes the need to change it on the other
- Conflicting cultures that value material well-being and comfort on the one hand and spiritual teachings about awe and gratitude on the other

Our Leaders Are Fallible

One of the challenges is that we are not aware of the millions of people taking action on a day-to-day basis. People often feel alone. Also, many people believe that significant change will only come if our business and political leaders act more responsibly. This leaves us off the hook for constructive action. However, the Bible warns us to not put too much faith in formal leaders because they are imperfect. When the Jewish people ask Samuel to appoint a king so they can emulate other nations, God tells Samuel to "warn them solemnly, and tell them about the practices of any king who will rule over them."[211] Samuel then describes all the harm that a king will cause them, and concludes by saying, "The day will come when you cry out because of the king whom you yourselves have chosen; and the Lord will not answer you on that day."[212] Our elected and corporate leaders often don't have the courage to take new actions until they see signals from consumers and voters like us about how to act.

Our faith tradition calls on us to step up from wherever we are. *Tikun olam* is part of our practice. Joining in to create a better shared future calls on us to step away from being a bystander and become an agent for change. When we realized that we were contributing to climate change through our food waste as a family, we declared that our family's kitchen would be waste free. We had to change some of our own habits of thought and action to accomplish this.

Personal Growth Helps Us Make Better Choices

Systems change asks us to develop certain character traits so we can make better choices.[213] Here are the personal character traits we have found to be

---

211 Samuel 8.9.

212 Samuel 8.18.

213 David Peter Stroh, *Systems Thinking for Social Change: A Practical Guide to Solving Complex Problems, Avoiding Unintended Consequences, and Achieving Lasting Results*, White River Junction, VT: Chelsea Green Publishing, 2015.

particularly helpful in creating systems change:

Awareness. Knowing yourself and your habitual patterns, seeing more of the whole of which you are a part, and understanding how you might unwittingly be contributing to the very situation you want to change.

Curiosity. Being open to learning, particularly in the face of failing to achieve what you really care about.

Courage. Finding the strength to take risks for a new outlook or action. Taking a stand for the integrity and sustainability of the whole in the face of seemingly more expedient alternatives. Going even further and asking: What might I or we have to give up in order for the whole system to succeed?

Vision. Listening for what moves you and what is being called for by the world around you. Imagining a better world that might seem to be impossible to achieve. Working for what you deeply care about and remembering, in the words of Vaclav Havel, that "Hope is definitely not the same thing as optimism. It is not the conviction that something will turn out well, but the certainty that something makes sense, regardless of how it turns out."[214]

Respect. Assuming that everyone is doing the best they can with what they know at the time.

Compassion. Recognizing that at some level all of us are unaware of the harm we do, and that limited awareness is a source of suffering.

Patience. Developing the patience and persistence to continue to act in the face of uncertainty and time delays.

Flexibility. Balancing the ability to stay on course with the flexibility to adjust in the face of new information.

> *Consider if one trait especially calls to you to focus on first.*

We started by increasing our *awareness* of our actions. We noticed that when we were moving too fast we made poor choices. As we sought change in the present moment, difficult thoughts arose such as: I don't have time for this. This isn't making any difference. Or, I just don't have the energy to do something

---

214 Vaclav Havel, *Disturbing the Peace: A Conversation with Karel Huizdala,* New York: Vintage Books, 1991.

different. Thoughts and behaviors are so highly habitual that we might not even notice them. Instead, we chose to notice that we were throwing leftovers away instead of freezing them, buying too much food when we become enticed by special deals, and storing unlabeled food in the back of the fridge and forgetting about it.

Once we became more aware, we used our *curiosity* to get interested on two levels: the inner and the outer levels. On the personal side, we got interested in our own patterns of thought, and we could see that haste led to food waste. As we sought to reduce our family's food waste, we found a lot of contradictions in our lives. We didn't want hectic last-minute cooking, but we did it a lot because we wanted to work until right before dinner. We wanted to buy less at the grocery store, but we still bought too much — in haste, without a plan, just in case. We didn't want to get food on the table with irritation and even exasperation, but we didn't see an alternative when we were hungry, tired, and cranky.

And then we started to see ourselves as part of the system, not outside it. Holding a *vision* for a better future for us and our planet is high leverage for change. Let's imagine for a moment a future of steadily moderate weather. Massive hurricanes have died down, and we imagine with great relief the calming of these extreme weather events. We can imagine the planting of massive numbers of trees all over the world, and perhaps we can imagine a healthier world population with a truly workable food system. Not only did we affirm these aspirations in our own minds, but we started talking to people and communicating that a better future is possible. That took *courage* as well.

We recognized that we were trying to resolve conflicting values without determining which were the most important to us. We began to engage in small practices that enabled us to stop in the midst of those day-to-day decisions and remember what was important. It also took *courage* to decide to shift our priorities. We began to steward our own food. We stopped letting it rot. We paid more attention to how much food we prepared. We served ourselves less and scraped less food down into the trash. We labeled and dated any leftovers so we would eat them in a timely way.

As part of this, we slowed down. We tasted our food. Savoring deliciousness provides a significant source of pleasure. It cut into our rapid-pace lifestyles. It interrupted that underlying pulse of never done, never enough. We learned to stop pushing so hard and, in so doing, we found small ways to treasure our lives and our sources of energy. And we stopped just talking about our climate panic — we now do something real to offset it every day.

As we talk to more people, we discover there are whole groups of people who also want to affirm a positive future. And then, because we now see ourselves as part of the system, we ask ourselves: What else can we do today to bring this future into reality? Just for today, we'll plan meals ahead and make a shopping list so we don't buy too much food. We see that we have the *patience* and the community orientation to make this change, and we'd like to do it again tomorrow, and then we work on the old patterns that arise. As we continue to develop *self-compassion*, we become more adept at working with the inner interferences to change. We might hear ourselves say: Ah, it doesn't matter. I'm too busy to figure this out. Very gently we reaffirm that our new choices count and that we really want that better future, and so today you and I will both make some choices that will bring about a future of steadier weather, cooling oceans, and the restoration of ice in the Arctic and Antarctica.

We contribute to a better future by beginning with our greatest source of leverage: ourselves. We see ourselves as an essential part of the systems we want to change. We increase our awareness of our own choices, thinking, and behavior. We courageously assess the extent to which we are part of the problem, not just part of the solution. And in doing so, we cultivate new insights, choices, thoughts, and actions that are more closely aligned with the world we want to create. And when we do this for ourselves, we naturally reach out in more effective ways to others — our friends and families, neighbors, communities, and the larger systems to which we belong.

As the historian Howard Zinn said, "We don't have to engage in grand, heroic actions to participate in the process of change. Small acts, when multiplied by millions of people, can transform the world."[215] We can eliminate food waste and transform the world, bite by bite. And in the process, we can discover the power and satisfaction of contributing to a better world.

---

215 Howard Zinn, *You Can't Be Neutral on a Moving Train: A Personal History of Our Times*, Boston: Beacon Press, 1994.

Epilogue

I'm crafting this epilogue on the first day of the month of Elul, when Jewish tradition invites us to a daily practice of hearing the awakening call of the shofar in advance of the High Holy Days.

Stories, too, have the power to awaken. They can awaken the soul and return us to our inner wisdom — especially Hasidic stories. In the wake of October 7 and the ensuing year filled with pain alongside valiant nobility, I'm ending this book with one of my favorite Hasidic stories.

I hope this story awakens for you an insight from the previous chapters and inspires you to act on it to draw meaning, joy, and blessing to yourself and those around you. May this contribute, even if a little, to connecting Heaven and Earth.

First, a modicum of background about two characters in the story.

Elijah the Prophet

The biblical Elijah was a zealot and a loner who lived, according to tradition, in the ninth century BCE. At the end of his life, "Elijah went up to Heaven in a whirlwind" in a fiery chariot but never actually died.[216] His departure was only temporary. The Torah's final prophet promised that Elijah will return to Earth to herald the coming of a new era of a healed world through reconnecting parents and children to each other: "I will send you Elijah the Prophet before the coming of the great and awesome day of God, and he will return the hearts of parents to their children and the hearts of children to their parents."[217]

But between Elijah's departure more than three thousand years ago and his forthcoming return to bring about a better world, Elijah transformed from a zealot to a humble, loving, caring peacemaker who visits every bris, every family at the end of Shabbat, and every Passover Seder. The sages speak of him roaming the world to help people in need[218] and visiting great sages to teach mystical Torah secrets. One of those sages was the Baal Shem Tov.

---

216 II Kings 2:11.

217 Malachi 3:23-24.

218 See for example Babylonian Talmud Brachot 58a, Taanit 21a, Kidushin 40a, Sanhedrin 108a-109a.

The Baal Shem Tov

The Baal Shem Tov was the founder of the Hasidic movement. Born in eighteenth-century Ukraine as Israel ben Eliezer, he became a legend in his own time. Healers at the time were called *Baal Shem*, Master of the (divine) Name, which is how he became known as the Baal Shem Tov.

Miraculous tales of his wisdom, insight into human nature, and healing powers spread through Eastern Europe. His close followers and students, called his *Hasidim,* prayed and learned with him and accompanied him on wondrous journeys.

A Story of Meeting Elijah[219]

One of the Baal Shem Tov's *Hasidim* in the town of Mezhibuzh (in current-day Ukraine) was particularly enthralled by his rebbe's encounters with Elijah the Prophet. The Baal Shem Tov often related mystical teachings he received in encounters and visions with prophets, including Elijah.

So this *Hasid* began to implore the Baal Shem Tov to help him to also have an encounter with Elijah the Prophet. But the Baal Shem Tov kept telling him that he would need to wait until he was ready.

Finally, the Baal Shem Tov agreed.

"If you want to meet Elijah, I'll tell you what to do. Speak with your wife about fitting timing, because you'll need to take a significant journey, nearly a week's time. Then travel to the city of Minsk in Belarus. When you get there, find the local market and fill a wagon with food — bread, fish, fruit, vegetables, grain, chicken, meat, wine — and buy generously. Then follow the road to the outskirts of town. Just before the forest begins is a dilapidated house. Find that house, but don't knock on the door immediately. Stand and listen carefully. When you hear a fitting signal, you will know what to do. This plan can have you meeting Elijah."

The *Hasid* was beside himself with excitement and headed home to speak with his wife. She understood how meaningful this once-in-a-lifetime chance to meet Elijah was to her husband and offered him her blessing.

So the *Hasid* set off and did as the Baal Shem Tov had told him. When he got to Minsk, he filled a large wagon with plenty of good food from the market, then

---

219 This rendition of the oft-told story is adapted from two wonderful books: Eliezer Shore, *Meeting Elijah: True Tales of Eliyahu Hanavi,* Jerusalem: Tehiru Press, 2020; and Yitzhak Buxbaum, *The Light and Fire of the Baal Shem Tov,* London: The Continuum International Publishing Group, 2008.

a few hours before Shabbat he found the broken-down house at the edge of town. He stood by the ramshackle door, listening carefully. Inside, he heard children crying. After some time, he heard a child say, "Mommy, we're hungry! We haven't eaten anything since breakfast yesterday. How can we celebrate Shabbat with no food?" He heard the woman sighing and answering, "Oy, my children, let's trust in God to send us what we need!"

"This must be my sign!" thought the *Hasid* and he knocked on the door. A disheveled woman opened the door with several young children clinging to her. "I'm passing through town and need a place to stay for Shabbat."

"I'm sorry," said the woman, "my husband is sick, and we don't have food even for our own family."

"Don't worry," he said, "I brought food for all of us."

The woman looked behind him at the wagon and her eyes lit up. She welcomed him in and quickly began preparing food. He came in, gave the children some fruit, and played with them while the woman cooked for Shabbat.

He was there for two nights, waiting to see Elijah the Prophet. His eyes kept darting after every small sound in anticipation. He did not even sleep. How could he sleep? How often do you get a chance to meet Elijah the Prophet? But nothing happened. No special knock on the door, no mystical encounter.

On Sunday morning he parted from the family and headed back to Mezhibuzh with a heavy heart.

He returned to the Baal Shem Tov and said, "Master, I did not see Elijah the Prophet."

"Did you do everything I told you?" asked the Baal Shem Tov.

"I did." he said.

"And you didn't see him?"

"No, Rebbe."

"Then I suggest that you do the trip again," said the Baal Shem Tov. "Go back and do what you did last time, filling a wagon with food and heading to the same house, arriving well before sunset. Don't knock, but wait by the door until you hear a clear sign."

With complete trust in his rebbe, the *Hasid* spoke again with his wife, explaining this would be his last try. After listening to the full story, she bid him good luck. Once more he set out for Minsk, arriving there on Friday morning. Once again, he brought a wagon with Shabbat supplies and made his way to the dilapidated house at the edge of town.

This time, the *Hasid* arrived earlier and stood in front of the door, listening.

Inside he heard children crying, "Mommy, we're hungry! We haven't eaten the whole day!"

"Children!" said the mother. "Do you remember you were crying last Shabbat? And I told you, 'Trust in God to send us Elijah the Prophet who'll bring you food!' Wasn't I right? Didn't Elijah come and bring you food and stay with us for two days? Let's hope that God sends us Elijah again this week to bring you food."

The *Hasid* smiled with joy and understanding. Thinking of his rebbe, the Baal Shem Tov, he shook his head slowly with eyes shining. He knocked on the door, gently opened it, and brought in the wagon of food.

Acknowledgments

This book would not have come to life without the vision and support of Helen and David Zalik and the leadership of Amanda Abrams, the executive director of the Zalik Foundation. Helen and David imagined a book that offers Jewish wisdom on issues most relevant to contemporary life, and Amanda adroitly helped envision how to bring that vision into being. Many thanks also to Susan Kramer, who participated in these critical formative planning conversations.

My deep appreciation goes to the members of Momentum's Education Advisory Panel, under the leadership of Manette Mayberg, who helped form the structure of the book. Dr. Erica Brown's idea to draw on multiple authors for each chapter was particularly instrumental.

Profound gratitude goes to each of the trailblazing contributors for sharing their rich experience and insights. It has been an honor and a privilege to journey with you. Your stories and teachings testify to the diverse beauty and wonder of the human spirit.

It is a privilege to have benefited from the support of gifted editors with hearts as brilliant as their minds. Rachel Sales supported several authors to craft their article from interviews or lectures they had given. Deborah Meghnagi Bailey did a first round of editing on most of the articles. Adrienne Gold Davis and Jessica Berkowitz provided a sounding board at critical junctures; in addition, Adrienne helped shape the introductions to the first two sections, while Jessica drafted the introduction to the chapter *Contributing to a Better Future*. Chaya Lester did a first round of editing on the introductions, and Deena Glickman the second. Both elevated them remarkably. Wendy Bernstein enthusiastically served as the book's final copy editor.

Thanks to the encompassing support from the Momentum global movement for being the greenhouse for Jewish initiatives that has nourished this project. This includes Momentum Board members for setting the organization's mission and priorities that underlie the book; Ben Pery and the executive leadership team for tirelessly working to make everything Momentum thrive; Orit Mitzner for championing the book's completion as a priority; and the remarkable Momentum staff who assiduously bring initiatives to life. Much appreciation for Lior Krinsky, Faryn Beirman, and Yuval Koslovsky, for skillfully managing the nuts and bolts of this project; the Momentum participants whose survey responses guided the selection of the book's topics; and the advance readers whose feedback helped hone the work — Fran Kritz, Lori Brockman, Orit Mitzner, Andrea Mail, Jeanie Milbauer, Dafna Berman, Jenn Fechter, and Dasee Berkowitz.

Ira Ginzburg, your design sensibility makes each page sing! Thank you also to Anna Hacco and Shaked Zirman on Ira's team, who collaborated with her on the design work. A special thank you to Avshalom Eshel, a talented calligrapher, artist, and *sofer stam*, who, on very short notice, worked for hours with a generous heart to craft the Hebrew calligraphy on the book's section openers and cover.

Matthew Miller, Ashirah Firszt, Carly Meltz, Alex Drucker, and the entire team at Magid / Koren Publishers, thank you for believing in this book from the outset and bringing decades of experience to its publishing and distribution.

I'm grateful to my teachers and learning partners. I thank my parents, Dr. Yael Zif z"l and Dr. Jehiel Zif, who set me on a path of seeing life as a canvas to beautify through living wondrously; and my parents-in-law, Sara Kreger z"l and Jerry Kreger z"l, who added music and joyful choral harmony, literally. I thank our children, Shir, Maor Eden Oman, and Ma'ayan Hodaya; our sons-in-law, Dor and Yonatan Gad; and my husband, Dr. David Ziv-Kreger, for a journey of awe and the delight of learning and growing together. David, your deep wells of wisdom and support in all aspects of life and partnership in wondrous living have made me forever grateful. I dedicate my work on this book to you with a prayer that we merit many more awesome years together.

God, You are the source not only of the deepest awe and love but of all wonder. With gratitude beyond words, I thank You and pray that the nectar of Your closeness spreads around the world inspiring healing and wholeness.

Finally, thank you, dear reader. This book was created with you in mind, with the hope that you will find inspiration in the chapters that are most meaningful to your life and that you will roll up your sleeves, encouraged to make your life and the life of your family and community more wondrous. You are here with a role to play! May the mosaic of voices in this book support you to elevate current reality into an even more awesome future.

About the Editor

About the Editor

Ronit Ziv-Kreger serves as Momentum's director of education. With a PhD from MIT, she has more than twenty-five years of experience in designing and leading large-scale educational initiatives. Since coming to Momentum in 2016, her responsibilities have included collaboratively advancing bold ideas and overseeing data-driven success in fostering positive impact for communities, institutions, families, and individuals. The author and editor of two other Momentum Publications — *Year of Growth* and *Soul Full: Gateways to Jewish Prayer* — she enjoys collaborating with the global Jewish community in creating learning resources and publications that foster unity without uniformity. Ronit lived her formative years in both Israel and Boston. She is the mother of three adult children, and she lives with her husband in the Boston area. She loves to hike, garden, and study Torah.

About Momentum

Momentum empowers women to change the world through Jewish values that transform them, their families, and their communities. Since launching in 2008, and in strong partnership with the government of Israel and over four hundred and forty community organizations in thirty-six countries around the world, Momentum has welcomed more than twenty-three thousand mothers on a yearlong journey that includes a week-long immersive Israel experience as part of a journey of growth that lasts a year or longer in their home community. The Momentum library of programming also includes the Yomm app for Jewish women, ongoing community and regional leadership development fellowships, and a robust digital content library of accessible webinars and podcasts that have reached upwards of five million people across the globe.